Mathematics for Economics and Business

Mathematics for Economics and Business

Rebecca Taylor and
Simon Hawkins

McGraw-Hill
Higher Education

London Boston Burr Ridge, IL Dubuque, IA Madison, WI New York San Francisco
St. Louis Bangkok Bogotá Caracas Kuala Lumpur Lisbon Madrid Mexico City
Milan Montreal New Delhi Santiago Seoul Singapore Sydney Taipei Toronto

Mathematics for Economics and Business
Rebecca Taylor and Simon Hawkins

ISBN-13 978-0-07-710786-4
ISBN-10 0-07-710786-1

 **McGraw-Hill
Higher Education**

Published by McGraw-Hill Education
Shoppenhangers Road
Maidenhead
Berkshire
SL6 2QL
Telephone: 44 (0) 1628 502 500
Fax: 44 (0) 1628 770 224
Website: www.mcgraw-hill.co.uk

British Library Cataloguing in Publication Data
A catalogue record for this book is available from the British Library

Library of Congress Cataloguing in Publication Data
The Library of Congress data for this book has been applied for from the Library of Congress

Acquisitions Editor: Mark Kavanagh
Development Editor: Hannah Cooper
Marketing Manager: Vanessa Boddington
Senior Production Editor: James Bishop

Cover design by Fielding Design Limited
Printed and bound in Great Britain by Bell & Bain Ltd Glasgow

ISBN-13 978-0-07-710786-4
ISBN-10 0-07-710786-1

Brief Table of Contents

Preface   *viii*
Guided tour   *ix*
Technology to enhance learning and teaching   *x*
Acknowledgements   *xiii*

1 Mathematical review   *1*
2 Linear equations   *27*
3 Linear equations: further topics   *59*
4 Linear programming   *89*
5 Finance and growth   *117*
6 Non-linear equations and principles of differentiation   *153*
7 Marginal concepts and optimization   *191*
8 Partial differentiation   *215*
9 Integration   *247*
10 Matrices   *275*

Index   *309*

Detailed Table of Contents

Preface viii
Guided tour ix
Technology to enhance learning
and teaching x
Acknowledgements xiii

1 Mathematical review 1
1.1 Introduction 2
1.2 The arithmetic operators 2
1.3 Fractions 4
1.4 Percentages 7
1.5 Powers 12
1.6 Logarithms 16
1.7 Basic rules of algebra 17
Answers to quick problems 22

2 Linear equations 27
2.1 Introduction 28
2.2 Co-ordinates 28
2.3 Linear form 29
2.4 Equation of a line 34
2.5 Intersection 38
2.6 Application of linear equations
in economics 44
Answers to quick problems 56

3 Linear equations: further topics 59
3.1 Introduction 60
3.2 Simultaneous linear equations
with more than two unknowns 60
3.3 Market equilibrium and
changes in supply or demand 66
3.4 Cost, volume and profit
analysis 71
3.5 Effects of a per unit tax 73
3.6 Macroeconomic models 76
Answers to quick problems 86

4 Linear programming 89
4.1 Introduction 90
4.2 Graphing inequalities 90
4.3 Graphing simultaneous linear
inequalities 95
4.4 The objective function 98
4.5 Unbounded feasible regions 104
4.6 Application of linear
programming in economics 105
Answers to quick problems 113

5 Finance and growth 117
5.1 Introduction 118
5.2 Arithmetic progressions 119
5.3 Geometric progressions 123
5.4 Practical applications: simple
and compound interest 129
5.5 Practical applications:
investment appraisal 132
5.6 A further practical application:
economic growth 140
Answers to quick problems 144

**6 Non-linear equations and principles
of differentiation** 153
6.1 Introduction 154
6.2 Functions with more than one
independent variable 154
6.3 Factorization 160
6.4 The quadratic formula 163
6.5 Economics application of
quadratic equations 168
6.6 Basic principles of differentiation 173
6.7 The simple derivative 173
6.8 The sum rule and the
difference rule 180
6.9 The product rule 182
6.10 The quotient rule 185
6.11 The chain rule 186
Answers to quick problems 188

7 Marginal concepts and optimization 191
7.1 Introduction 192
7.2 Marginal functions 192
7.3 Demand, total revenue and
marginal revenue 193
7.4 Total and marginal cost 197
7.5 Production 198
7.6 Consumption and savings 202
7.7 Second-order derivatives 203
7.8 Optimization 205
7.9 The use of optimization in
economics 210
Answers to quick problems 213

8 Partial differentiation 215
8.1 Introduction 216
8.2 Functions of two variables 216
8.3 Partial derivatives 217

8.4   Second-order partial derivatives   *219*
8.5   Changes to independent and
       dependent variables   *221*
8.6   Partial elasticity   *223*
8.7   Partial differentiation and
       marginal functions   *225*
8.8   Unconstrained optimization   *231*
8.9   Constrained optimization   *237*
8.10   Lagrange multipliers   *240*
       Answers to quick problems   *244*

9   Integration   *247*
9.1   Introduction   *248*
9.2   Indefinite integration   *249*
9.3   Integrating $\frac{1}{x}$ *252*
9.4   Integrating using exponentials
       (e^x)   *253*
9.5   Integrating expressions with
       multiple terms   *254*
9.6   Application of indefinite
       integration   *255*
9.7   Definite integrals   *260*
9.8   Applying definite integrals:
       consumer surplus   *265*
9.9   Applying definite integrals:
       producer surplus   *267*

9.10   Definite integrals using
       exponentials   *267*
       Answers to quick problems   *269*

10   Matrices   *275*
10.1   Introduction   *276*
10.2   Definitions, notation and
       operations   *276*
10.3   Vectors   *279*
10.4   Adding and subtracting
       matrices   *280*
10.5   Dealing with 'zero matrices'   *282*
10.6   Scalar multiplication of
       matrices   *282*
10.7   Multiplying matrices   *284*
10.8   Matrix inversion   *287*
10.9   Application of 2×2 matrices
       and inversions: solving
       economic equations   *290*
10.10 Inversions of 3×3 matrices   *292*
10.11 Application of 3×3 matrices
       and inversions: solving
       economic equations   *293*
10.12 Cramer's rule   *300*
       Answers to quick problems   *304*

Index   *309*

Preface

The American economist Heilbroner once said that, 'Mathematics has given economics rigour, but alas, also mortis' and that might be a surprising and bold opening to a textbook which has both 'mathematics' and 'economics' in its title. But, in a way, Heilbroner was right to imply that too often mathematics can overtake the economics leaving us with long pages of equations which are perfectly described but which we cannot relate to the world we all observe and experience. Both authors are economists and both have a passion for teaching and learning. As students, both authors have sat through hours of dreary lectures of mathematics which threw little if any light on the fascinating, dynamic and puzzling world of business and economics. It was against this backdrop that we set about creating a textbook which genuinely provided an interesting and engaging introduction to the world of business and economics *through* mathematics, and not the other way around.

The book is aimed at students who are embarking on a course of economics or business at first or second year undergraduate level and no mathematical proficiency is presumed beyond perhaps having undertaken a GCSE. The techniques we cover can be applied to a wide variety of related undergraduate modules and topics including accounting and finance, operational research, pure mathematics, statistics, marketing and geography.

Readers should feel that the mathematics here is a tool or perhaps a 'way-in' to better understand the contemporary problems in the world of business and economics, rather than an end in itself. In this way, we hope to secure the rigour but avoid any of the mortis.

Guided tour

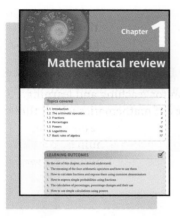

Learning outcomes

Each chapter opens with a set of learning outcomes, summarizing the mathematical knowledge, skills and understanding you should acquire from each chapter.

Student notes

Student notes are provided in boxes within each chapter. These are a useful quick reference tool, summarizing key terms and providing tips to help understanding.

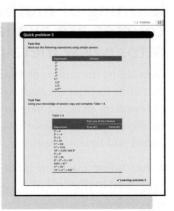

Examples

Each chapter provides worked examples, to consolidate learning and demonstrate the mathematical principles as applied in an economic context.

Quick problem boxes

Each chapter includes quick problem boxes to test your understanding and application of the mathematical principles taught in that chapter. Answers are provided at the end of each chapter so you can check your progress and see where you may need to refer back to the chapter to fill in any gaps in understanding.

Technology to enhance learning and teaching

Visit www.mcgraw-hill.co.uk/textbooks/taylor **today**

Online Learning Centre (OLC)

After completing each chapter, log on to the supporting Online Learning Centre website. Take advantage of the study tools offered to reinforce the material you have read in the text, and to develop your knowledge of mathematics for economics and business in a fun and effective way.

Resources for students include:

- *Self-test questions*
- *Weblinks*
- *Excel-based exercises*
- *Practice examination questions*

Also available for lecturers:

- *PowerPoint slides*
- *Seminar exercises*
- *Additional questions*
- *Teaching solutions*

me:таl

Further resources to support the teaching and learning of mathematics for economics and business courses are available via the METAL project website: http://www.metalproject.co.uk

Directed by the author of this text, Dr Rebecca Taylor, METAL is a HEFCE funded FDTL5 project that aims to *enhance teaching and learning* by providing lecturers and students with a selection of resources that will help to engage Level 1 students more fully and enthusiastically in mathematics for economics, through the provision of an accessible and fully interactive toolkit of varied and flexible resources. These resources include:

- An online question bank of mathematics teaching and assessment materials specifically applied to the field of economics.
- Fifty video units that relate mathematical concepts to the field of economics.

- Ten teaching and learning guides that provide an extensive bank of teaching activities (large and small groups) covering all aspects of Level 1 Mathematics for Economics.
- Fifleen case studies for use in structions/tutorials.
- An interactive website to present the teaching and learning resources, to facilitate distance learning and to foster students' autonomy and ownership of the learning process.

Custom Publishing Solutions: Let us help make our content your solution

At McGraw-Hill Education our aim is to help the lecturer find the most suitable content for their needs and the most appropriate way to deliver the content their students Our **custom publishing solutions** offer the ideal combination of content delivered in the way which suits lecturer and students the best.

The idea behind our custom publishing programme is that via a database of over two million pages called Primis, www.primisonline.com, the lecturer can select just the material they wish to deliver to their students:

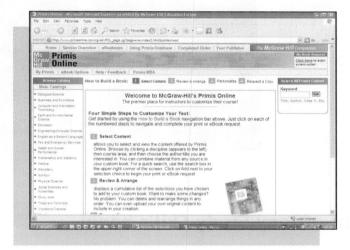

Lecturers can select chapters from:

- textbooks
- professional books
- case books – Harvard Articles, Insead, Ivey, Darden, Thunderbird and BusinessWeek
- Taking Sides – debate materials

Across the following imprints:

- McGraw-Hill Education
- Open University Press
- Harvard Business School Press
- US and European material

There is also the option to include material authored by lecturers in the custom product – this does not necessarily have to be in English.

We will take care of everything from start to finish in the process of developing and delivering a custom product to ensure that lecturers and students receive exactly the material needed in the most suitable way.

With a Custom Publishing Solution, students enjoy the best selection of material deemed to be the most suitable for learning everything they need for their courses – something of real value to support their learning. Teachers are able to use exactly the material they want, in the way they want, to support their teaching on the course.

Please contact *your local McGraw-Hill representative* with any questions or alternatively contact Warren Eels e: *warren eels@mcgraw-hill.com*.

Make the grade!

30 per cent off any Study Skills book!

Our Study Skills books are packed with practical advice and tips that are easy to put into practice and will really improve the way you study. Topics include:

- Techniques to help you pass exams
- Advice to improve your essay writing
- Help in putting together the perfect seminar presentation
- Tips on how to balance studying and your personal life

www.openup.co.uk/studyskills
Visit our website to read helpful hints about essays, exams, dissertations and much more.

Special offer! As a valued customer, buy online and receive 30 per cent off any of our Study Skills books by entering the promo code **getahead**

Acknowledgements

Our thanks go to the following reviewers for their input at various stages in the text's development:

Kevin Albertson, Manchester Metropolitan University

Tony Conibear, London Metropolitan University

Marco Ercolani, Birmingham University

Hilary Lamaison, Brunel University

Paul Latreille, University of Wales, Swansea

Jason Laws, Liverpool John Moores University

Tony Miller, Newcastle University

Kay Pollock, Kingston University

Cristina Santos, The Open University

Rob Simmons, Lancaster University

Mark Voorneveld, Stockholm School of Economics.

Both authors would like to acknowledge the comments which reviewers have helpfully provided. Thanks must also go to David Milnes for working through the problem sets and offering advice on how worked examples and answers could be clarified. Simon Hawkins would like to thank Claire and Sam and Alice for their understanding – when he was ensconced in his study when he really should have been doing family things – and to Jean and David Cheesman for their unfailing support. Rebecca Taylor would like to thank Chris, Larissa and Zachary for being so understanding, and Michael and Maureen Taylor for their support and interest in this project.

Chapter 1

Mathematical review

Topics covered

1.1 Introduction   2
1.2 The arithmetic operators   2
1.3 Fractions   4
1.4 Percentages   7
1.5 Powers   12
1.6 Logarithms   16
1.7 Basic rules of algebra   17

LEARNING OUTCOMES

By the end of this chapter, you should understand:

1. The meaning of the four arithmetic operators and how to use them

2. How to calculate fractions and express them using common denominators

3. How to express simple probabilities using fractions

4. The calculation of percentages, percentage changes and their use

5. How to use simple calculations using powers

6. The basic rules governing powers and roots and how to rearrange and solve expressions

7. How to calculate logarithms and use logarithmic expressions

8. The rules of algebra and how to use them.

1.1 Introduction

Business and economics is all around us and shapes our everyday lives. We are confronted by decisions, choices and issues which at their core are often to do with business and economics issues. How many hours do we choose to work each week? How much money are we prepared to accept for our services to an employer? Should we save some of our salary or should we spend it all?

Many of our choices are informed by mathematics, although we may not even know it.[1] The more complex or advanced the problem so we often find that the mathematics becomes more overt or explicit. The point here is that to really understand and solve business and economics issues we need to have a confident and secure understanding of the underlying mathematics. This needs to be put into a practical context: we should use mathematics to help us understand what is going on, not to confuse or dazzle people; it is a tool to illuminate and solve business and economic problems.

This first section focuses on some of the 'mathematical fundamentals' which you will need to understand business and economics. As your mathematical proficiency grows, so too will your capacity to think independently and critically about these concepts and your understanding of which concepts and methods to apply.

1.2 The arithmetic operators

'Arithmetic operators' simply refers to the nut and bolts of all basic mathematics: addition (+), subtraction (−), multiplication (×) and division (÷). You will recognize these operators and understand their function, and will probably be able to use them confidently.

You will need to be aware that different words or 'synonyms' can be used to describe the same mathematical operator.

Look at the list in Table 1.1 which summarizes some of the most common alternative words or expressions.

Table 1.1

Addition (+)	Subtraction (−)	Multiplication (×)	Division (÷)
Adding	Taking away	Times	Share
Adding-up	Minus	Product	Apportion
Summing (shown by Σ)	Deduction		Attribute
Summation	Take-off		Allocate
Totalling	Less		
Accumulating			

---

[1] Consider for example when a pedestrian chooses to cross a road. The pedestrian will be unaware that their decision to cross will be determined by their brain's continuous assessment of risk, taking into the likelihood of being hit by a vehicle against the need to cross the road and make good progress with their journey. It is only once these two factors have been balanced out that the pedestrian crosses the road.

Note that multiplication can also be denoted by a '·', i.e. $a \cdot b$, and simply as ab. These are equivalent to $a \times b$

Multiplication and division are closely linked: you can divide by multiplying by the reciprocal. Put another way:

$$a/b = a \times (1/b) = (1/b) \times (a/1)$$

Example:
You are asked to divide 7 by $^1/_4$. This could be solved by either:

$7/1 \div {}^1/_4$ or,

$7/1 \times 1/4$

Quick problem 1 gives you an opportunity to practise using the four operators.

Quick problem 1

Using your knowledge and understanding of the four operators complete each line by filling in the missing item(s) in Table 1.2. The first line has been done for you

✔ **Learning outcome 1**

Table 1.2

Figure	Operator (+, −, ×, ÷)	Figure	Equals	Answer
5	×	31	=	155
	+	17	=	125
	÷	57.5	=	230
−4	−		=	−10
13	÷	2	=	
16		5	=	80
	÷	4	=	169
169	+		=	150
346	÷		=	173
567		383	=	

Although the four arithmetic operators are basic mathematical tools, it is because they are so fundamental that you need to be able to use them with confidence and fluency. Simple calculations involving addition, subtraction, multiplication and division are the foundations of higher and more advanced calculations. Look at the table in the student note below to get a feel for the types of simple business calculations that you might encounter.

Many business and economics problems can be simply and routinely solved using the four arithmetic operators. The quadrants below provide brief lists of typical day-to-day calculations.

Addition	**Subtraction**
Adding the incomes of a husband and wife to calculate their joint household income.	Subtracting tax and National Insurance payments from a worker's salary to calculate their net income.
Adding together the spending of government departments to calculate total government spending.	Subtracting inflation from a pay rise to calculate the value of the real pay award.
Summing the tax payments of all workers in an economy to calculate the tax revenue which a government receives over a period of time.	Taking away the amount of money paid by a customer to a supplier to arrive at the final amount outstanding.
Multiplication	**Division**
Calculating the revenue a firm receives from the sales of a particular product by multiplying the price of the product by the quantity sold.	Calculating a salaried worker's hourly wage by dividing their total annual salary by the number of hours worked in a year.
Calculating the tax liability of a corporation by multiplying the taxable profits by the tax rate.	Calculating a company's solvency by dividing current assets by current liabilities.
Calculating a worker's daily wage by multiplying their hourly wage rate by the number of hours worked.	Calculating the dividend per share by dividing total profits by the number of shares in circulation.

1.3 Fractions

Fractions are a simple but powerful concept which can be used to express numbers as parts or elements of another number. For example the fraction '$1/4$' literally means 'one out of four identically sized parts'. In effect, the middle line which divides the top number from the bottom represents a division.

Fractions are usually expressed as 'proper fractions' with the top number (or numerator) smaller than the number underneath (or denominator). For example, $1/4$, $1/2$ and $3/4$ are all proper fractions. Sometimes, though, fractions are written or expressed in a way that can look a little odd: the numerator can be larger than the denominator. Fractions which are represented in this way are called 'improper fractions'. e.g. $7/3$ or $9/16$.

We see fractions in our everyday lives although we may not consciously register this. Look at the following examples of common fractions we encounter.

- England were widely quoted by bookmakers at 7/1 to win the World Cup in 2006.
- The Bank of England has been lobbied by business leaders to cut interest rates by at least $^1/_2$ per cent at the next meeting of the Monetary Policy Committee.
- Of all of the respondents in a large US based survey in December 2006 who said that they do not use debit cards, close to one fourth cited concerns about fraud or identity theft.[2]
- In 2006, the BBC reported that, 'One third of China is suffering from acid rain caused by rapid industrial growth.'[3]
- A poll of 461 children by ChildLine in 2006 revealed the single most popular pledge children picked for their parents in 2007 was for them to give up smoking, with one in six 11-year-olds having it top of their wish list.

Where else have you seen fractions quoted?

Fractions are usually stated in their lowest common form. This means, that where it is possible, it is often preferable to reduce a fraction using the lowest and simplest numbers we can. For example, it is easier to see that 214/428 is really $^1/_2$. This requires looking for common denominators. Common denominators are numbers which can be used to divide both the denominator and numerator. In the example above, the common denominator was 2.

Look at examples below which show how fractions can be re-expressed using the highest common denominator.

Examples

Fraction	Highest common denominator	Re-expression
12/15	3	4/5
20/60	20	1/3
23/69	23	1/3
44/176	44	1/4
102/119	17	6/7
11/121	11	1/11
42/147	21	2/7

[2] Source: Mintel.
[3] Source: BBC.

Quick problem 2

Test your understanding of fractions and how they can be re-expressed using Table 1.3. Which fraction in the left-hand column can be matched with which re-expression in the right-hand column? Copy Table 1.3 and draw a line to match the two.

Table 1.3

Fraction	Re-expression
20/80	1/8
7/56	1/4
14/98	1/21
26/65	1
4/84	1/7
5/165	3/8
12/12	3/2
21/56	1/33
369/246	2/5

✔ **Learning outcome 2**

Fractions can be particularly useful when we are trying to measure the likelihood or probability of an event occurring. Economists use probability to try and make reasoned judgements on what might happen in the future. For example, an investment company will want to look at the probability of stocks and shares rising and then, on the basis of that assessment, make a careful decision on how they should invest. In effect, these firms are gambling using mathematical models to assess probabilities or likelihoods. If their judgements are proved correct their dividend or payout can be millions of dollars.

We can illustrate this idea of assessing and expressing likelihood or probability by using a simple fairground game.

Quick problem 3

The owner of a large fairground is considering whether to introduce a new game. The game is essentially a variation of darts. The board is made of 12 identically sized triangles (see Figure 1.1) with each individual triangle being right-angled and with a base of 10 cm and a height of 6 cm.

Task One
Calculate the total area (in cm²) of:

(a) All of the black triangles

(b) The area of the board.

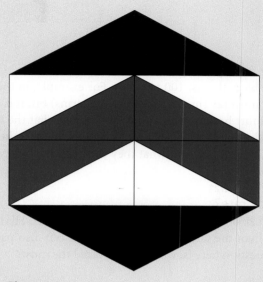

Remember that the area (A) of a right-angled triangle is calculated by multiplying half of the height (H) by the base (B).

Or,

$A = \frac{1}{2}BH$

Figure 1.1

Task Two
(a) What fraction of the board is while?
(b) What fraction of the board is green and black?

Task Three
If the game owner decides that anyone who hits a green area is a winner what is the chance that someone who chooses to play will be a winner on their first throw?

Task Four (extension task)
(a) In pairs use the Internet to research where fractions are used to describe an economic or business issue. You might find a simple search such as 'economics fractions' will be productive.
(b) Summarize your research in a simple mindmap or spider diagram. You might want to use 'Freemind' a free web-based mind mapping utility available at http://prdownloads. sourceforge.net/freemind/FreeMind-Windows-Installer-0_8_0.exe?download

✔ **Learning outcomes 2 and 3**

1.4 Percentages

A percentage is a simple but powerful concept which is closely linked to fractions. Put simply, a percentage simply allows a part or a proportion to be expressed as a fraction of 100. In its simplest form a percentage is calculated as:

Percentage calculation $= \alpha/\beta \times 100\%$

where:

α is the numerator

β is the denominator.

One strength of using percentages is that proportions and fractions can be easily compared because they are converted to the same base, that is, 100 per cent. For example, in the simple example below we can see who pays the most tax (in crude or absolute terms) but it is not easy to see which person is being *taxed* the most because we cannot easily infer what the different tax proportions are. Put another way, using a percentage allows us to see who faces the highest percentage or incidence of taxation, taking into account what they earn and what they have to pay to the government as tax.

Example: Who faces the highest tax rate?

A farm worker earns a modest salary of £20 000 per year and he pays £6000 in tax. His boss, the farm owner, earns considerably more than the farm worker at £150 000 but also pays more money in tax at £40 000 per year. The question here is, who is being taxed the most?

Tax rate (%) = (Tax paid/income) × 100%

Farm worker tax rate = £6000/£20 000 × 100% = 30%

Farm owner tax rate = (£40 000/£150 000) × 100% = 26.7%

Conclusion

The fact that the farm owner pays more tax in terms of pounds sterling (£) is more than offset by the fact that he earns considerably more than his farm worker. In effect, the percentage calculation translates the salaries into a common base of 100 and then expresses the tax paid as a proportion of the base. Because we have a common base – the figure of 100 – we can compare the tax paid on a like-for-like basis. In this case, the farm owner pays more 'tax pounds' but taking into account their salaries, we can see he is actually taxed at a lower rate for each pound earned than his farm worker. This concept is linked to ideas of 'average rate of taxation' and 'marginal rate of taxation'.

Percentages are very useful when looking at the rate of taxation which individuals and businesses face. The average rate of taxation simply describes how much total tax is paid as a percentage of total income.

The marginal rate of taxation is a more meaningful measure because it looks at how much tax would be paid if a person or firm earned an additional £1 (as salary or revenue). It is often argued that a high rate of marginal rate of tax can dissuade people from working hard because a relatively high proportion of the extra (or marginal) income they earn will go straight to the government in the form of tax.

You could explore this idea by researching these related topics:

- Average rate of taxation
- Marginal rate of taxation
- The Laffer curve (which hypothesises a link between the tax rate, the effect on workers' productivity and the government's tax revenue).

Student note

We have seen that simple percentages make it easier for us to make assessments or inferences about fractions and proportions. They can also be very useful when looking at rates of change: how one variable changes in response to another.

Look at Figure 1.2 which summarizes data which an economist has collated on five countries. Her research covers two specific time periods: 1995 and 2005.

Data for 1995

	Unemployment (millions)	Inflation (% per annum)	Population (millions)	GDP (£ billions)
Country A	5	1	125	2125
Country B	3	3	100	1250
Country C	2	2	57	1311
Country D	13	4	250	5000
Country E	6	1	165	2640

Data for 2005

	Unemployment (millions)	Inflation (% per annum)	Population (millions)	GDP (£ billions)
Country A	4	2	130	2125
Country B	3	4	190	1250
Country C	3	1	59	1311
Country D	12	6	234	5000
Country E	8	3	176	2640

Figure 1.2 Summary of economic data

This data might be useful but at the moment it is very difficult to draw any meaningful conclusions. For example, we cannot easily tell which country has the highest unemployment rate or how the unemployment rate has changed over the time period. Nor can we judge how the size of each economy (as measured by gross domestic product or GDP) has moved over time. To do this we need to apply percentages and percentage changes.

Student note

A percentage change measures the absolute change that has occurred and then divides this by the original number. This gives a single measurement on how big the difference is relative to the original figure.

We can express this use a simple mathematical expression:

Percentage change $= [(P_1 - P_0)/P_0] \times 100\%$

where:

$P_1 =$ the new figure
$P_0 =$ the original figure
$(P_1 - P_0) =$ the change or difference.

Example

Using Figure 1.2, we can calculate the percentage change in unemployment for Country A.

$P_0 = 5$ million
$P_1 = 4$ million

$$\begin{aligned} \text{Percentage change} &= [(4 - 5)/5] \times 100\% \\ &= -1/5 \times 100\% \\ &= -20\% \end{aligned}$$

Conclusion
Unemployment has fallen in country A by 20 per cent over the period 1995 to 2005.

This calculation does not measure the change in the unemployment *rate*. To do this we need to take account of the size of the population.

Unemployment rate (%) $=$ [Unemployment/population] $\times 100\%$

Country A:

Unemployment rate in 1995 $= [5/125] \times 100\% = 4\%$
Unemployment rate in 2005 $= [4/130] \times 100\% = 3.1\%$

The unemployment rate has fallen from 4% in 1995 to 3.1% in 2005.

Student note

A rate of percentage change can provide some insights into how business and economic variables such as unemployment, inflation, sales revenues or exchange rates are changing over time.

They can be calculated simply by looking at how percentage changes have themselves moved over time. Look back at the above example to see how this can give a slightly different picture of how business and economic conditions might be changing.

Rates of change can also be expressed using differentials where rates of increase are shown by positive figures and, conversely, rates of decrease are negative numbers. This is explored in Chapter 8, 'Partial differentiation'.

Quick problem 4

You will need to refer to Figure 1.2.

Task One

(a) Which country experienced the biggest positive change in unemployment?

(b) What was the percentage change?

Task Two
Which country had the biggest unemployment rate (unemployment as a proportion of the total population) in 1995 and what was the figure?

Task Three
Look at the GDP for country E. If the percentage change in GDP over 1995 to 2005 was 7 per cent, what was GDP in 2005?

Task Four
Why are percentage changes sometimes more useful than a simple percentage?

✔ **Learning outcome 4**

The base figure

The figure '4' is the power, index or 'replicator'

Figure 1.3

1.5 Powers

A power describes how many times the base figure should be multiplied by itself as illustrated in Figure 1.3.

Thus,

$$3^4 = 3 \times 3 \times 3 \times 3$$

$$\alpha^4 = \alpha \times \alpha \times \alpha \times \alpha$$

Using powers in business and economics is a time-saving tool which allows mathematical relationships to be expressed in a convenient shorthand. Powers are widely used in a range of business and economics contexts including:

- Calculating compounded figures such as interest payments on a mortgage
- Working out areas or volumes, e.g. the volume of a sphere is measured by $4/3 \ \Pi r^3$ when r in the radium
- Estimating the expected return from an investment project (net present values)
- Calculating the value of a pension in times of high and sustained inflation.

Student note

If you are using powers you need to understand a few rules about how they work.

Rule 1: The meaning of replication

$$\alpha^n = \alpha_1 \times \alpha_2 \times \alpha_3 \times \ldots \alpha_n$$

Rule 2: The negative power rule

$$\beta^{-n} = 1/\beta^n$$

Notice that a 'negative power' means, in effect, the reciprocal but with the negative sign removed. So:

$$2^{-3} = 1/2^3 = 1/[2 \times 2 \times 2] = 1/8$$

Quick problem 5

Task One

Work out the following expressions using simple powers:

Expression	Answer
3^3	
5^3	
6^4	
6^6	
7^3	
11^3	
4.5^3	
2.2^2	
$4.4^{4.4}$	

Task Two

Using your knowledge of powers copy and complete Table 1.4.

Table 1.4

	Tick one of the columns	
Expression	True (✔)	False (✔)
$2^2 = 4$		
$2^2 = -4$		
$3^3 = 9$		
$3^4 = 18$		
$3^{-2} = 1/9$		
$4^{-2} = 1/16$		
$10^2 = 4.641\ 588\ 8^3$		
$9^2 = 4^3$		
$12^3 = 36$		
$8^3 = 2^9 = 2 \times 16^2$		
$6561 = 81^{-2}$		
$4^{-2} = 16^{-1}$		
$12^{-3} = 2^{-2} \times 432^{-1}$		

✔ **Learning outcome 5**

Rule 3: The logarithmic rule

We will look at logarithms in more detail below. You will need to know:

If

$$\alpha^{\beta} = \gamma,$$

then

$$\beta \times \ln \alpha = \ln \gamma$$

Where ln α is the natural logarithm of α.

You can check this using the following:

We can see that $3^4 = 3 \times 3 \times 3 \times 3 = 81$

If rule 3 is correct we should expect that: $4 \times \ln 3 = \ln 81$

First, $4 \times \ln 3 = 4.39$

Then, $\ln 81 = 4.39$ check

Rule 4: Powers and roots

A root can be seen as the opposite of a power.

The third root of 216 tells us 'Which number when multiplied by itself three times equals 216'. In this case the third root of 216 is 6 (check that $6 \times 6 \times 6 = 216$).

We can show this using the root sign $\sqrt{}$ and inserting n to show the root. For example, the third root of 216 would be shown as:

$$\sqrt[3]{216} = 6$$

We can check this since 6^3 should be equal to 216.

So, if

$$\alpha^{\beta} = \gamma$$

then

$$\sqrt[\beta]{\gamma} = \alpha$$

A common use of powers is to articulate how the output (Q) of a firm is related to the amounts of labour (L) and capital (K) it uses. This expression is known as a production function and is typically shown in the form:

$$Q = f(K, L)$$

Using powers we can sometimes describe the production function as follows:

$$Q = K^{\alpha} L^{\beta}$$

where α and β are powers which we believe to explain how amounts of labour and capital shape or determine the total output which a firm produces. A 'special case', called the Cobb-Douglas production, is sometimes described in textbooks.

Making sense of powers using the Cobb-Douglas production function

The Cobb-Douglas production function is specified as:

$$Q = K^{\alpha} L^{\beta}$$

where $\alpha = (1 - \beta)$.

This particular specification means that:

- Holding L constant, each extra unit of capital (K) we use will increase output (Q) by K^{α} units
- Holding K constant, each extra unit of labour (L) we use will increase output (Q) by L^{β} units
- If you add or sum the two powers together they come to 1 (since $\alpha + \beta = (1 - \beta) + \beta = 1$)

Quick problem 6

Task One

You are told that a company manufacturing cars has the following production function: $Q = K^{\alpha}$. The factory uses only robots so there is no labour (L).

Using this formula, copy and complete Table 1.5.

Table 1.5

	α	Q		α	Q		α	Q
$K = 5$	0	1	$K = -1$	0	+1	$K = 0.1$	0	1
	1			1			1	
	2			2			2	
	3	125		3			4	0.0001
	4			4				
	5			5				
	6			6	+1			

Task Two

The car company has employed a team of consultants to advise on whether it has specified the production function correctly. The team have considered four possible production functions:

(i) $Q = K^{\alpha}$

(ii) $3Q = 4K^{\alpha}$

(iii) $3K = 2Q^{\alpha}$

(iv) $3\alpha^2 = Q/K$

The team need to rearrange these functions to make α the subject in each case.

✔ **Learning outcome 6**

1.6 Logarithms

Logarithms are a useful mathematical tool and are closely related to powers (see section 1.5). Logarithms are particularly useful when analysing rates of change and growth. The spider diagram in Figure 1.4 gives some examples of how business and economics issues can be analysed using logarithms.

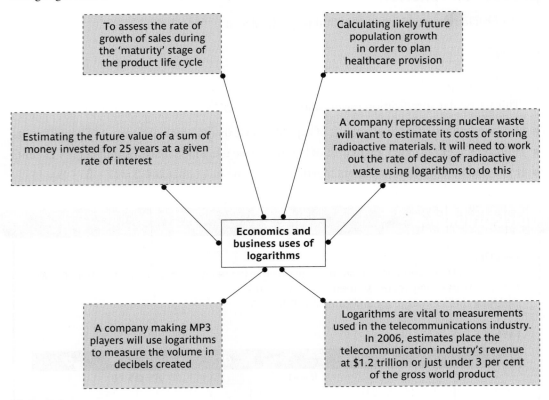

Figure 1.4

Logarithms follow four basic rules. We use the notation **ln** which is based on natural logarithms or log to the base e:

$\ln(ab) = \ln a + \ln b$

$\ln(a/b) = \ln a - \ln b$

$\ln a^b = b \times \ln a$

$\ln e = 1$

where e is a natural constant as 2.718.

Student note

Quick problem 7

An economist is researching the link between unemployment (in thousands) and inflation (percentage per annum) and collates the following data.

Inflation (% per year) I	Unemployment (thousands of people) U
5	22.4
8	45.3
12	83.1
14	104.8
20	178.9
30	328.6

(i)   Graph this data using graph paper or a spreadsheet package.

(ii) Show that the economist is correct to believe that the function is $U = a \times I^b$.

(iii) Can you use your graph to estimate the values of a and b?

(iv) Using the logarithmic rules, solve the following logarithmic equations:
   (a) $3^x = 5$
   (b) $3^{x+1} = 120$
   (c) $7^{x+1} = 2^{3-x}$

✔ **Learning outcome 7**

1.7 Basic rules of algebra

The term 'algebra' can be quite off-putting: it is not obvious what is being referred to, what it means or even what the context might be. Algebra is a simple mathematical tool and much of its power and usefulness lies in the fact that it is straightforward. In many ways, algebra is really a language; a way of expressing ideas in a universal shorthand which everybody can understand regardless of their culture, ethnicity or mother tongue: we can all understand what is being said without the need for a translator!

Sometimes algebra can seem quite abstract or lofty; something which concerns academics or mathematicians rather than people involved in business or everyday work. This perception is explicable but completely false. The principles of algebra and mathematical expression under-pin virtually every facet of our lives including:

- Air traffic control computers calculating arrival times and distances of aeroplanes
- Pit stop strategy for Formula 1 cars
- Working out the best time to sell a second-hand car
- Deciding when to reorder stock and how much, e.g. a bakery ordering flour using just-in-time production
- Estimating how much money a water company loses through leaky pipes

- Trying to work out for how long you should fix your mortgage rate before switching to a variable rate product
- Working out how much it will cost to transport fruit (how many spherical oranges can be packed into a cuboid lorry?)
- Creating realistic forecasts of costs and revenue to arrive at break-even points.

Student note

Algebra is really about translating numbers into letters or expressions. Once we have learnt the rules of algebra we can change, manipulate and solve these expressions and draw conclusions about a business or economic issue.

The basic rules are summarized below.

Rule 1: Addition and subtraction
    If

$$\alpha + \beta = \gamma$$

then

$$\alpha = \gamma - \beta$$

or

$$\beta = \gamma - \alpha$$

Rule 2: Multiplication and division
    If

$$\alpha\beta = \gamma$$

then

$$\alpha = \gamma/\beta$$

or

$$\beta = \gamma/\alpha$$

Rule 3: Powers (see above)
(i) $\beta^{-n} = 1/\beta^n$
(ii) If

$$\alpha^\beta = \gamma$$

then

$\beta \times \ln \alpha = \ln \gamma$

where $\ln \alpha$ is the natural logarithm of α.

(iii) If

$\alpha^{\beta} = \gamma$

then

$\sqrt[\beta]{\gamma} = \alpha$

Examples

An international space agency is planning to land a robot on Mars. The scientists produce a simple map of Mars and identify three zones upon which the robot could successfully land (Figure 1.5).

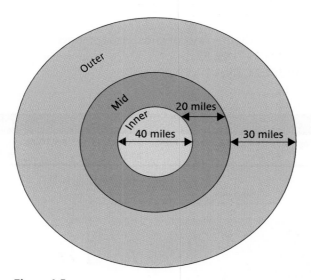

Figure 1.5

The zones are drawn as concentric circles (using the same middle point of the circle). The width of the outer zone is 30 miles, the next (mid) zone 20 miles and the inner zone has a diameter of 40 miles.

The scientists decide they need to:

(i)   Calculate the area of each zone

(ii)   Work out the percentage of each zone as a proportion of the total area

(iii) The scientists look at another area based on four identical "inner zone" circles from Figure 1.5. Calculate the area around the circles in Figure 1.6.

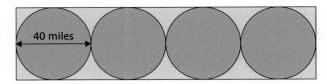

Figure 1.6

Calculation

(i)   Let A denote the area of a circle, and *r* denote the radius of a circle.
      Then

$$A = \Pi r^2$$

Area of whole = $\Pi \times 70^2$ = 15 393.8 miles^2

Area of mid and inner = $\Pi \times 40^2$ = 5026.55 miles^2

Area of inner = $\Pi \times 20^2$ = 1256.64 miles^2

Area of mid = Area of mid and inner − Area of inner
              = 5026.55 − 1256.64
              = 3769.91 miles^2

Area of outer = Area of whole − Area of mid − Area of inner
              = 15 393.8 − 5026.55
              = 10 367.25 miles^2

(ii)   **Table 1.6**

	Red	Yellow	Blue
Area as percentage of total	10 367.25/15 393.8 × 100% **67.3%**	3769.91/15 393.8 × 100% **24.5%**	1256.64/15 393.8 × 100% **8.2%**

(iii)

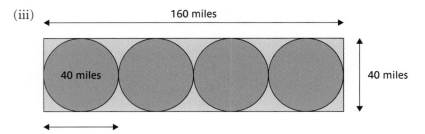

Figure 1.7

Area of rectangle = base × height = 160 × 40 = 6400 miles^2

Area of circles = $4\Pi r^2$

Area around the circles = 6400 − ($4 \times \Pi \times 20^2$) = 6400 − 5026.55 = 1373.45 miles^2

End of examples

You can see from these examples that algebra is useful because of the simplicity it provides for mathematical expression. We can easily reorder expressions such as the one needed to calculate the pink area and we only have to introduce the actual figures until the very end.

Quick problem 8

Task One

We are told that Claire's income is determined by three separate activities: her salary of £35 000, her part-time babysitting for which she charges £8.00 per hour and the small income she receives from the government as a grant for her child. The grant is worth £5000 per year.

Create a simple algebraic formula which could be used to calculate her total annual income.

Task Two

Graph the income for Claire using graph paper or spreadsheet software.

Task Three

Claire's total income is taxed at 22 per cent. Write a simple algebraic expression for her post-tax income.

Task Four

(a) Claire is delighted to be told she will receive a salary rise of 5 per cent next year. What will her post-tax income formula be now?

(b) If Claire is told she will receive a 5 per cent salary rise every year for h years, what will the new formula for her post-tax income be?

✔ **Learning outcome 8**

Answers to quick problems

Quick problem 1

Table 1.7

Figure	Operator (+, −, ×, ÷)	Figure	Equals	Answer
5	×	31	=	155
108	+	17	=	125
13 225	÷	57.5	=	230
−4	−	6	=	−10
13	÷	2	=	**6.5**
16	×	5	=	80
676	÷	4	=	169
169	+	**−19**	=	150
346	÷	2	=	173
567	+	383	=	**950**

Quick problem 2

Table 1.8

Fraction	Re-expression
20/80	1/8
7/56	1/4
14/98	1/21
26/65	1
4/84	1/7
5/165	3/8
12/12	3/2
21/56	1/33
369/246	2/5

Quick problem 3

Task One

(a)   120 cm^2

(b)   360 cm^2

Task Two

(a)   1/3

(b)   2/3

Task Three

1/3

Quick problem 4

Task One

(a) Country C.

(b) 50 per cent increase in unemployment.

Task Two
Country D with 5.2 per cent.

Task Three
GDP is £2824.8 million.

Task Four
A percentage change allows us to see how a fraction or proportion has moved over time. This can be useful when looking at economic variables such as unemployment rate or inflation when we are interested in just the absolute or exact figure but rather how it has moved. Without this sense of movement or change it can be difficult to make a judgement or inference on what is really going on. For example, an inflation figure of 12 per cent per year might look quite high but if in previous years inflation had been 30 per cent or more then we can see that the percentage fall has been significant and that it could be on a downward trend.

Quick problem 5

Task One

Expression	Answer
3^3	27
5^3	125
6^4	1 296
6^6	46 656
7^3	343
11^3	1331
4.5^3	91.13
2.2^2	4.84
$4.4^{4.4}$	677.94

Task Two

Expression	Tick one of the columns	
	True ($\checkmark$)	False ($\checkmark$)
$2^2 = 4$	$\checkmark$	
$2^2 = -4$		$\checkmark$
$3^3 = 9$		$\checkmark$
$3^4 = 18$		$\checkmark$
$3^{-2} = 1/9$	$\checkmark$	
$4^{-2} = 1/16$	$\checkmark$	
$10^2 = 4.641\ 588\ 8^3$	$\checkmark$	
$9^2 = 4^3$		$\checkmark$
$12^3 = 36$		$\checkmark$
$8^3 = 2^9 = 2 \times 16^2$	$\checkmark$	
$6561 = 81^{-2}$		$\checkmark$
$4^{-2} = 16^{-1}$	$\checkmark$	

Quick problem 6

Task One

Table 1.9

	α	Q		α	Q		α	Q
$K = 5$	0	1	$K = -1$	0	+1	$K = 0.1$	0	1
	1	5		1	−1		1	0.1
	2	25		2	+1		2	0.01
	3	125		3	−1		4	0.0001
	4	625		4	+1			
	5	3125		5	−1			
	6	15 625		6	+1			

Task Two

(i) $\alpha = \ln Q / \ln K$

(ii) $\alpha = \ln 3Q / \ln 4K$

(iii) $\alpha = \ln 3K / \ln 2Q$

(iv) $\alpha = \sqrt{(Q/3K)}$

Quick problem 7

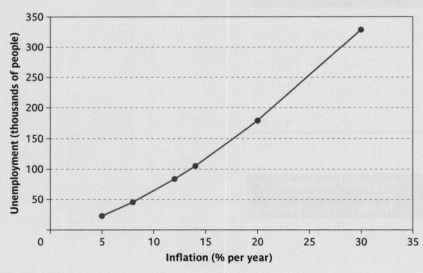

Figure 1.8

(iii) $a = 2, b = 1.5$

(iv) (a) $x = 1.465$
     (b) $x = 3.358$
     (c) $x = 0.05$

Quick problem 8

Task One

Let:

Y = Claire's total annual income

S = Claire's annual salary

B = Claire's income from babysitting

G = Claire's government grant

n = the number of hours Claire babysits in a year

Then:

$Y = S + B + G$

$Y = £35\ 000 + 8n + £5000$

$Y = £40\ 000 + 8n$, or

$Y = 8(£5000 + n)$

Task Two

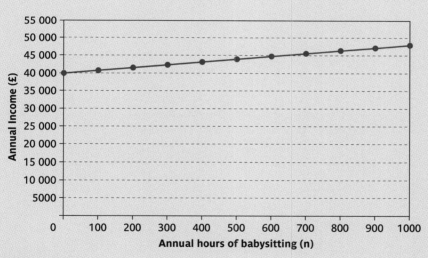

Figure 1.9

Task Three

$Y = 0.78(40\ 000 + 8n)$

$Y = 31\ 200 + 6.24n$

Task Four

(a) $Y = (1.05 \times 31\ 200) + 6.24n$

   $Y = 32\ 760 + 6.24n$

(b) $Y = (31\ 200 \times 1.05^h) + 6.24n$

Chapter 2

Linear equations

Topics covered

2.1 Introduction   28
2.2 Co-ordinates   28
2.3 Linear form   29
2.4 Equation of a line   34
2.5 Intersection   38
2.6 Applications of linear equations in economics   44

LEARNING OUTCOMES

By the end of this chapter, you should understand:

1. What co-ordinates are and how they are plotted on a graph

2. How co-ordinates are used to plot a linear equation

3. The general form of a linear equation

4. How to derive the equation of a line using given co-ordinates

5. How to sketch a linear equation using a given equation of a line

6. How to find the intersection point of two lines using four different equilibrium methods

7. How the derivation and graphing of linear equations can be applied to economic and business issues.

2.1 Introduction

Many key economic concepts can be analysed by considering the relationship between variables. What, for example, is the relationship between the quantity of a good consumers are willing to purchase and the price? This is a demand relationship. How much will suppliers offer for sale as price varies? This is a supply relationship. How do consumers distribute their expenditure between different goods when the level of income is constrained by the family budget? What happens to firms' costs of production as output is increased, and what happens to their revenue? What conclusions can we then draw about the relationship of firms' output to their profits?

We can gain insights into all of these and many other economic relationships through an understanding of *linear equations*, the subject matter of this chapter.

2.2 Co-ordinates

The two straight lines shown in Figure 2.1 (in bold) are referred to as '**axes**'. The vertical line is the y axis and the horizontal line is the x axis. The point at which these two lines intersect is known as the **origin**. Values can be assigned to the x and y axes as illustrated in Figure 2.1.

Note that the positive x values are on the horizontal axis to the right of the origin and the negative x values are on the horizontal axis to the left of the origin. Note also that the positive y values are on the vertical axis above the origin and the negative y values are on the vertical axis below the origin.

The intersection of the two lines creates four quadrants as illustrated in Figure 2.1. A point in any of these quadrants is made up of two values, an x value and a y value with the co-ordinates

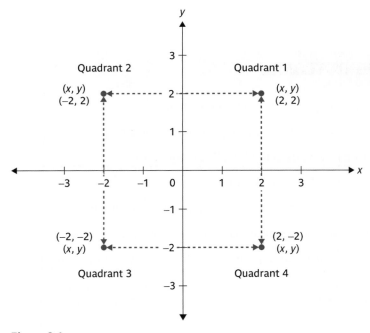

Figure 2.1

of a given point being expressed as (x, y). Depending on the location of the point the x and y values will either be positive or negative. Note that in Figure 2.1 a point has been added to each quadrant. The different combinations are as follows:

(2, 2): quadrant 1

(−2, 2): quadrant 2

(−2, −2): quadrant 3

(2, −2): quadrant 4.

Consider the point (−2, 2) in Figure 2.1. The first value in the brackets is the x value which indicates that the point will be located either directly above or below the value of −2 on the x axis. The second figure in the bracket is the y value which indicates that the point will be located in the positive section of the y axis at a value of 2. It is therefore easy to plot the point by locating the position on the graph that is in line with $x = -2$ and $y = 2$.

Student note

Quick problem 1

On a set of x and y axes plot the following points:

(1, 6), (−2, −7), (−4, 5), (6, −4), (3, 8)

✔ **Learning outcome 1**

2.3 Linear form

Linear form describes the most simple type of line that you will plot. When a group of co-ordinates are used to create a graph that is a straight line, the equation is said to be a linear equation.

A linear equation takes the form:

$$y = \mathrm{m}x + \mathrm{c}$$

where:

y = the dependent variable

x = the independent variable

c = the intercept: the value of y when $x = 0$. This is the point at which the line crosses the y axis

m = the slope (the steepness) of the line, also know as the gradient.

Since the value of x is chosen randomly, x is called an independent variable. However the value of y *depends* on the value of x, so y is called the dependent variable.

Student note

In mathematics we use x to represent our independent variable and we use y to represent our dependent variable. In this case x is measured on the horizontal axis and y is measured on the vertical axis. In economics this relationship is also shown through price (P) and quantity (Q) in the form of demand and supply equations where Q is usually measured on the horizontal axis and P is usually measured on the vertical axis. The linear equation showing the relationship between supply and demand is written as $P = aQ + b$. In this case:

P = the dependent variable, i.e., price is dependent on the quantity demanded/supplied

Q = the independent variable, i.e., different quantities chosen at random

b = the intercept: the value of P when $Q = 0$. This is the point at which the demand or supply curve crosses the price axis (the vertical axis)

a = the slope (the steepness) of the line.

Note that the above notation shows price (P) expressed in terms of quantity (Q). The demand and supply equations can also be written showing quantity (Q) expressed in terms of price (P). This is done by rearranging the equation (see Chapter 1, section 1.4 for explanation). In this case the general form of the equation will read $Q = (1/a)P - b$. Examples at the end of this chapter provide you with the opportunity to use both forms of the demand and supply equations.

These demand and supply equations are very basic in that they assume that supply and demand depend entirely on the price of the good that is demanded/supplied. More realistically, Q depends on various other factors including the price of alternative goods and consumer income. These more complicated equations will be considered later.

When sketching a line, select two or three values for the independent variable (x) and then calculate the value of the corresponding dependent variable (y). These co-ordinates will then enable you to sketch the straight line.

Example

For the linear equation $y = 3x + 2$, you can choose random values of x and then calculate the associated values of y. These x and y combinations give specific co-ordinates that can be plotted on a graph, as in Figure 2.1. For example:

When $x = 1$ $\Rightarrow$ $y = 3(1) + 2$ $\Rightarrow$ $y = 5$ $\Rightarrow$ $(x, y) = (1, 5)$

When $x = 2$ $\Rightarrow$ $y = 3(2) + 2$ $\Rightarrow$ $y = 8$ $\Rightarrow$ $(x, y) = (2, 8)$

When $x = 5$ $\Rightarrow$ $y = 3(5) + 2$ $\Rightarrow$ $y = 17$ $\Rightarrow$ $(x, y) = (5, 17)$

Each of these combinations give a pair of co-ordinates that represent one point on a graph. As each *y* value was calculated using a random *x* value and the same intercept (**b** = 2) and slope (**m** = 3), each set of co-ordinates represents a point on the same line. The three co-ordinates from the example above are (1, 5), (2, 8) and (5, 17). These points can now be plotted on a graph (Figure 2.2).

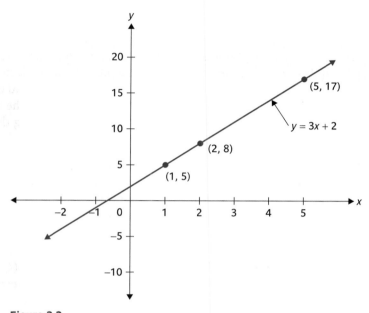

Figure 2.2

You only need to find two points for a given linear equation in order to be able to plot the graph. The straight line that you draw to connect the two points then includes all the different combinations of *x* and *y* values that are associated with that equation.

Student note

Example

Given the linear equation $y = 3x - 9$, find two sets of co-ordinates and graph the line:

When $x = 2$ $\Rightarrow$ $y = 3(2) - 9$ $\Rightarrow$ $y = -3$ $\Rightarrow$ $(x, y) = (2, -3)$

When $x = 5$ $\Rightarrow$ $y = 3(5) - 9$ $\Rightarrow$ $y = 6$ $\Rightarrow$ $(x, y) = (5, 6)$

By plotting these two points on a graph and joining the points with a straight line (Figure 2.3) you will have graphed the linear equation $y = 3x - 9$.

You are not restricted to selecting random values for x and then calculating the associated value of the dependent variable (y). You can also input values for y and then calculate the associated value for x.

It is often easiest to find the two co-ordinates on a line by setting each of x and y equal to zero and then working out the corresponding value of the other variable. For example, given the equation $y = 3x - 9$, instead of selecting two values for x and then calculating the corresponding value for y, you could instead do the following:

When $x = 0$ $\Rightarrow$ $y = 3(0) - 9$ $\Rightarrow$ $y = -9$ $\Rightarrow$ $(x, y) = (0, -9)$

When $y = 0$ $\Rightarrow$ $0 = 3x - 9$ $\Rightarrow$ $9 = 3x$ $\Rightarrow$ $x = 3$ $\Rightarrow$ $(x, y) = (3, 0)$

This has successfully given you two points on the line $y = 3x - 9$ which enables you to graph that line. It is interesting to note that when you use this technique you are finding the two points at which the line crosses the axes, i.e., if $y = -9$ when $x = 0$, it means that the line crosses the y axis (the vertical axis) at a value of $y = -9$. Likewise, if $x = 3$ when $y = 0$, it means that the line crosses the x axis (the horizontal axis) at a value of $x = 3$.

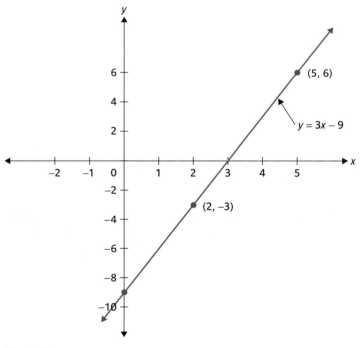

Figure 2.3

Example

Given the supply function $P = 6Q - 4$, find two sets of co-ordinates and graph the line.

When $Q = 2$ $\Rightarrow$ $P = 6(2) - 4$ $\Rightarrow$ $P = 8$ $\Rightarrow$ $(Q, P) = (2, 8)$

When $Q = 4$ $\Rightarrow$ $P = 6(4) - 4$ $\Rightarrow$ $P = 20$ $\Rightarrow$ $(Q, P) = (4, 20)$

When graphing a demand or supply equation you only need to consider the first quadrant of the graph (refer back to Figure 2.1). This is because quadrants 2, 3 and 4 all include a negative co-ordinate. As neither price nor quantity can be negative, the points and the demand/supply equations will only be drawn in that first quadrant. The graph therefore only shows the curve as it appears in quadrant 1. This is further illustrated in Figure 2.4.

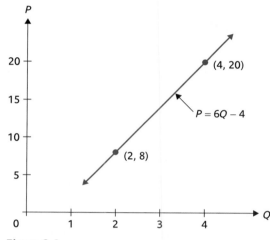

Figure 2.4

As price and quantity are measured in different units, the scales along the two axes do not need to be the same. You should label each of the axes in a way that can best represent the points that you want to plot.

Student note

Quick problem 2

Given the following linear equations, find two sets of co-ordinates associated with each line and graph the line:

$y = 4x - 8$

$y = -2x + 1$

$P = 4Q + 6$

$P = -2Q - 9$

✔ **Learning outcome 2**

2.4 Equation of a line

You can now plot a given linear equation by randomly selecting two x values and finding the associated y values. But what if you are instead given two sets of co-ordinates and want to use these to derive the equation of the line? You need to know how to calculate the slope (**m**) and the intercept (**c**) in order to derive the equation of the line that passes through the co-ordinates that you have been given.

Slope

The slope of the line is the coefficient associated with x; it is the change in the value of y resulting from a one-unit increase in the value of x. Referring back to the equation $y = 3x - 9$, we can calculate that when $x = 4$, $y = 3$. If we now increase the value of x by 1, to $x = 5$, then we can calculate that $y = 6$. The change in y as a result of a one-unit increase in x is $6 - 3 = 3$ which means that the slope is 3. This is confirmed by the fact that the coefficient of x in the equation is 3. The following shows you how to calculate the value of the slope if you have two sets of co-ordinates but do not yet know the equation of the line associated with these points.

First, it is useful to be familiar with the different types of slope that you might encounter. If **m** = 0 then the slope of the line is zero and the line will be horizontal. If **m** is positive (**m** > 0) then the slope of the line is positive and the line will be upward sloping. If **m** is negative (**m** < 0) then the slope is negative and the line will be downward sloping. Finally, a vertical line has a slope of infinity. In this case a vertical line would appear as $x = a$ (where a is a constant). Note that the equation of a vertical line does not involve y; x is equal to a for all values of y. Each of these scenarios is illustrated in Figure 2.5.

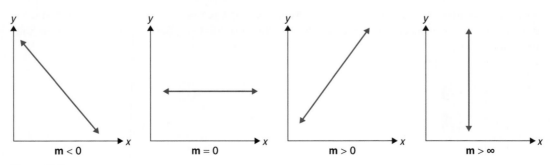

Figure 2.5

The value of the slope increases as the line rotates counter clockwise. For example, a downward sloping line has a negative slope. This slope becomes zero as the line becomes horizontal, and the slope becomes positive as the line rotates again and becomes upward sloping. The value of the slope continues to increase until the line becomes vertical at which stage the value of the slope is infinity.

Note, though, that the slope of any given linear equation (the slope at any point along the straight line) is fixed.

The slope is calculated by dividing the change in the value of y by the change in the value of x.

Equation

$$\frac{\text{Change in the value of } y}{\text{Change in the value of } x} = \frac{y_2 - y_1}{x_2 - x_1}$$ This shows the difference between your two y values divided by the difference between your two x values.

If you are given two sets of co-ordinates, (2, 3) and (1, 5), you need to label each set in order to correctly apply the slope formula. In this case the co-ordinates will be labelled as follows:

(0, 2)   and   (3, 4)
(x_1, y_1) (x_2, y_2)

This information can now be used to calculate the slope of your line:

$$\frac{y_2 - y_1}{x_2 - x_1}$$

It does not matter which co-ordinates are labelled x_1 and y_1 or x_2 and y_2 but you cannot have a value for x_1 and a value for y_2 in the same bracket. To calculate the slope correctly you must keep the associated x and y values together.

Example

Given the co-ordinates $(0, 2)$ and $(3, 4)$, find the slope of the line.

In this example $x_1 = 0$, $y_1 = 2$, $x_2 = 3$, and $y_2 = 4$.

Using the equation given above, the slope of the line is equal to:

$$(4 - 2)/(3 - 0) = 2/3.$$

The slope is positive which indicates that the line will be upward sloping.

You now have a value for the slope (**m**) and can write the linear equation as $y = 2/3x + c$. By substituting one set of co-ordinates from above into the equation you can calculate a value for the intercept (**c**). Note that you can use either $(0, 2)$ or $(3, 4)$.

Substituting $(3, 4)$ into $y = 2/3x + c$:

$$4 = 2/3(3) + c$$

$$4 = 2 + c$$

$$c = 2$$

Therefore the equation of the line passing through the points $(0, 2)$ and $(3, 4)$ is $y = 2/3x + 2$.

Student note

You can substitute any co-ordinates into the linear equation as long as they represent a specific point on the line. This can be confirmed by repeating the above calculation of the intercept (**c**) using point $(0, 2)$:

$$2 = 2/3(0) + c$$

$$2 = 0 + c$$

$$c = 2$$

Example

Find the equation of the line passing through the points $(2, 3)$ and $(1, 5)$.

In this example $x_1 = 2$, $y_1 = 3$, $x_2 = 1$, and $y_2 = 5$. Therefore the slope of the line is equal to:

$$(5 - 3)/(1 - 2) = 2/(-1) = -2.$$

The slope is negative which confirms that the line is downward sloping.

You now have a value for the slope (**m**) and can write the linear equation as $y = -2x + c$. By substituting one of your co-ordinates from above into the equation you can calculate a value for the intercept (**c**). Note that you can use either $(2, 3)$ or $(1, 5)$.

Substituting $(1, 5)$ into $y = -2x + c$:

$5 = -2(1) + c$

$5 = -2 + c$

$c = 7$

Therefore the equation of the line passing through the points $(2, 3)$ and $(1, 5)$ is $y = -2x + 7$.

Example

Looking specifically at price and quantity, if price is £5 per unit when quantity demanded is 20 units, and price is £7 per unit when quantity demanded is 34 units, find the equation for the demand curve.

If $P = 7$ when $Q = 20$, then one point on the demand curve is $(20, 7)$.

If $P = 5$ when $Q = 34$, then a second point on the demand curve is $(34, 5)$.

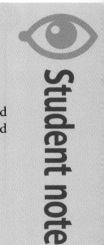

Notice that the value of quantity (Q) comes first in the brackets. This is because Q is measured on the horizontal axis. If, instead, price (P) was measured on the horizontal axis then you would write P as the first value in the bracket and Q as the second value.

Student note

Using the same technique as in the previous examples, you first need to find the slope of the demand curve and you can do this by using the slope equation. We will label our first set of co-ordinates Q_1 and P_1 and our second set of co-ordinates Q_2 and P_2.

$(20, 7)$ and $(34, 5)$

(Q_1, P_1) (Q_2, P_2)

The slope equation measures the difference in the y values (or the term measured on the vertical axis) divided by the difference in the x values (or the term measured on the horizontal axis). Thus in this example the slope equation would measure the difference in price divided by the difference in quantity. Written as an equation the slope can be calculated as:

$(5 - 7)/(34 - 20) = -2/14 = -0.14.$

In this example the slope is negative which indicates that the demand curve is downward sloping.

Using either pair of co-ordinates, (20, 7) or (34, 5), you can now calculate the value of the intercept by plugging a value for price and quantity into the demand equation:

$P = aQ + b$

$5 = -0.14(34) + b$

$5 = -4.76 + b$

$b = 9.76$

Therefore the demand equation that relates to the two points given above is:

$P = -0.14Q + 9.76.$

Quick problem 3

Find the equation of the line passing through each of the given sets of co-ordinates:

(a) (2, 4), (6, 8)

(b) (−1, 4), (3, 8)

(c) (−6, −3), (−2, 9)

(d) If quantity supplied is 10 units when price is £3 per unit, and quantity supplied is 15 units when price is £4 per unit, find the equation of the supply curve.

✔ **Learning outcomes 3, 4 and 5**

2.5 Intersection

In mathematics and economics we usually use two or more lines to illustrate or explain the relationship between different factors. If we can find the point at which these two lines intersect, then this gives us more information about the given situation.

The intersection between two lines is of fundamental importance in the understanding of economic theory. It shows the point at which the quantity demanded is exactly equal to the quantity supplied of a given product (Figure 2.6). Excess supply exists when the quantity supplied exceeds the quantity demanded at a given price, while excess demand exists when the quantity demanded exceeds the quantity supplied at a certain price. In cases where the market is self-correcting, prices will increase or decrease so as to move to a point of equilibrium.

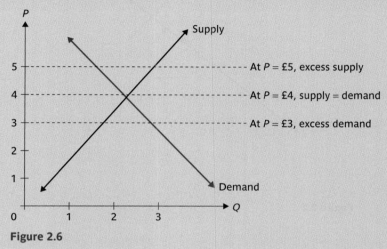

Figure 2.6

There are four methods for finding the intersection point between two linear equations. Each of these is demonstrated below. Ultimately it does not matter which method you use to find the equilibrium point (the point at which the two lines intersect) but it is useful to be practised in all methods as the different techniques are useful in applications presented in later chapters.

2.5.1 Graphically

Graphing your two lines will immediately give you a visual picture of the linear equations and provide you with some insight into the approximate intersection point. The main problem with this method is that it is not an efficient way to find an exact intersection point because the process occurs through trial and error; eventually you will hit on the combination of x and y values that fits both lines (the intersection point) but this may take a long time.

Example

Find the point of intersection of the following two linear equations:

(1) $y = 3x + 4$

(2) $y = -4x + 25$

(1) When $x = 1, y = 7$
     When $x = 2, y = 10$

(2) When $x = 1, y = 21$
     When $x = 2, y = 17$

The solution is (3, 13). See Figure 2.7.

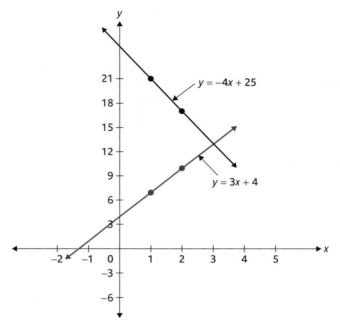

Figure 2.7

Note that graphing the two lines has not given you the exact co-ordinates of the point at which the two lines intersect but it has shown you approximately where that intersection point will be. You can then use trial and error to find the x and y values that fit both equations.

Example
Find the point of intersection of the following two linear equations:

(1) $y = 4x + 8$

(2) $y = 4x - 3$

(1) When $x = 1$, $y = 12$
     When $x = 2$, $y = 16$

(2) When $x = 1$, $y = 1$
     When $x = 2$, $y = 5$

See Figure 2.8.

The budget constraint equation takes the form $M = P_x X + P_y Y$ where:

M = total income or budget

P_x = the price of good X

P_y = the price of good Y

X = the quantity demanded of good X

Y = the quantity demanded of good Y.

The budget constraint shows a linear relationship between these factors and as such its graph is a straight line.

Student note

Example

A firm has a budget of £3000 to spend on the two goods X and Y. Good X costs £50 per unit and good Y costs £30 per unit. The budget constraint for this firm can be written as:

$3000 = 50X + 30Y$

$M = P_x X + P_y Y$

Graphing the budget constraint can be done by selecting different quantities of good X or Y and working out the associated quantity that would be demanded of the other good. For example: if the firm purchased 12 units of good X, how many units of good Y could they purchase given their budget of £3000:

$3000 = 50(12) + 30Y$

$3000 = 600 + 30Y$

$2400 = 30Y$

$Y = 80$

Therefore, if the firm purchased 12 units of good X then they would have enough of their budget left to also purchase 80 units of good Y.

In order to graph the equation it is useful to find the points at which the budget constraint intersects the X and Y axes. This can be done by working out how many units of good X would be purchased if the firm decided not to buy any units of good Y, and vice versa. For example: if the firm does not buy any units of good Y then on a budget of £3000:

$$3000 = 50X + 30(0)$$

$$3000 = 50X$$

$$X = 60$$

The firm can purchase 60 units of good X.

If the firms instead decides not to buy any units of good X then on a budget of £3000:

$$3000 = 50(0) + 30Y$$

$$3000 = 30Y$$

$$Y = 100$$

The firm can purchase 100 units of good Y.

Measuring good X on the horizontal axis and good Y on the vertical axis you can now draw the budget constraint (Figure 2.9).

Figure 2.9 shows that the firm can split the budget between goods X and Y. All the different combinations of X and Y that can be purchased with £3000 are shown by all the different points along the budget constraint.

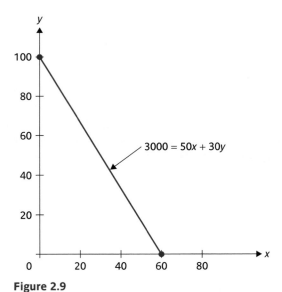

Figure 2.9

Remember that graphs that illustrate these simple economic concepts use only one quadrant rather than the four that are used when considering more general mathematical equations. This is because in economics we are looking at the relationship between two key variables which cannot be negative. As quadrants 2, 3 and 4 show one or both values to be negative, many examples in economics are shown only in the first quadrant where the values of both variables are positive.

Calculating the slope of the budget constraint

The equation for the slope of the budget constraint is:

$-P_x/P_y$

where P_x is the price of good X which is measured on the horizontal axis and P_y is the price of good Y which is measured on the vertical axis.

In the example, the price of good X is £50 per unit and the price of good Y is £30 per unit. Therefore the slope of the budget constraint is:

$-50/30 = -5/3$ or -1.67

The reason that the equation for the slope of the budget constraint is different from the equation for the slope of other linear equations is due to the form in which the equation is presented. Note that if you rearranged the terms in your budget equation so that the equation was presented in the form $y = \mathbf{m}x + \mathbf{c}$ you would find that the value of the slope ($\mathbf{m}$) is expressed as $-P_x/P_y$.

Example

$M = P_x X + P_y Y$

$P_y Y = M - P_x X$

$Y = M/P_y - P_x X/P_y \rightarrow M/P_y$ is the point at which the budget constraint crosses the Y axis (the value of Y when $X = 0$). Therefore M/P_y is the intercept ($\mathbf{c}$) as presented in our previous linear equation. $-P_x/P_y$ is the term associated with X which is always the slope ($\mathbf{m}$). Therefore the value of the slope in a budget constraint equation is always $-P_x/P_y$.

Quick problem 8

If a consumer has an income of £160 to spend on the two goods X and Y whose prices are £20 and £5 each, respectively:

(a) Determine the consumer's budget constraint.

(b) Calculate the slope of the consumer's budget constraint.

(c) Graph the consumer's budget constraint.

(d) Explain what happens to the slope of the consumer's budget constraint if P_y increases to £10 per unit. Show the new budget constraint on your graph.

(e) Explain what happens to the slope of the consumer's budget constraint if total income decreases to £100.

2.6.2 Supply and demand

Table 2.1

The Demand Curve	The Supply Curve
The demand curve shows the relation between price and quantity demanded, holding other things constant.	The supply curve shows the relation between price and quantity supplied, holding other things constant.

Source: Begg (2003: 28)

The demand and supply equations can be graphed using the information in Table 2.2. To plot the demand curve first identify the relevant co-ordinates, i.e., when price is 0.00, 200 bars of chocolate are demanded. Therefore the associated co-ordinate is (200, 0). Alternatively, when the price per bar is £0.10, 160 bars of chocolate are demanded giving a co-ordinate of (160, 0.10).

Supply co-ordinates are determined in the same way. Referring to Table 2.2, when price is £0.00, the quantity supplied is 0 giving a co-ordinate of (0, 0.00). When the price is £0.30, the quantity supplied is 80 giving a co-ordinate of (80, 0.30).

The full list of co-ordinates related to the demand and supply of chocolate bars at given prices can therefore be written as in Table 2.3. These co-ordinates can then be used to plot the demand and supply curves on a graph (Figure 2.10).

Table 2.2 The demand and supply for chocolate bars at different prices

Price (£/bar)	Demand (no. of bars)	Supply (no. of bars)
0.00	200	0
0.10	160	0
0.20	120	40
0.30	80	80
0.40	40	120
0.50	0	160

Table 2.3

Demand	Supply
(200, 0)	(0, 0.00)
(160, 0.10)	(0, 0.10)
(120, 0.20)	(40, 0.20)
(80, 0.30)	(80, 0.30)
(40, 0.40)	(120, 0.40)
(0, 0.50)	(160, 0.50)

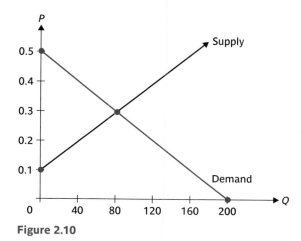

Figure 2.10

Deriving the demand and supply equations

Using any two of the co-ordinates related to the demand curve you can derive the associated demand equation for chocolate bars. Referring back to section 2.4 you know that the demand equation takes the form $P = aQ + b$. The two co-ordinates chosen randomly to derive the demand equation are:

(160, 0.10) and (40, 0.40).

(Q_1, P_1) (Q_2, P_2)

First, calculate the slope:

$(P_2 - P_1)/(Q_2 - Q_1)$

$(0.40 - 0.10)/(40 - 160) = 0.30/(-120) = -0.0025$

Which gives a linear equation of $P = -0.0025Q + b$

In order to find the intercept term **b** we again use one set of co-ordinates chosen at random:

$0.40 = -0.0025(40) + b$

$0.40 = -0.1 + b$

$b = 0.5$

Giving a demand equation of:

$P = -0.0025Q + 0.5$

If you plug any quantity into the above demand equation you will get the associated price. This price and quantity will represent one point along your demand curve.

  Similarly you can find the equation of the supply curve. Using any two of the co-ordinates related to the supply curve you can derive the associated supply equation for chocolate bars. Referring back to section 2.4 you know that the supply equation takes the form $P = aQ + b$. The two co-ordinates chosen randomly to illustrate this situation are:

$(80, 0.30)$ and $(160, 0.50)$
(Q_1, P_1) (Q_2, P_2)

First, calculate the slope of the equation:

$(P_2 - P_1)/(Q_2 - Q_1)$
$(0.50 - 0.30)/(160 - 80) = 0.20/80 = 0.0025$

This slope now gives you a supply function of $P = 0.0025Q + b$.

  Again, using one set of co-ordinates chosen at random you can calculate the value of the intercept (**b**).

$0.30 = 0.0025(80) + b$

$0.30 = 0.2 + b$

$b = 0.1 \rightarrow$ remember that this is the point at which the supply curve crosses the vertical axis. You can confirm that this is the case by referring to Figure 2.10.

  The supply function can therefore be written as:

$P = 0.0025Q + 0.1$

If you plug any quantity into the above supply function you will get the associated price. This price and quantity will represent one point along your supply curve.

Student note

Note in this case that the slope of the supply function has the same value as the slope of the demand function but the slope of the supply function is positive (showing that the supply curve is upward sloping) while the slope of the demand equation is negative (showing that the demand curve is downward sloping).

Finally, you need to find the equilibrium point – the values of P and Q at the point where the supply and demand curves intersect. You can do this using any of the four methods discussed previously. For the purposes of this example we will equate the equations:

$P = -0.0025Q + 0.5 \rightarrow$ demand equation

$P = 0.0025Q + 0.1 \rightarrow$ supply equation

$-0.0025Q + 0.5 = 0.0025Q + 0.1$

$-0.005Q = -0.40$

$Q = 80.$

Substituting $Q = 80$ into both the supply and demand equations gives a price of £0.30 which means that the demand and supply equations intersect at point (80, 0.30). This is the point at which there is no excess demand or supply; the quantity supplied is exactly equal to the quantity demanded.

As discussed previously, supply and demand are often expressed as a function of Q in terms of P (as opposed to a function of P in terms of Q as illustrated in this example). One form is simply the inverse of the other so you can easily rearrange your equations to express them in the form that you find most applicable to a given situation.

In the example above, the demand and supply curves were calculated from the data on chocolate bars and price is expressed as a function of quantity. If, instead, you wanted to have quantity expressed as a function of price you could rearrange the equations as follows:

$P = -0.0025Q + 0.5 \quad \rightarrow$ demand equation

$0.0025Q = -P + 0.5$

$Q = -400P + 200 \quad \rightarrow$ demand equation

$P = 0.0025Q + 0.1 \quad \rightarrow$ supply equation

$-0.0025Q = -P + 0.1$

$Q = 400P - 40 \quad \rightarrow$ supply equation

Student note

Quick problem 9

Supply and demand data for lamps are show in Table 2.4:

Table 2.4

Price (£/unit)	Demand (no. of units)	Supply (no. of units)
10	10	3
12	9	4
14	8	5
16	7	6
18	6	7
20	5	8

(a) Calculate the supply and demand equations for lamps.

(b) Provide a graphical representation of the supply and demand equations.

(c) Calculate the exact point at which these two lines intersect.

2.6.3 The demand function

It was mentioned in section 2.3 that a demand equation is not very realistic if it shows the quantity demand to be entirely dependent on the price of that good. It is more realistic to have a function that acknowledges that there are other factors that influence the amount that the consumer demands of a particular good. There are a number of factors that can be included but for the purposes of this example we will settle on two: the consumer's total income (Y) and the price of an alternative good (P'). The demand function for a particular good can then be presented as:

$$Q = f(P, Y, P')$$

This indicates that the quantity demanded depends on three different factors. The demand equation would therefore be written as:

$$Q = a + bP + cY + dP'$$

If the parameters **a**, **b**, **c** and **d** are all fixed then the equation could be presented as:

$$Q = 100 - 3P + 0.01Y + 0.4P'$$

If the consumer's total income (Y) was £1000 and the price of the alternative good (P') was £10 per unit:

$$Q = 100 - 3P + 10 + 4$$

$$Q = 114 - 3P$$

Note that when income and the price of the alternative good are fixed, then the demand equation is of the same form as those studied earlier in this chapter. Therefore the simplest form of a demand equation is the one in which all factors apart from the price of the good are fixed.

If any of the variables change this would alter the relationship between the quantity demanded and the price of the good. For example, if Y were to change from £1000 to £2000 while P' remained unchanged, the relationship between price and quantity would change to:

$$Q = 100 - 3P + 20 + 4$$

$$Q = 124 - 3P$$

This shows that a rise in income would cause more of the good to be demanded at any given price. Graphically this would cause the demand curve to shift out as illustrated in Figure 2.11.

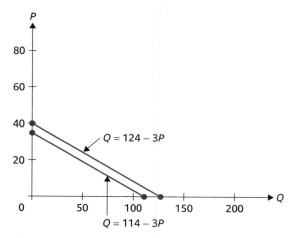

Figure 2.11

Quick problem 10

If the demand for good X is:

$$Q = 350 - 5P + 0.025Y + 0.6P'$$

where P is the price of the good, Y is the consumer's total income and P' is the price of an alternative good:

(a) Rewrite the demand function if income is fixed at £2000 and the price of the alternative good is fixed at £15 per unit. Graph the demand function.

(b) Explain how the relationship between quantity demanded and price would change if the price of the alternative good increased to £25 per unit.

(c) Illustrate the new demand curve on the graph from part (a).

2.6.4 Break-even point (total cost and total revenue)

Now consider a situation in which a firm wants to calculate the exact level of output at which it breaks even; the point where its total revenue is exactly equal to its total costs (the total amount that the firm pays out to make a given number of units of a good).

The firm's total revenue (TR) is equal to the total quantity that the firm sells (Q) multiplied by the price per unit of that good (P). **Therefore $TR = PQ$.**

The firm's total costs are made up of:

(a) Fixed costs (FC) which are overhead costs that must be paid no matter how many units of the good are produced.

(b) Variable costs (VC) which are a cost per unit of the good produced ($VC(Q)$).

Therefore the firm's total costs can be expressed as: $TC = FC + VC(Q)$.

Example

Assume that a firm can sell as many units of its product as it can manufacture in a month at £18 each. It has to pay out £240 in fixed costs in addition to a variable cost of £14 for each unit produced. How much does the firm need to produce to break even?

Referring to the information above, the firm has fixed costs of £240 and a variable cost of £14 per unit produced. The firm's total costs can therefore be expressed as:

$TC = 240 + 14Q$

If price per unit is equal to £18 then the total revenue function for this firm is:

$TR = 18Q.$

The firm breaks even when $TR = TC$. That is, when everything the firm makes (TR) is equal to everything that the firm pays out in production costs (TC). The break-even point is therefore when $TR = TC$, or when $18Q = 240 + 14Q$.

Rearranging this equation gives:

$4Q = 240$

$Q = 60.$

Therefore the firm breaks even when it sells 60 units of good X.

To find the value of total revenue and total cost at the break-even point you need to substitute the value of $Q = 60$ back into either function.

$TR = 18Q$

$TR = 18(60) = 1080$

$TC = 240 + 14Q$

$TC = 240 + 14(60)$

$TC = 1080$

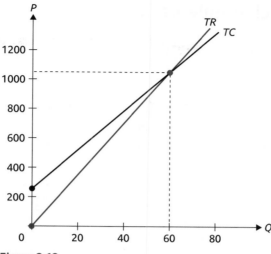

Figure 2.12

You can now graph these two linear equations and show the point of intersection on the graph (Figure 2.12).

Quick problem 11

A firm's fixed costs are constant at £500 regardless of how many units of good X they produce. The firm also has variable costs of £9 per unit produced. Product X sells for £13 per unit.

(a) Calculate the number of units of good X the firm needs to produce in order to break even.

(b) Graph the firm's total revenue and total cost functions.

✔ **Learning outcome 7**

Answers to quick problems

Quick problem 1

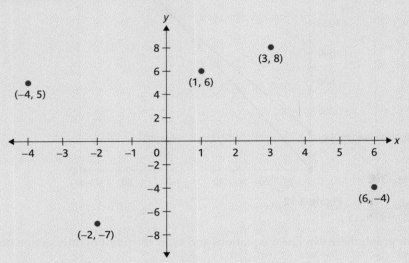

Figure 2.13

Quick problem 2

(1, −4), (4, 8)

(0, 1), (3, −5)

(0, 6), (3, 18)

(0, −9), (−4, −1)

Quick problem 3

(a) $y = x + 2$

(b) $y = x + 5$

(c) $y = 3x + 15$

(d) $P = 0.2Q + 1$

Quick problem 4

(−1, −17)

Quick problem 5

(2, 1)

Quick problem 6

(−1, −17) and (2, 1)

Quick problem 7

(−0.25, −0.5) and (1.5, 5)

Quick problem 8

(a) $160 = 20x + 5y$

(b) Slope $= -4$

(c) When $x = 0$, $y = 32$
     When $y = 0$, $x = 8$

(d) Slope $= -2$

(e) Nothing because total income does not affect the slope of the line.

Quick problem 9

(a) Demand: $P = -2Q + 30$
     Supply: $P = 2Q + 4$

(b)

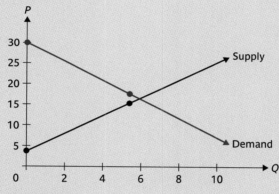

Figure 2.14

(c) (6.5, 17)

Quick problem 10

(a) $Q = 409 - 5P$

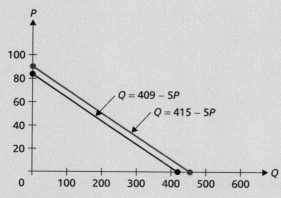

Figure 2.15

(b) $Q = 415 - 5P$. This shows that a rise in the price of the alternative good would result in more of this good being demanded at any given price.

(c) Refer to dashed line on graph in part (a). An increase in P' would cause the demand curve to shift out.

Quick problem 11

(a) The firm breaks even when $Q = 125$. At this point total revenue and total cost equal £1625.

(b) Total revenue: when $Q = 0$, $TR = 0$
     when $Q = 125$, $TR = 1625$

Total cost: when $Q = 0$, $TC = 500$
     when $Q = 125$, $TC = 1625$

Chapter **3**

Linear equations: further topics

Topics covered

3.1 Introduction	*60*
3.2 Simultaneous linear equations with more than two unknowns	*60*
3.3 Market equilibrium and changes in supply or demand	*66*
3.4 Cost, volume and profit analysis	*71*
3.5 Effects of a per unit tax	*73*
3.6 Macroeconomic models	*76*

LEARNING OUTCOMES

By the end of this chapter, you should understand:

1. How to solve simultaneous linear equations with three unknowns

2. How to solve additional supply and demand problems related to economics

3. How to use different techniques to solve problems related to revenue, cost and profit

4. How to deal with per unit taxes and to solve associated problems

5. How to solve macroeconomic models.

3.1 Introduction

The previous chapter introduced the concepts of supply and demand and provided an explanation of how to solve simultaneous linear equations with two unknowns. Such techniques are useful when they are applied to specific economic applications such as budget constraints and price/quantity issues. However, there are a number of other types of questions that you will need to be able to tackle which are more complex than those covered in Chapter 2. For instance, solving simultaneous linear equations with more than two unknowns is important in the study of economics. Macroeconomic models, per unit taxes, and a firm's revenue, cost and profit decisions are also key issues in economics which will be explored further in this chapter.

The structure of this chapter is slightly different from all others in this text. The number of actual concepts to be learned is minimal. This chapter focuses on the application of previously learned mathematical concepts to more complex economic issues. Therefore this chapter builds largely on short explanations with numerous examples and practice exercises to show the use of mathematical concepts in a variety of different economic scenarios.

3.2 Simultaneous linear equations with more than two unknowns

A set of simultaneous equations may have a unique solution, no solution or infinitely many solutions. There is no solution when there is no set of values that will satisfy all equations. This occurs when the two or three lines given are parallel; the fact that the lines never intersect means that there is no solution to the simultaneous system of equations. A set of simultaneous equations has infinitely many solutions when the two or three equations are actually equations of the same line. For instance, if the two equations are given as:

$$x + y = 4 \tag{3.1}$$

$$2x + 2y = 8 \tag{3.2}$$

then equation (3.2) is simply equation (3.1) multiplied through by 2. In this case all values assigned to x are going to give the same values for y in each equation. In this case there are said to be infinitely many solutions to the same system of equations. Finally, a unique solution refers to the case where there is just one set of values that satisfies all given equations. It is this situation that we will explore further in this chapter.

In Chapter 2, we covered the three methods for solving linear equations where there were only two equations, each with only two unknown variables. These methods included substitution, row operation and equating the equations. An equation with more than two unknowns becomes much more complicated to solve. This concept forms the basis of this first section. Simultaneous linear equations with more than two unknowns can still be solved using the substitution method, but you need to include a number of additional steps which are outlined in the example below.

When you are solving a problem with more than two unknown variables it is best to follow a set of specific steps. These steps are listed below and will be identified in each of the problems that are covered in this section.

1. Number each of your initial equations.
2. Select two of the initial equations and multiply one or both of these equations through by a number that will result in the coefficient of one of the unknowns being the same in both equations.
3. Add or Subtract one equation from the other in order to eliminate one unknown.
4. Using the same technique, eliminate the same unknown variable from the third initial equation that you have not yet used. This can then be combined with either of the other initial equations.
5. Using the two new equations each with two unknowns solve for one of the unknowns using the row operation method learned in Chapter 2.
6. Substitute the value of the first unknown back into either of your equations with only two unknowns to solve for the second unknown.
7. Finally, substitute the values for the two unknowns into any of the initial three equations to obtain the value of the third unknown. You can then plug all three values into each of the initial equations to check that all calculations are correct.

Refer to each of these steps as you work through the example below to ensure that you understand each part of the process.

Example

$$x + 12y + 3z = 120$$

$$2x + y + 2z = 80$$

$$4x + 2y + 6z = 219$$

Find the value of x, y and z that makes each of these equations true.

Step 1
Number your equations to keep track of them properly through each of the subsequent steps.

$$x + 12y + 3z = 120 \tag{3.3}$$

$$2x + y + 2z = 80 \tag{3.4}$$

$$4x + 2y + 6z = 219 \tag{3.5}$$

Step 2
Choose two of the three equations and multiply one or both of the equations through by a number(s) that will make one of the coefficients (either x, y or z) equal in each of the two equations.

$$(3.3) \times 2 \quad 2x + 24y + 6z = 240 \tag{3.6}$$

$$(3.4) \qquad 2x + y + 2z = 80$$

1. Remember to multiply through the whole equation by the chosen value, i.e., values on both sides of the equal sign.
2. You should number any new values or equations that form part of your calculations so that you can keep track of the different steps. Note that when equation (3.3) is multiplied through by 2 (above) the new equation is labelled as equation (3.6).

Step 3
Subtract one equation from the other in order to eliminate one unknown.

$$(3.6) - (3.4) \quad 23y + 4z = 160 \tag{3.7}$$

You have now eliminated x from two of the three equations.

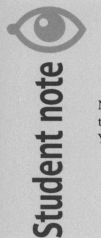

Notice that equation (3.4) was subtracted from equation (3.6) in order to eliminate x. If one of the x coefficients had been negative you would have added the two equations together instead. You should use whatever operation is necessary to eliminate one unknown.

Step 4
Now eliminate x from equation (3.5) by subtracting or adding it to either one of the remaining equations. Again, select either equation (3.3) or equation (3.4) and multiply through one or both equations to get the coefficient of x the same in both equations.

$$(3.5) \qquad 4x + 3y + 6z = 219$$

$$(3.4) \times 2 \qquad 4x + 2y + 4z = 160 \tag{3.8}$$

$$(3.5) - (3.8) \quad y + 2z = 59 \tag{3.9}$$

It does not matter which equations you select, or which unknown you first eliminate, as long as once you have started the process you remain consistent throughout the calculation of the solution.

Step 5

Equations (3.7) and (3.9) now only have two unknowns (y and z) so you can solve for either of these unknowns by using any of the techniques learned in Chapter 2. For the purpose of this example we will use the row operation method.

(3.7)	$23y + 4z = 160$	
(3.9) $\times 2$	$2y + 4z = 118$	(3.10)
(3.7) $-$ (3.10)	$21y = 42$	
	$y = 2$	

Step 6

Substitute $y = 2$ into either equation (3.7) or (3.9):

(3.9) $2 + 2z = 59$

Solve for z:

$2z = 57$

$z = 28.5$

Step 7

Finally, substituting $y = 2$ and $z = 28.5$ into any of your original equations ((3.3), (3.4) or (3.5)) enables you to calculate the value of x. For the purpose of this example the values of y and z have been substituted into equation (3.3).

(3.3) $x + 12(2) + 3(28.5) = 120$

Solve for x:

$x + 24 + 85.5 = 120$

$x + 109.5 = 120$

$x = 10.5$

Example

$4x + 5y - 2z = 125$

$-x - 3y + 7z = 95$

$5x - 4y - 3z = 64$

Find the value of x, y and z that makes each of these equations true.

Step 1
Number the initial equations:

$4x + 5y - 2z = 125$ (3.11)

$-x - 3y + 7z = 95$ (3.12)

$5x - 4y - 3z = 64$ (3.13)

Step 2
Multiply through any two of your initial equations by any number(s) that will make the coefficient of one of the unknowns the same.

In this example, equation (3.11) is multiplied through by 3 and equation (3.12) is multiplied through by 5. This makes the coefficient of y in each of the two equations equal to 15.

Student note

At this point it does not matter that the signs are different, i.e., +15 versus −15, you just need to ensure that the coefficients have the same value. The fact that the signs are different means that in order to eliminate y you will add the two equations together (see step 3) rather than subtracting them (as you did in step three of the previous example).

$(3.11) \times 3$ $12x + 15y - 6z = 375$ (3.14)

$(3.12) \times 5$ $-5x - 15y + 35z = 475$ (3.15)

Step 3
Add or subtract one equation from the other. In this example you can eliminate y by adding the two equations together to give you equation (3.16).

$7x + 29z = 850$ (3.16)

Step 4
Eliminate y from the third equation by combining it with either of the two equations already used. Multiply one or both of the equations through to make the coefficients of y equal.

$(3.12) \times 4 \quad -4x - 12y + 28z = 380$ (3.17)

$(3.13) \times 3 \quad 15x - 12y - 9z = 192$ (3.18)

Add or subtract one equation from the other to eliminate y.
    To eliminate y from these equations you can subtract equation (3.18) from equation (3.17) to get equation (3.19).

$-19x + 37z = 188$ (3.19)

Step 5
Solve for one of the two remaining unknowns by combining equations (3.16) and (3.19).

$(3.16) \quad 7x + 29z = 850$

$(3.19) \quad -19x + 37z = 188$

$(3.16) \times 19 \quad 133x + 551z = 16\,150$ (3.20)

$(3.19) \times 7 \quad -133x + 259z = 1316$ (3.21)

Add the two equations together to eliminate x and solve for z:

$810z = 17\,466$

$z = 21.5$

Step 6
Substitute the value of z into either equation (3.16) or (3.17) to solve for x:

$(3.16) \quad 7x + 29(21.5) = 850$

Solve for x:

$7x + 623.5 = 850$

$7x = 226.5$

$x = 32.35$

Step 7
Substitute the values of x and z into any of the initial equations to obtain the value for y:

$(3.12) \quad -x - 3y + 7z = 95$

Solve for y:

$-32.35 - 3y + 7(21.5) = 95$

$-32.35 - 3y + 150.5 = 95$

$118.15 - 3y = 95$

$-3y = -23.15$

$y = 7.72$

Quick problem 1

Solve the following system of simultaneous equations for x, y and z.

$x - 3y + 4z = 5$

$2x + y + z = 3$

$4x + 3y + 5z = 1$

✔ **Learning outcome 1**

3.3 Market equilibrium and changes in supply or demand

As discussed in Chapter 2 the market equilibrium is found by equating the demand and supply equations (refer to Chapter 2, section 2.6.3 for reference and quick problems). The following example offers an additional illustration of the calculation of market equilibrium.

Demand: $Q_d = 96 - 4P$

Supply: $Q_s = 8P$

Market equilibrium is the point at which these two lines intersect, a point which can be solved for using any of the three methods learned in Chapter 2.

For the purposes of this example we will equate the equations:

$96 - 4P = 8P$

$96 = 12P$

$P = 8$ is the price of the good when the quantity demanded is equal to the quantity supplied.

If $P = 8$, then $Q_s = 8(8) = 64$. And when $P = 8$, $Q_d = 96 - 4(8) = 64$. Therefore the point $(8, 64)$ is the market equilibrium.

The following section takes this concept one step further and considers the effect on the market equilibrium when either the supply or demand for the good changes.

The quantities of a good demanded and supplied are assumed to be dependent on a number of factors all of which (except price) are assumed to remain constant when we draw simple demand and supply curves. Changes in any of these factors (other than price) will cause a shift in either the demand or supply curve.

For example, demand is not entirely dependent on price. It is also influenced by factors such as a consumer's income (M) and the price of an alternative good (P_a). Thus a more realistic demand equation might look as follows:

$$Q_d = 96 - 4P + 0.1M + 0.3P_a$$

When income and the price of an alternative good are fixed (say at $M = 2500$ and $P_a = 60$) the demand equation becomes:

$$Q_d = 96 - 4P + 0.1(2500) + 0.3(60)$$

$$Q_d = 364 - 4P$$

If either M or P_a subsequently change (either increase or decrease), then the demand curve will shift to the right or left. Note that the new demand curve will be parallel to the old demand curve. This is evident if you examine the example above. Changes in M or P_a both change the intercept of the demand equation but not the slope (the coefficient of price (P)). With a new intercept but the same slope the new demand curve will be parallel to the old demand curve (Figure 3.1).

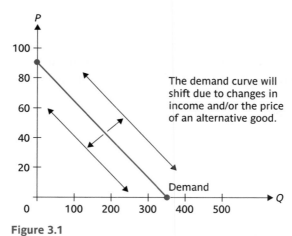

Figure 3.1

However, a demand curve can also change its slope, i.e., pivot/rotate rather than shift. This occurs when, for example, there is a change in tastes which may cause twice as much to be demanded at any given price.

If the demand curve is given as $Q = 55 - 5P$ and there is a change in tastes that results in twice as much of the good being demanded, then the new demand curve, denoted as Q_d' will be:

$$Q_d' = 2Q = 110 - 10P$$

Note that the slope of the demand curve has now changed and the new demand curve has a different slope, thus causing the curve to pivot/rotate.

Example

For the demand and supply functions listed below, show the effect of a 20 per cent increase in demand for the product.

Demand: $Q_d = 110 - 5P$
Supply: $Q_s = 6P$

First, you can graph the demand and supply curves using the techniques covered in Chapter 2.

Demand: When $P = 0$, $Q_d = 110$
When $Q_d = 0$, $P = 22$

Supply: When $P = 0$, $Q_s = 0$
When $Q_s = 60$, $P = 10$

The market equilibrium for this good can be found by any of the three methods also covered in Chapter 2 (substitution, equating the equations or row operation).

Setting the two equations equal to each other:

$$110 - 5P = 6P$$

$$110 = 11P$$

$$P = 10$$

When $P = 10$, $Q_s = Q_d = 60$.

Thus supply and demand are equal at the point $P = 10$ and $Q_s = Q_d = 60$.

The supply and demand curves and the market equilibrium are illustrated in Figure 3.2.

If demand now increases by 20 per cent the new demand equation will be written as:

$$Q'_d = 1.2Q_d = 1.2(110 - 5P)$$

$$Q'_d = 132 - 6P$$

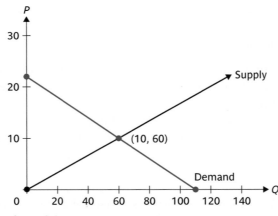

Figure 3.2

Note that to increase demand by 20 per cent you have to multiply the equation through by 1.2. If you multiplied through by 0.2 (20 per cent) then you would only get 20 per cent of your original figure. Using 1.2 (120 per cent) means that you retain the full amount that you already have and increase that amount by 20 per cent.

Notice that both the intercept and the slope of the demand curve have changed, so the demand curve is going to pivot/rotate.

When $P = 0$, $Q_d = 132$

When $Q_d = 0$, $P = 22$

The new market equilibrium is:

$132 - 6P = 6P$

$132 = 12P$

$P = 11$

When $P = 11$, $Q'_d = 132 - 6(11)$

$Q'_d = 66$

This new curve and equilibrium are illustrated in Figure 3.3 which shows the effect of a change in demand.

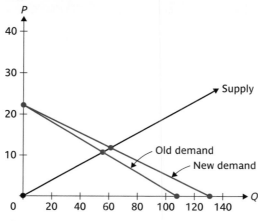

Figure 3.3

Example

Now consider the situation in which, instead of a percentage increase in demand, the consumer's income increased by 40 per cent. Given the demand equation outlined earlier, $Q_d = 96 - 4P + 0.1M + 0.3P_a$, and assuming that income was initially £2500 and the price of the alternative good is £60, consider the effect on demand of this increase in income.

$$Q_d = 96 - 4P + 0.1M + 0.3P_a$$

$$Q'_d = 96 - 4P + 0.1(2500)(1.4) + 0.3(60)$$

$$Q'_d = 96 - 4P + 350 + 18$$

$$Q'_d = 464 - 4P$$

In this case the intercept has changed while the slope (-4) has stayed the same. Therefore the new demand curve will have shifted (due to the change in the intercept) but will be parallel to the old demand curve (due to the value of the slope staying the same). This situation is illustrated in Figure 3.4.

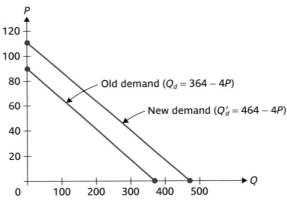

Figure 3.4

Quick problem 2

(a) For the following demand and supply functions show the effect on the market equilibrium of a 25 per cent increase in demand for the product.

Demand: $Q_d = 120 - 10P$

Supply: $Q_s = 8P$

(b) For the following demand and supply functions show the effect of a 65 per cent increase in the price of the alternative good.

Demand: $Q_d = 145 - 12P + 0.25M + 0.2P_a$

Supply: $Q_s = 12P - 25$

where $M = £1000$ and $P_a = 50$.

✔ **Learning outcome 2**

3.4 Cost, volume and profit analysis

Linear equations can also be used to analyse situations involving cost, volume and profit. In Chapter 2 you learned how to find the break-even point for a firm by calculating its total revenue and total cost. This analysis can now be taken a step further to include profit, variable costs and average variable costs.

Student note

It is necessary to consider how the different parts fit together:

$\pi = TR - TC$: Profit is equal to total revenue minus total cost

$TR = P \cdot Q$: Total revenue is equal to price multiplied by quantity

$TC = FC + VC$: Total cost is equal to fixed cost plus variable cost

$AVC = (VC)/Q$: Average variable cost is equal to variable cost divided by quantity

$VC = AVC \cdot Q$: Variable cost is equal to average variable cost multiplied by quantity

Example

A firm has fixed costs of £555, average variable costs of £12 and is selling a specific good at a price of £17 per unit.

(a) Find an expression for profit in terms of its level of sales, Q.

(b) What is the value of Q that will achieve the profit target of £195?

(c) At what sales level does the firm break even?

(d) Illustrate this situation on a diagram.

(a) Find an expression for profit in terms of sales, Q
Referring to the equalities in the above *student note*:

$$\pi = TR - TC = (P \cdot Q) - (FC + VC)$$

where $VC = AVC \cdot Q$
Therefore

$$\pi = (P \cdot Q) - FC - (AVC \cdot Q)$$

$$\pi = 17Q - 555 - 12Q$$

$$\pi = 5Q - 555$$

which is the expression for profit in terms of sales, *Q*.

(b) *What is the value of Q that will achieve the profit target of £195?*
Rewrite the above equation to express Q in terms of π:

$\pi + 555 = 5Q$

$Q = (\pi + 555)/5$

Substituting the profit target of £195 then enables you to solve for the quantity that needs to be sold (Q) in order to achieve this target.

$Q = (195 + 555)/5 = 150$

Therefore sales of 150 units (Q = 150) are required to achieve the profit target of £195.

(c) *At what sales level does the firm break even?*
Referring back to Chapter 2, section 2.6.4, a firm breaks even when π = 0. Therefore substituting π = 0 into the above expression $Q = (\pi + 555)/5$ would give:

$Q = (0 + 555)/5 = 111$

The firm breaks even when quantity sold is equal to 111 units.

(d) *Illustrate this situation on a diagram*
In order to illustrate this situation you need to graph TR and TC and indicate the point at which these two lines intersect (which is the point at which π = 0 and the firm breaks even).
       Thus we need two points for the linear TR curve and two points for the linear TC cost curve.

$TR = P \cdot Q = 17Q$

When Q = 0, TR = 0
When Q = 111, TR = 1887

$TC = FC + VC = 555 + 12Q$

When Q = 0, TC = 555
When Q = 111, TC = 1887

With two points for each of total revenue and total cost we can now plot the linear equations and show the break-even point graphically (Figure 3.5).

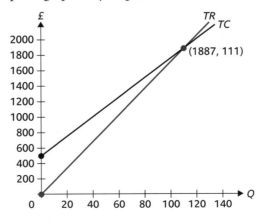

Figure 3.5

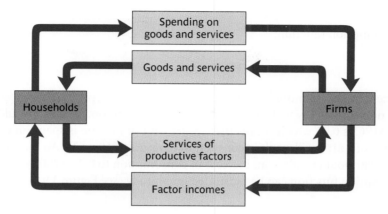

Figure 3.8 Begg, D, Fischer, S and Dornbusch, R. Foundations of Economics, 2nd Edition, London, 2003.

The circular flow diagram in Figure 3.8 shows the relationship between households and firms.

3.6.1 The household: consumption and savings

First, it is important to understand the consumption and savings functions. A typical linear consumption function will take the form:

$C = aY + b$ (consumption function)

where a and b are both greater than 0. The intercept, b, is the level of consumption that would take place if no income was earned, i.e., when $Y = 0$. This is known as autonomous consumption. The slope of the consumption function, a, is known as the marginal propensity to consume (MPC). The MPC is the proportion of total income spent on consumption. For instance, if the consumption function is defined as $C = 0.4Y + 20$ and income is £100, then the consumer has autonomous consumption of £20 which is the amount they would spend (consume) even if they had no income (presumably this would come out of their savings). They would also consume £40 of their earned income (0.4(£100) = £40). The remaining £60 of earned income would then be allocated to savings. This is why income, Y, is said to be made up of two main components, consumption, C, and savings, S.

Thus when we say that the MPC is 0.4 (or that 40 per cent of income is spent on consumption) this means that the other 60 per cent is savings. Thus the value of consumption added to the value of savings will equal the total income, Y.

$Y = C + S$ (income identity)

You can also think of the marginal propensity to consume (MPC) as the increase in consumption as a result of an increase in income. Using the consumption function above, $C = 0.4Y + 20$, if income is initially £100 then £40 is consumed and £60 is saved (ignoring autonomous consumption for the moment). If income then rises to £120 then £48 will be consumed and £52 will be saved. That is consumption rises by £8 and savings fall by £8.

Example

Given the consumption function:

$$C = 0.25Y + 10$$

we can deduce that autonomous consumption is 10 (the intercept, b). This means that if the person earns no income they will still spend £10 on consumption. This £10 would come from savings. The MPC is 0.25 which means that 25 per cent of income is spent on consumption. Thus an income of a £100 will result in consumption of £25 + £10 = £35. An increases in income from £100 to £200 would result in an increase in consumption to 0.25(£200) + £10 = £60.

The consumption function can be illustrated graphically (see Figure 3.9).

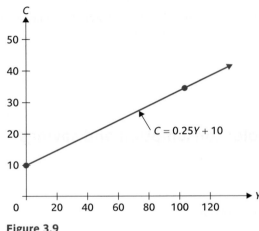

Figure 3.9

$$C = 0.25Y + 10$$

The slope, or marginal propensity to consume, a, is 0.25 and the intercept, or autonomous spending, b, is £10.

When $Y = 0$, $C = 10$
When $Y = 100$, $C = 35$

The savings function can be derived from the consumption function and the income identity given above.

If $C = 0.25Y + 10$, and $Y = C + S$, then you can substitute one equation into the other to obtain:

$$Y = \underbrace{0.25Y + 10}_{C} + S \quad (Y = C + S)$$

$Y - 0.25Y = 10 + S$ (collect the like terms on the left-hand side of the equation)

$0.75Y = 10 + S$ (combine the like terms)

$S = 0.75Y - 10$ (rearrange the equation to express savings, S, in terms of income, Y).

If you have Y on the left-hand side of the equation and $0.25Y$ on the right-hand side of the equation you can combine these two terms. Y is actually a simplified version of the term $1Y$ so by moving $0.25Y$ over the left-hand side and subtracting it from $1Y$ you will get $1Y - 0.25Y = 0.75Y$.

Thus the savings function represents everything remaining from total income that was not consumed, i.e., 75 per cent of income is saved ($0.75Y$), minus the value of autonomous savings (which was £10 in the example above).

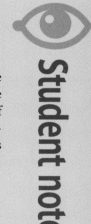

The value of the coefficient, in this case −£10, represents autonomous savings which is the value of savings when income (Y) is equal to zero. It is negative because if income is zero then the consumer is going to have to withdraw money from savings in order to maintain some level of consumption. Note that in the consumption function this value is called autonomous consumption while in the savings function it is called autonomous savings. Either way it represents the value that would be consumed (taken from savings) if the person had no income.

The savings function also has a coefficient and a slope. The coefficient in this example is −10 (autonomous savings) and the slope is 0.75. The slope represents the proportion of income that is saved rather than consumed and is called the marginal propensity to save (MPS). Note that the MPS is actually equal to 1 − MPC. This is because the MPC and the MPS must add up to one to account for total income.

The slope of both the consumption and savings functions is positive (both curves are upward sloping). This is because there is a positive relationship both between consumption and income and between savings and income. Thus as income increases, so does consumption and so does savings.

As was the case with the consumption function, the savings function can be illustrated on a graph (Figure 3.10).

$S = 0.75Y - 10$

When $Y = 0$, $S = -10$
When $Y = 100$, $S = 65$

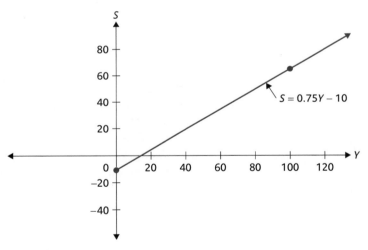

Figure 3.10

Quick problem 5

Determine the savings functions that correspond with the following consumption functions:

(a) $C = 0.6Y + 25$

(b) $C = 0.35Y + 45$

✔ **Learning outcome 5**

3.6.2 The firm: consumption and investment

The identity $Y = C + S$ relates specifically to the household. Now we can look at an identity that relates to firms. Firms split their income, Y, between consumption, C, and investment, I. Thus the equivalent identity for firms would be $Y = C + I$.

If the amount of investment is fixed then you can calculate the equilibrium level of income. For example, if the firm has a marginal propensity to consume (MPC) of 0.75, autonomous consumption of £10 and a fixed investment level of £25:

$C = 0.75Y + 10$

$I = 25$

In equilibrium income equals expenditure, hence:

$Y = C + I$

$Y = (0.75Y + 10) + 25$

$Y = 0.75Y + 35$

$0.25Y = 35$

$Y = 140$

Now substitute $Y = 140$ into the consumption function:

$C = 0.75(140) + 10 = 115$

This then gives the equilibrium level of income and consumption. This equilibrium can also be found graphically (Figure 3.11) by plotting expenditure against income on the same graph where aggregate expenditure is equal to $C + I$ (as above). The 45° line (called such because it lies at 45 degrees from both axes) is the line which shows all the points where expenditure and income are in balance. Equilibrium income is then the point of intersection of this line and the aggregate expenditure line, $C + I$.

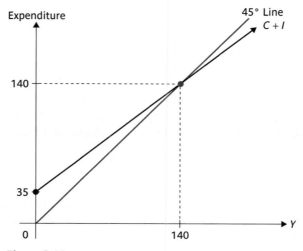

Figure 3.11

Quick problem 6

Determine the firm's equilibrium levels of income and consumption which correspond to the consumption and investment information below. Illustrate each equilibrium on a graph.

(a) $C = 0.6Y + 25$, $I = 20$

(b) $C = 0.35Y + 45$, $I = 100$

✔ **Learning outcome 5**

3.6.3 Government activity, taxation and trade

We will now combine the household and firm information and, to make the situation more realistic, we will include government spending (G), taxation (T) and trade (exports, X, and imports, M). In this section the household will represent all consumers and the firm will represent all firms. We will then use the information about consumption, expenditure, investment, government spending, taxes and trade to find the equilibrium national income.

Government spending

Including government spending expands the firm's income identity to:

$$Y = C + I + G$$

At this stage government spending, like investment, is normally assumed to be a fixed amount.

Taxation

We also include taxation in our identity which is combined with income in the household consumption function. This is because taxation affects the income of each consumer (reducing total income). Therefore a consumer's income is not actually Y, as stated previously, but $Y - T$, where T represents taxation. This introduces the concept of 'disposable income' denoted as Y_d ($= Y - T$). We can now write the consumption function as:

$$C = aY_d + b$$

where $Y_d = Y - T$. If the tax is a lump sum then this will simply be subtracted from Y to give Y_d. However if tax is a proportion of income then $Y_d = tY$.

We use the information in this section to work out the equilibrium level of national income. National income, represented as Y, is made up of total consumption (which is a function of disposable income) plus government spending and investment. The following example best illustrates how the different parts work together in the calculation of national income.

Example

Given

$C = 0.75Y_d + 50$ (now we are considering National Income we are grossing together all individual consumption and thus the units have increased also so that 50 is in fact £50 million)

$T = 0.25Y$　　　　(tax is a proportion of income with $t = 0.25$)

$G = £25$ million

$I = £30$ million

find the equilibrium level of national income.

$Y = C + G + I$　　　　　　　(income identity)

$Y = 0.75Y_d + 50 + 25 + 30$　(substitute given values into identity)

$Y_d = Y - T$

$Y_d = Y - 0.25Y$　　　　　　(incorporate taxation to calculate disposable income)

$Y_d = 0.75Y$

$C = 0.75(0.75Y) + 50$　　　(substitute value for disposable income into consumption function)

$C = 0.56Y + 50$

$Y = 0.56Y + 50 + 25 + 30$　(substitute consumption into income identity)

$0.44Y = 105$　　　　　　　(gather like terms together)

$Y = 238.6$　　　　　　　　(simplify and solve for Y)

This indicates that the equilibrium level of national income is £238.6 million

Quick problem 7

Determine the equilibrium level of national income given:

$C = 0.8Y_d + £20$ million

$T = 0.4Y + £10$ million

$G = £30$ million

$I = £40$ million

✔ **Learning outcome 5**

Trade – Exports and Imports

Finally we should include trade transactions in our calculations because all countries engage in some form of trade which affects their level of national income. Note that a country that engages in trade is referred to as an 'open' economy and a country that does not engage in trade is described as a 'closed' economy.

Imports, denoted as M, add to a country's spending as the country is paying for goods that they are importing from another country.

Exports, denoted as X, add to a country's income as the country is being paid for goods that they export.

The trade identity is expressed as $(X - M)$ and can either be positive or negative.

If $(X - M) > 0$ then the value of exports is larger than the value of imports and the country is said to have a trade surplus. In this case the country is earning more from its exports than it is paying out for the purchase of imports and so the overall trade balance is positive.

If $(X - M) < 0$ then the value of imports is larger than the value of exports and the country is said to have a trade deficit. In this case the country is paying more for imports than it is earning for its exports and so the overall trade balance is negative.

Exports and imports are easily incorporated into the national income identity:

$Y = C + I + G + X - M$ (we add exports because they represent earnings and subtract imports because they represent spending)

The following example will clarify the calculation of equilibrium national income for an economy open to trade.

Example
Determine the equilibrium level of national income given:

$C = 0.6Y + £120$ million

$I = £45$ million

$G = £634$ million

$X = £160$ million

$M = 0.45Y + £8$ million

$Y = C + I + G + X - M$ (theory)

$Y = 0.6Y + 120 + 45 + 634 + 160 - 0.45Y - 8$ (substitute all given values into the income identity)

Student note

Imports are often presented as a two part equation which includes marginal propensity to import (MPM) and a level of autonomous spending on imports. The MPM shows the proportion of income that is spent on imports and represents the slope of the import function. The intercept is autonomous spending on imports and illustrates the fact that even with no income the country would still spend a certain amount on imports (financed from savings).

The import equation is subtracted from the national income identity because imports represent spending. Always ensure that you subtract *both parts* of the import equation, i.e., a common error is to apply the minus sign to the first part of the equation and to retain the addition of the second part (autonomous imports). It is important to remember that the minus sign must be multiplied through the whole of the import equation when incorporating it into the national income identity.

$Y - 0.15Y = 951$ (gather like terms together and simplify)

$0.85Y = 951$

$Y = 1118.82$ (solve for Y)

The equilibrium level of national income is £1118.82 million.

Example
Calculate the equilibrium level of income given:

$C = 0.65Y + £70$ million

$I = £50$ million

$G = £125$ million

$X = £80$ million

$M = 0.4Y + £20$ million

$Y = 0.65Y + 70 + 50 + 125 + 80 - (0.4Y + 20)$

$Y = 0.65Y + 70 + 50 + 125 + 80 - 0.4Y - 20$

$Y = 0.25Y + 305$

$Y - 0.25Y = 305$

$0.75Y = 305$

$Y = £228.75$

The equilibrium level of national income is £228.75 million.

Quick problem 8

Determine the equilibrium level of national income given:

$C = 0.75Y + £50$ million

$I = £25$ million

$G = £105$ million

$X = £60$ million

$M = 0.2Y + £25$ million

✔ **Learning outcome 5**

Answers to quick problems

Quick problem 1

$x = 3, y = -2, z = -1$

Quick problem 2

(a) Before increase in demand: market equilibrium at $P = £6.67, Q = 53.33$
     After increase in demand: market equilibrium at $P = £7.32, Q = 58.5$

(b) Before increase in Pa: market equilibrium at $P = £17.92, Q = 190$
     After increase in Pa: market equilibrium at $P = £18.19, Q = 193.25$

Quick problem 3

(a) $\pi = 5Q - 450$
(b) $Q = 135$
(c) $Q = 90$

(d)
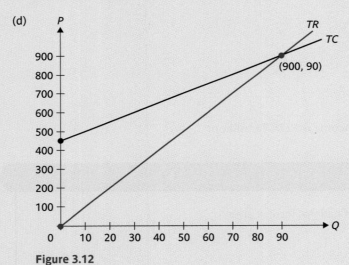

Figure 3.12

Quick problem 4

(a) $P = £5.6$, $Q = 32.8$

(b) See (d) below

(c) $P = £7.6$, $Q = 8.8$

(d)

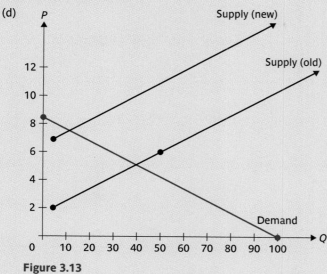

Figure 3.13

Quick problem 5

(a) $S = 0.4Y - £25$

(b) $S = 0.65Y - £45$

Quick problem 6

(a) $Y = £112.5$

(b) $Y = £223$

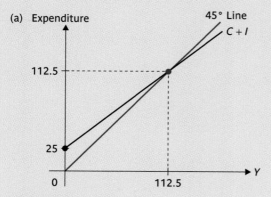

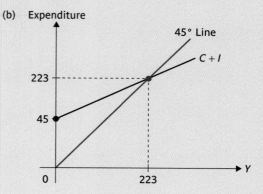

Figure 3.14

Quick problem 7

Y = £157.69

Quick problem 8

Y = £477.78 million

Chapter 4

Linear programming

Topics Covered

4.1 Introduction   90

4.2 Graphing inequalities   90

4.3 Graphing simultaneous linear inequalities   95

4.4 The objective function   98

4.5 Unbounded feasible regions   104

4.6 Application of linear programming in economics   105

LEARNING OUTCOMES

By the end of this chapter, you should understand:

1. How to graph linear inequalities

2. How to identify a feasible region defined by linear inequalities

3. How to calculate the points that define a feasible region

4. How to solve linear programming problems graphically

5. How to identify a linear programming problem that has no, or multi-, solutions

6. How to use objective functions and constraints

7. How to calculate a maximum or minimum point.

4.1 Introduction

There are many situations in which it is necessary to be able to identify the specific bundle of goods that offers the optimal benefit to the supplier or consumer. For example, if a supplier can only produce a certain number of goods A and B, then that supplier needs to be able to identify the combination that will maximize his or her profits and/or minimize his or her costs. Likewise, if a consumer has a tight budget and wants to buy some of each good available, he or she will want to maximize the amount that he or she can consume with the budget available.

These optimal bundles of goods are calculated through a process called *linear programming* which will be explained throughout this chapter. The following sections will outline how to identify the constraints faced by both consumer and producer, the concepts of cost minimization and profit maximization and the use of objective functions to identify the optimal bundle for the consumer and/or producer.

4.2 Graphing inequalities

As explained in Chapter 2, a linear equation of the form

$2x + 3y = 7$

can be expressed on a graph by substituting values for x and y that make the left-hand side of the equation equal to the right-hand side. For example:

If $x = 2$, then $y = 1$ because $2(2) + 3(1) = 7$, or

If $x = 5$, then $y = -1$ because $2(5) + 3(-1) = 7$.

Thus $(2, 1)$ and $(5, -1)$ are both points on the line $2x + 3y = 7$. This line can be graphed as in Figure 4.1.

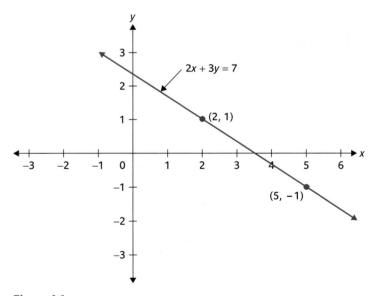

Figure 4.1

We know that < (less than), ≤ (less than or equal to), > (greater than) and ≥ (greater than or equal to) can all be used to express a linear inequality involving two variables. Each of these symbols is used to illustrate the fact that the left-hand side of the equation is not equal to the right-hand side. The simplest form of a linear inequality is presented as:

$x \leq y$

We need to identify at least two points in order to graph this inequality. Consider the situation in which $x = y$. In this case you can easily identify two sets of co-ordinates.

Student note

When graphing each of the constraints, we first have to plot the associated lines. This means that by replacing the symbols <, ≤ , < or ≥ with an equal sign (=) you can find co-ordinates that fall on the actual line. You can then consider the inequality to identify which side of the line is to be excluded.

For example:

When $x = 2$, $y = 2$

When $x = 5$, $y = 5$

Therefore the points (2, 2) and (5, 5) can be used to draw the straight line $x = y$. This is shown in Figure 4.2.

We can now identify the area that illustrates the original inequality $x \leq y$; the area where the value of x is either less than or equal to the value of y. This area is on or above the line $x = y$ and is illustrated in Figure 4.3.

Shading identifies the area that is excluded by the inequality. In Figure 4.3 the area above the line is the area illustrated by the inequality while the area below the line is shaded because it is excluded by the expression $x \leq y$.

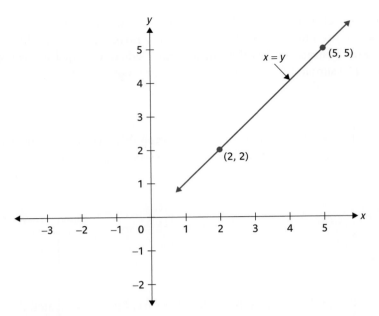

Figure 4.2

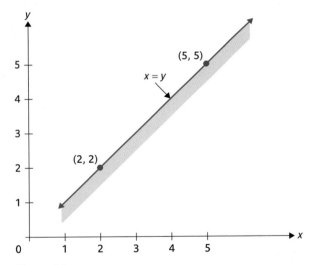

Figure 4.3

A bold line with shading either above or below represents an inequality that includes the values on the line; inequalities that state that one unknown is greater than/less than *or equal to* another unknown, i.e., $x \leq y$. Alternatively, an inequality that states that one unknown is simply less than (<) or greater than (>) another unknown is represented by a dashed line. This means that the values *on the line* are not included. These two scenarios are illustrated in Figure 4.4.

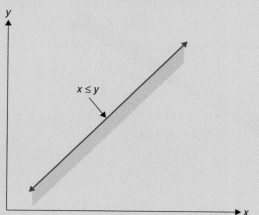
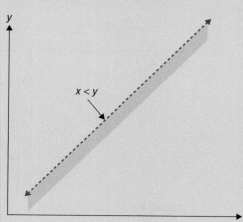

Figure 4.4

Remember that the area that is *excluded* by the inequality is shaded.

Student note

Example

Illustrate the inequality $5x - 2y > 30$.

The easiest way to graph this inequality is to first consider the line represented by $5x - 2y = 30$. Referring to the technique used in Chapter 2, you would consider two specific points for x and then calculate the corresponding values for y. For example:

When $x = 1$,

$5(1) - 2y = 30$

$-2y = 25$

$y = -12.5$

Therefore $(1, -12.5)$ is one point on the line $5x - 2y = 30$.

When $x = 4$,

$5(4) - 2y = 30$

$20 - 2y = 30$

$-2y = 10$

$y = -5$

Therefore $(4, -5)$ is another point on the line $5x - 2y = 30$.

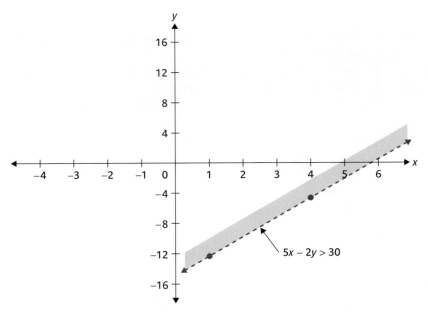

Figure 4.5

We are now able to graph the line $5x - 2y = 30$ using these two sets of co-ordinates (Figure 4.5).

Note that as the inequality states that $5x - 2y$ is greater than 30 (but not equal to it), the line illustrating this inequality is dashed rather than solid.

Shading is then used to illustrate the area that is excluded by the inequality. In this example the shaded area is to the left of the line as the inequality states that for all values of x and y, $5x - 2y$ is greater than 30.

Example

Illustrate the inequality $6x \geq 4y$.

First, replace the $\geq$ with an equal sign and find two sets of co-ordinates on the line.

For the equation $6x = 4y$:

When $x = 2$, $y = 3$, so $(2, 3)$ is one point on the line $6x = 4y$.

When $x = 4$, $y = 6$, so $(4, 6)$ is another point on the line $6x = 4y$.

The line will be solid because the inequality includes the possibility that $6x$ is equal to $4y$, and the shaded area will be to the left of the line as the inequality states that we are looking for values of x and y that make $6x$ greater than $4y$.

This example is illustrated in Figure 4.6.

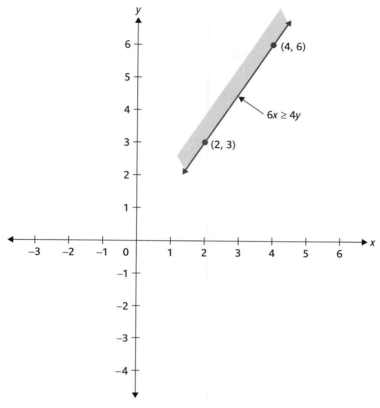

Figure 4.6

Quick problem 1

Illustrate each of the following inequalities on a set of axes:

(a) $3x \leq y$

(b) $4x + 6y \geq 12$

(c) $2x - 5y < 20$

(d) $4x > 9y$

✔ **Learning outcome 1**

4.3 Graphing simultaneous linear inequalities

By graphing two or more linear inequalities we can identify a *feasible region* which consists of values of x and y that satisfy several inequalities at the same time. We find this region by sketching each of the linear inequalities onto the same graph.

Unless otherwise stated you should assume that there are always two additional constraints. These are:

$x \geq 0$

$y \geq 0$

These constraints indicate that the values of x and y are greater than zero, so we only need to consider points that lie in the first quadrant. This is represented graphically by shading the area below the x axis and to the left of the y axis. Shading these areas excludes any negative values for x and y in the identified feasible area. This is illustrated in Figure 4.7.

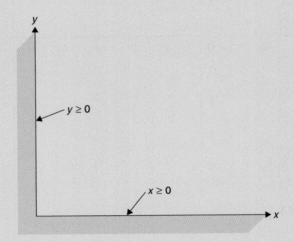

Figure 4.7

Example
Illustrate the following inequalities on the same graph:

$2x + 4y \leq 16$

$5x + 15y \leq 45$

First you must find two sets of co-ordinates for each of the inequalities and then you need to graph the inequalities to identify the feasible area.

Convert the above inequality into an equation of a line by replacing $\leq$ with $=$. Then plug random values for either x or y into the equation to find the associated value of y or x. For instance, by plugging a value of $x = 0$ into the equation $2x + 4y = 16$, you can calculate that:

$2(0) + 4y = 16$

$4y = 16$

$y = 4$

Therefore one point on the line $2x + 4y = 16$ is $(0, 4)$. Two points on each of the lines will then enable you to graph these lines, shade the side of the line excluded by the associated inequality, and define the feasible region. Two sets of co-ordinates for each of the constraints in this problem are:

$2x + 4y = 16$	$5x + 15y = 45$
$(0, 4)$	$(0, 3)$
$(8, 0)$	$(9, 0)$

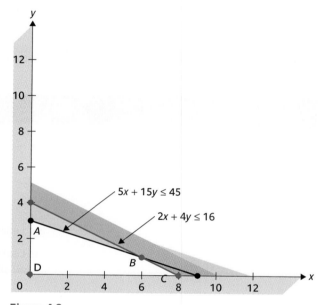

Figure 4.8

Figure 4.8 presents the two lines on the same graph and uses shading to illustrate the area excluded by each of the inequalities.

Remember that you need to include the two additional inequalities of $x \geq 0$, and $y \geq 0$.

The previous example shows that several lines/inequalities can be illustrated on the same graph. The non-shaded area that is created by graphing the linear inequalities is the feasible region and is defined by the points of intersection of the different inequalities. In Figure 4.8, the area $ABCD$ defines the feasible region created by the inequalities $2x + 4y \leq 16$, $5x + 15y \leq 45$, $x \geq 0$, and $y \geq 0$.

Note that points A, B, C and D are all the points where two lines intersect. In the example above, point A is simply the intersection point of $5x + 15y \leq 45$ and $x = 0$. Substituting $y = 0$ into the first equation confirms that the two lines intersect at point $(0, 3)$.

Point C is the intersection of $2x + 4y \leq 16$ and $y = 0$. Substituting $y = 0$ into the first equation confirms that the two lines intersect at point $(8, 0)$.

Point D is the intersection of $x = 0$ and $y = 0$ which is simply the origin, defined as $(0, 0)$.

Finally, Point B is the intersection of $2x + 4y = 16$ and $5x + 15y = 45$. The point of intersection can be calculated as follows:

Rearrange $2x + 4y = 16$ and express it as

$x = (16 - 4y)/2$

$x = 8 - 2y$

Substituting $x = 8 - 2y$ into $5x + 15y = 45$ gives:

$5(8 - 2y) + 15y = 45$

$40 - 10y + 15y = 45$

$5y = 5$

$y = 1$

Substituting $y = 1$ into either of the original equations will yield $x = 6$. Therefore $(6, 1)$ is the point of intersection of lines $2x + 4y = 16$ and $5x + 15y = 45$.

Quick problem 2

Sketch the following inequalities and use shading to illustrate the feasible region. Calculate the points that define the feasible region.

(b) $5x + 3y \leq 30$; $7x + 2y \leq 28$; $x \geq 0$; $y \geq 0$

(b) $2x + 5y \leq 20$; $x + y \leq 5$; $x \geq 0$; $y \geq 0$

✔ **Learning outcome 2**

✔ **Learning outcome 3**

4.4 The objective function

As discussed in the introduction to this chapter, linear programming is used to find the combination of x and y that will maximize or minimize some objective function. In economics we are usually looking to maximize profit or to minimise costs. In order to do this we need to add an additional element to our linear programming exercise. The *objective function* represents the profits, costs, budget, spending, etc. that we want to either maximize or minimize. The purpose of the objective function can best be illustrated through an example.

Example
Maximize

$-x + y$ (objective function)

subject to the constraints:

$3x + 4y \leq 12$

$x \geq 0$

$y \geq 0$

First, find two co-ordinates on the line associated with the first inequality.

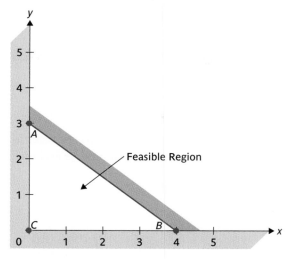

Figure 4.9

$3x + 4y = 12$

$(0, 3)$

$(4, 0)$

Second, graph the three inequalities using shading to illustrate the feasible area (Figure 4.9).

Third, identify each of the points that make up the feasible area – the points of intersection of each pair of lines. Point A is one point that defines the feasible area and represents the interse tion between $3x + 4y = 12$ and $x = 0$. When $x = 0$, $y = 3$, so point A is defined as $(0, 3)$. Point B is another point that defines the feasible area and represents the intersection between $3x + 4y = 12$ and $y = 0$. When $y = 0$, $x = 4$, so point B is defined as $(4, 0)$. Finally, C is a third point that defines the feasible area and represents the intersection between $x = 0$ and $y = 0$. This would be the point $(0, 0)$. These three points illustrate all the intersections that make up the feasible area.

You now need to identify which of these three points maximizes the objective function. You do this by plugging each of the three co-ordinates into the objective function and calculating which combination gives you the highest value.

The objective function was give as $-x + y$.

Using point A $(0, 3)$: $-0 + 3 = 3$

Using point B $(4, 0)$: $-4 + 0 = -4$

Using point C $(0, 0)$: $-0 + 0 = 0$

Therefore, the objective function is maximised when $x = 0$ and $y = 3$ (point A).

Example

Using the same inequalities as Quick Problem 2(b),
Maximize $3x + 6y$, subject to the constraints:

$2x + 5y \leq 20$

$x + y \leq 5$

$x \geq 0$

$y \geq 0$

First, find two points on each of the lines associated with the first two inequalities. You do not need to find points associated with the non-negativity constraints because these are always defined in the same way.

$2x + 5y = 20$	$x + y = 5$
$(0, 4)$	$(0, 5)$
$(10, 0)$	$(5, 0)$

Second, graph the four constraints (on the same graph) and refer to the inequality symbols to identify which side of each of the associated lines should be excluded (shaded). This process is illustrated in Figure 4.10.

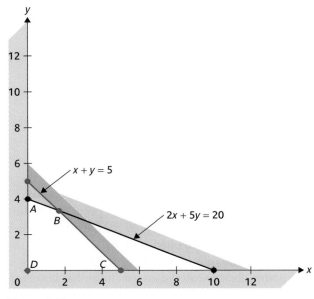

Figure 4.10

Third, identify the points of intersection that define the feasible area. In the graph in Figure 4.10 the points of intersection are labelled as A, B, C and D.

Point A represents the intersection between $2x + 5y = 20$ and $x = 0$. By substituting $x = 0$ into the first equation you can calculate that the co-ordinates of point A are $(0, 4)$.

Point C represents the intersection between $x + y = 5$ and $y = 0$. By substituting $y = 0$ into the first equation you can calculate that the co-ordinates of point C are $(5, 0)$.

Point D represents the intersection between $x = 0$ and $y = 0$ so has the co-ordinates $(0, 0)$.

Finally, point B represents the intersection between $2x + 5y = 20$, and $x + y = 5$. By solving these equations simultaneously you can find the values for x and y at which these two lines intersect. *To review the different methods for solving simultaneous equations see Chapter 2, section 2.5.*

In this case if $x + y = 5$, then $x = 5 - y$. Substituting this into $2x + 5y = 20$ gives:

$$2(5 - y) + 5y = 20$$

$$10 - 2y + 5y = 20$$

$$10 + 3y = 20$$

$3y = 10$

$y = 10/3$

The value of $y = 10/3$ can now be substituted into either of the equations to obtain the associated value for x. Therefore:

$x + (10/3) = 5$

$x = 5 - 10/3$

$x = 15/3 - 10/3$ (see Chapter 1, section 1.3 for the explanation of changing whole numbers into fractions)

$x = 5/3$

Therefore the point at which the two lines intersect is (5/3, 10/3) which represents point B.
We can list our points and co-ordinates as follows:

Point A (0, 4)

Point B (5/3, 10/3)

Point C (5, 0)

Point D (0, 0)

Together these points represent the feasible region. You must now substitute each of these co-ordinates into the original objective function ($3x + 6y$) in order to find out which set of x and y values maximises that objective function.

Point $A = 3(0) + 6(4) = 24$

Point $B = 3(5/3) + 6(10/3) = 25$

Point $C = 3(5) + 6(0) = 15$

Point $D = 3(0) + 6(0) = 0$

This tells us that the objective function is maximized when $x = 5/3$ and $y = 10/3$.
Both of the previous examples have involved the maximization of an objective function. The following example requires you to minimize an objective function. Note that the process is the same; the difference between minimizing and maximising is only relevant at the end of the question when you select the point in the feasible region that satisfies the objective function.

Example
Minimize $-5x + y$, subject to the constraints:

$4x + y \leq 8$

$-2x + 5y \leq 10$

$x \geq 0$

$y \geq 0$

First, find two points associated with each of the first two inequalities.

$4x + y = 8$

When $x = 0$, $y = 8$
When $x = 2$, $y = 0$

So two points associated with $4x + y = 8$ are $(0, 8)$ and $(2, 0)$.

$-2x + 5y = 10$

When $x = 0$, $y = 2$
When $x = 5$, $y = 4$

So two points associated with $-2x + 5y = 10$ are $(0, 2)$ and $(5, 4)$.

Plot the two lines on a graph and shade the areas that are excluded by the inequality (Figure 4.11). Remember to also identify the areas excluded by the inequalities $x \geq 0$ and $y \geq 0$.

This clarifies the feasible region which is identified as area *ABCD*. Note that each point that defines the feasible region is the intersection between two of the original inequalities.

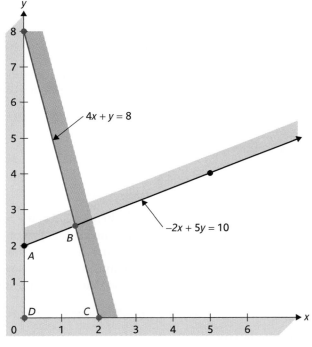

Figure 4.11

Each of points *A*, *B*, *C* and *D* is defined by a set of co-ordinates. These are calculated by finding the intersection point of the two associated lines. In this example these points are calculated as follows.

Point *A* represents the intersection between $-2x + 5y = 10$ and $x = 0$. By substituting $x = 0$ into the first equation you can calculate that the co-ordinates of point *A* are $(0, 2)$.

Point C represents the intersection between $4x + y = 8$ and $y = 0$. By substituting $y = 0$ into the first equation you can calculate that the co-ordinates of point C are $(2, 0)$.

Point D represents the intersection between $x = 0$ and $y = 0$, so has the co-ordinates $(0, 0)$.

Finally, Point B represents the intersection between the two lines $4x + y = 8$ and $-2x + 5y = 10$. By solving these equations simultaneously you can find the values for x and y at which these two lines intersect.

In this case, if $4x + y = 8$, then $y = 8 - 4x$. Substituting this into the equation $-2x + 5y = 10$ gives:

$-2x + 5(8 - 4x) = 8$

$-2x + 40 - 20x = 8$

$-22x + 40 = 8$

$-22x = -32$

$x = 16/11$

This value of x can now be substituted into either of the equations to obtain the associated value for y. Therefore:

$4(16/11) + y = 8$

$64/11 + y = 8$

$y = 8 - 64/11$

$y = 88/11 - 64/11$

$y = 24/11$

Therefore the point at which the two lines intersect is $(16/11, 24/11)$ which represents point B.

We can list our points and co-ordinates as follows:

Point A $(0, 2)$

Point B $(16/11, 24/11)$

Point C $(2, 0)$

Point D $(0, 0)$

Together these points represent the feasible region. You must now substitute each of these co-ordinates into the original objective function $(-5x + y)$ in order to find out which set of x and y values minimises the objective function.

Point $A = -5(0) + 2 = 2$

Point $B = -5(16/11) + 24/11 = -56/11 = -5.09$

Point $C = -5(2) + 0 = -10$

Point $D = -5(0) + 0 = 0$

This tells us that the objective function is minimized when $x = 2$ and $y = 0$.

Quick problem 3

Maximize $6x + 9y$ subject to:

$3x + 7y \leq 21$

$9x + 4y \leq 36$

$x \geq 0$

$y \geq 0$

Minimize $2x + 4y$ subject to:

$5x + 10y \geq 30$

$12x + 3y \geq 36$

$x \geq 0$

$y \geq 0$

✔ **Learning outcome 4**

4.5 Unbounded feasible regions

As discussed in Chapter 2 (section 2.5) sometimes there is no solution to a simultaneous linear equation problem. For example when the two lines are parallel, solving for the intersection point (no matter which way it is attempted) results in there being no solution. A similar situation can arise in linear programming. These are quite easy to identify once the linear equations have been graphed, as they will present themselves as unbounded areas which do not have a complete set of intersection points to define the feasible region.

One such case is illustrated in the following example.

Example
Maximize $12x - 3y$, subject to:

$2x + y \geq 14$

$3x - 4y \geq 12$

$x \geq 0$

$y \geq 0$

First, find two points associated with each inequality and plot the inequalities on a graph (Figure 4.12). Remember to shade the area on the side of the line that is excluded by the inequality.

Note that in this case the feasible region is not bounded on all sides. This leads to one of two possible conclusions. If you are trying to minimize an objective function then you can calculate all the intersection points and simply identify the set of co-ordinates that gives the lowest value.

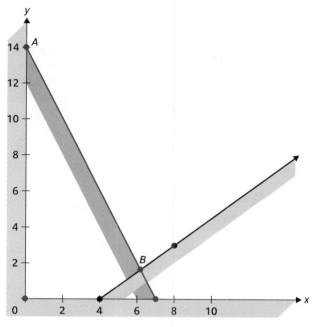

Figure 4.12

However, if you are trying to maximize the objective function then you will find that the unbounded feasible region does not give you an obvious maximization point. In this case we would conclude that the problem does not have a finite solution.

Quick problem 4

(a) Maximize $2x - 4y$, subject to:

$4x + 2y \geq 16$

$9x - 3y \geq 9$

$5x + 5y \geq 60$

$x \geq 0$

$y \geq 0$

(b) Minimize $2x - 4y$ subject to the same set of constraints.

✔ **Learning outcome 5**

4.6 Application of linear programming in economics

Linear programming is yet another key concept in the study of economics and the techniques learned in the beginning of this chapter can now be used to illustrate different types of economic applications. The application of these concepts is most easily presented in the form of examples, two of which are included below.

It is useful to identify a few additional points which bridge the gap between using linear programming as a mathematical concept and as an economics application.

First, linear programming problems that are used in economics are presented initially as written statements rather than as objective functions with clearly identifiable constraints. Therefore, an additional skill that must be practised at this stage is to be able to interpret the written question correctly so as to set out the initial elements. The interpretation of questions will be identified as a key step in the following two examples.

Second, it is useful to think of each question as having seven distinct steps. As long as you carefully follow each of the seven steps you should be able to complete each question correctly.

The seven steps are:

1. Identify the unknowns and label them x and y (or equivalent).

2. Write down an expression for the objective function in terms of x and y, and decide whether it needs maximizing or minimizing.

3. Write down all constraints on the variables x and y.

4. Write down any obvious constraints such as the non-negativity constraints which you may have forgotten about in (3).

5. Graph the constraints in order to find the feasible area.

6. Evaluate all the intersection points in the feasible area to solve for the maximum or minimum.

7. Check that the final answer makes sense as a solution to the original problem.

It will be useful to follow each of these steps as you work through the following linear programming questions.

Example

UNITY manufactures two models of DVD player, the Standard and the Deluxe. The production of the Standard is very straightforward involving four plastic components and 12 metal components. The production of the Deluxe is more complex involving the use of 18 plastic components and six metal components. There are 1296 plastic components and 1824 metal components ordered by the company every month and the company seeks to use up as many of the components each month as it can while still maximizing its profit. If the profit on a Standard is £55 and the profit on a Deluxe is £89, how should the manufacturer arrange production to maximize total profit?

Solution

First, you need to identify both the constraints and the objective function. For the purpose of this question we will refer to the Standard model as S and the Deluxe model as D.

The first constraint deals with the use of plastic components used in the production of both the Standard and Deluxe models of radio. The Standard model uses four plastic components and the Deluxe model uses 18 plastic components. The question also tells us that there are 1296 plastic components in total. So the constraint regarding the use of plastic components can be written as:

$$4S + 18D \leq 1296$$

The second constraint deals with the use of metal components and is constructed in the same way as the constraint for plastics. The standard model uses 12 metal components and the deluxe model uses six metal components so the constraint can be written as:

$$12S + 6D \leq 1824$$

Remember to add in the two non-negativity constraints to identify that S and D cannot be negative. These are:

$$S \geq 0$$

$$D \geq 0$$

Now you need to identify the objective function. This usually relates to either the profit that will be earned or the costs that will be incurred. In this question you are given the profit on each item which tells you that the objective function will be about maximizing profit and can be written as:

Maximize $55S + 89D$

You now need to graph each of the constraints and identify the feasible region. This has been done in Figure 4.13.

The feasible region is defined as A, B, C, D where each of the points represents the intersection of two constraints. We need to use these constraints to find out the co-ordinates of each of the points in the feasible region.

Point A represents the intersection between $4S + 18D = 1296$ and $S = 0$. By substituting $S = 0$ into the first equation you can calculate that the co-ordinates of point A are $(0, 72)$.

Point C represents the intersection between $12S + 6D = 1824$ and $D = 0$. By substituting $D = 0$ into the first equation you can calculate that the co-ordinates of point C are $(152, 0)$.

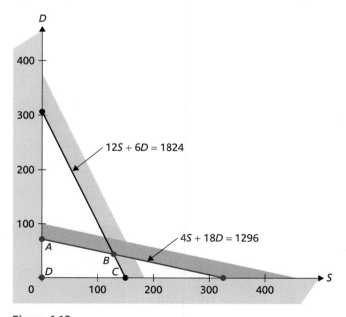

Figure 4.13

Point D represents the intersection between $S = 0$ and $D = 0$ so has the co-ordinates $(0, 0)$.

Finally, point B represents the intersection between the two lines $4S + 18D = 1296$ and $12S + 6D = 1824$. By solving these equations simultaneously you can find the values for S and D at which these two lines intersect.

Given the two equations:

$$4S + 18D = 1296 \tag{4.1}$$

$$12S + 6D = 1824 \tag{4.2}$$

$$12S + 54D = 3888 \quad (4.1) \times 3 \tag{4.3}$$

$$12S + 6D = 1824 \quad (4.2)$$

$$48D = 2064 \quad (4.3) - (4.2) \tag{4.4}$$

$$D = 43$$

Substituting $D = 43$ back into equation (4.1) gives:

$$4S + 18(43) = 1296$$

$$4S = 522$$

$$S = 130.5$$

Therefore, the point at which the two lines intersect is $(130.5, 43)$ which represents point B.

We can list our points and co-ordinates as follows:

Point A $(0, 72)$

Point B $(130.5, 43)$

Point C $(152, 0)$

Point D $(0, 0)$

Together these points represent the feasible region. You must now substitute each of these co-ordinates into the original objective function $(55S + 89D)$ in order to find out which combination of standard and deluxe radios will make the firm the highest profit.

Point $A = 55(0) + 89(72) = 6408$

Point $B = 55(130.5) + 89(43) = 11\ 004.5$

Point $C = 55(152) + 89(0) = 8360$

Point $D = 55(0) + 89(0) = 0$

This tells us that the objective function is maximized when the firm makes 130.5 (or 130) Standard radios and 43 Deluxe radios.

Example
A florist has decided to grow pansies and daisies in an attempt to increase the supply available at her store without incurring additional supplier costs. She does not have a lot of free time and

finds that in order to produce healthy, saleable plants she needs to spend 10 minutes per day tending each of the pansies plants and 15 minutes per day tending each of the daisies plants. She must fit this into a maximum of seven hours per week that she has free. Her allotment is quite large and she has worked out that if she only grows pansies plants then she could fit 50 into the total space available. Daisy plants though take up triple the space of pansy plants. Finally, she does not want to plant more than 10 pansy plants but would like to plant at least 12 daisy plants.

(a) If each pansy plant yields five flowers and each flower sells for £1.25 and if each daisy plant yields eight flowers with each flower selling for £2.50, how many of each flower should the florist plant in order to maximize her profit.

(b) If the daisies turn out to be very large, so that they yield 12 flowers instead of eight would the solution calculated in part (a) still hold?

(c) How would the solution change if the florist found that she only had five hours in total to dedicate to tending the flowers?

Solution (a)

First, you need to determine the constraints and the objective function from the above question. (This can often be the most difficult step!)

If you define a pansy plant as P and a daisy plant as D the first constraint will deal with the number of minutes that it takes for the florist to tend each plant. In this case the constraint would be:

$$10P + 15D \leq 420$$

The two are added together because they represent the amount of time that the florist would tend each plant, and the inequality is 'less than or equal to' 420 because this represents the seven hours that she has available for 'tending' in minutes (we express everything in minutes to keep the units consistent).

The next constraint deals with space. If the florist only grew pansy plants then she could plant up to 50 in the space available (hence the 'less than or equal to' sign). As a daisy plant takes up twice as much space as a pansy plant the second part of the constraint reads '+ 2D' to illustrate that if no pansy plants were grown then the florist could plant 25 daisy plants. Therefore, the space constraint is written as:

$$P + 2D \leq 50$$

Finally, there is a constraint on the number of pansy plants that she will grow. This is written as:

$$P \leq 10$$

And there is a constraint on the number of daisy plants that she can produce based on the fact that she wants to grow at least 12. This is written as:

$$R \geq 12$$

We also know that P will be ≥ 0 so we need to include this as a further constraint. We do not need to include $D \geq 0$ because we already have a constraint that states that $D \geq 12$.

The objective function relates to the maximisation of profit (as stated in the question). In this case each pansy plant yields five flowers and each flower sells for £1.25 so the profit for a pansy plant would be 5P(£1.25) or £6.25P. A daisy plant yields eight flowers and each flower sells for £2.50 so the profit on a daisy plant would be 8R(£2.50) or £20R. Therefore the objective function can be written as:

Maximize $6.25P + 20D$

The whole question can now be presented as:

Maximize $6.25P + 20D$

subject to:

$10P + 15D \leq 420$

$P + 2D \leq 50$

$P \leq 10$

$D \geq 12$

$P \geq 0$

The constraints can now be graphed as shown in Figure 4.14.

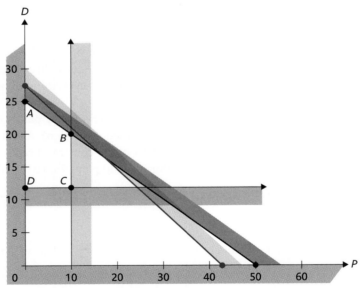

Figure 4.14

Note that the intersection points that define the feasible region have been labelled as A, B, C and D. Each of these points identifies the intersection of two of the constraints. Also note that in this example the first constraint ($10P + 15D \leq 420$) does not actually form one of the boundaries of the feasible region. This is not a problem and means that you are able to ignore this constraint when looking for the point of maximum profit.

The co-ordinates of the points that define the feasible region are:

Point A: intersection of $P + 2D \leq 50$ and $P \geq 0$. This gives co-ordinates of $(0, 25)$

Point B: intersection of $P + 2D \leq 50$ and $P \leq 10$. This gives co-ordinates of $(10, 20)$

Point C: intersection of $P \leq 10$ and $D \geq 12$. This gives co-ordinates of $(10, 12)$

Point D: intersection of $P \geq 0$ and $D \geq 12$ which gives co-ordinates of $(0, 12)$

Plugging each of these co-ordinates into the objective function gives:

Point A: £500.00

Point B: £462.50

Point C: £302.50

Point D: £240.00

This confirms that the florist will maximize her profit if she grows 25 daisy plants and no pansy plants.

Solution (b)

The solution would stay the same although the objective function would change and the florist's profit would increase. The new objective function would be:

Maximize $6.25P + 30D$

The florist would still maximize her profit by only growing daisy plants but would now make a total profit of £750.00.

Solution (c)

The change from seven hours to five hours means that the first constraint would now be written as:

$10P + 15D \leq 300$

The situation is illustrated in Figure 4.15.

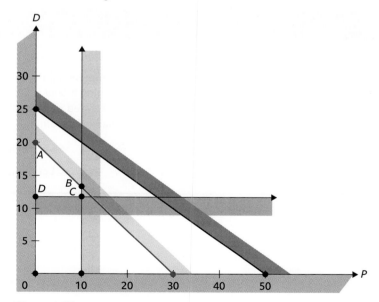

Figure 4.15

Note that the first constraint now forms part of the boundary of the feasible region so new intersection points need to be calculated. The points *A*, *B*, *C*, and *D* are illustrate in Figure 4.15 and are defined as:

Point *A*: the intersection between $10P + 15D = 300$ and $P = 0$. Point *A* has co-ordinates $(0, 20)$

Point *B*: the intersection between $10P + 15D = 300$ and $P = 10$. Point *B* has co-ordinates $(10, 13.3)$

Point *C*: the intersection between $P = 10$ and $D = 12$. Point *C* has co-ordinates $(10, 12)$

Point *D*: the intersection between $P = 0$ and $D = 12$. Point *D* has co-ordinates $(0, 12)$

Given the original objective function:

Maximize $6.25P + 20D$

The profit earned for each of these different combinations of pansies and daisies would be:

Point *A*: £400.00

Point *B*: £328.50

Point *C*: £302.50

Point *D*: £240.00

This confirms that the florist would still maximize her profits by growing only daisy plants but that as she has less time available she will need to reduce the number of plants that she grows from 25 to 20.

This demonstrates the use of linear programming in the field of economics where we need to be able to calculate how profits can be maximized, or how costs can be minimized, based on a selection of constraints.

Quick problem 5

A furniture manufacturer makes two types of chair: Dining and Lounge. The Dining model takes two hours of sanding and four hours of staining. The Lounge model takes two hours of sanding and three hours of staining. The profit margin on the Dining model is £42 while profit on the Lounge model is £46. How should the production be allocated to maximize profits if there are only 78 hours available for sanding and 96 hours available for staining?

✔ **Learning outcome 6**

✔ **Learning outcome 7**

Answers to quick problems

Quick problem 1

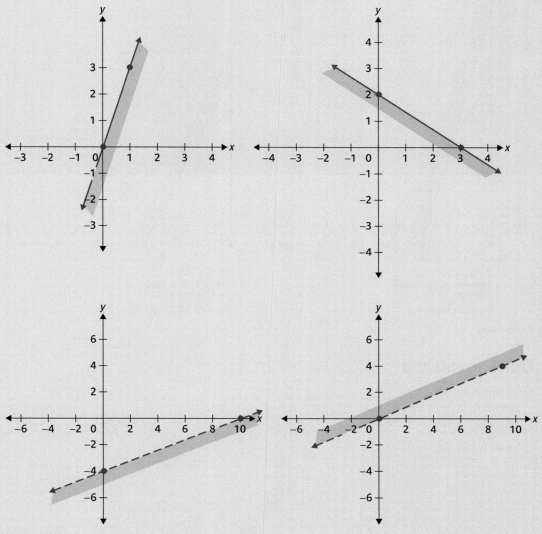

Figure 4.16

Quick problem 2

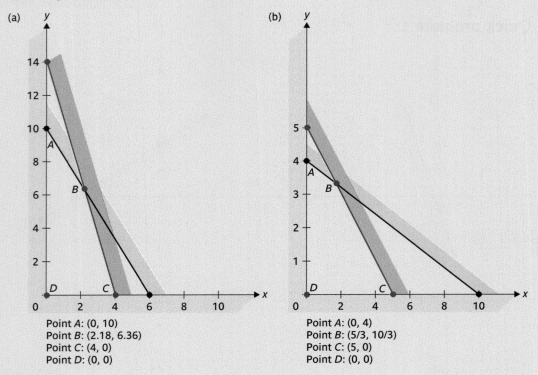

(a)

Point A: (0, 10)
Point B: (2.18, 6.36)
Point C: (4, 0)
Point D: (0, 0)

(b)

Point A: (0, 4)
Point B: (5/3, 10/3)
Point C: (5, 0)
Point D: (0, 0)

Figure 4.17

Quick problem 3

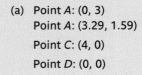

(a)   Point A: (0, 3)
      Point A: (3.29, 1.59)

      Point C: (4, 0)

      Point D: (0, 0)

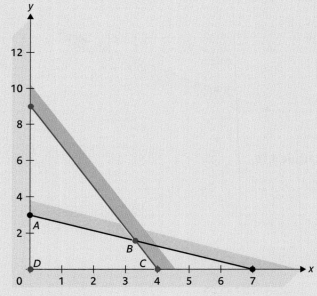

Figure 4.18

The objective function is maximized when $x = 3.29$ and $y = 1.59$ (point B), giving a total of 34.05.

(b) Point *A*: (0, 9)
     Point *B*: (2.57, 1.71)
     Point *C*: (6, 0)

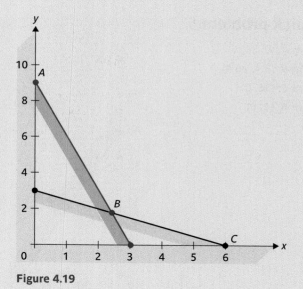

Figure 4.19

The objective function is minimized when $x = 2.57$ and $y = 1.71$ (point *B*), giving a total of 11.98.

Quick problem 4

(a) Point *A*: (4, 0)
     Point *B*: (2.2, 3.6)
     Point *C*: (3.75, 8.25)
     Point *D*: (12, 0)

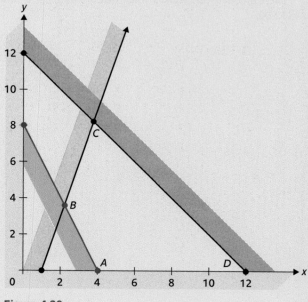

Figure 4.20

The objective function will be maximized when $x = 12$ and $y = 0$ (point *D*), giving a total of 24.

(b) The objective function will be minimized when $x = 3.75$ and $y = 8.25$ (point *C*), giving a total of −25.5.

Quick problem 5

Point *A*: (0, 32)
Point *B*: (8.4, 26.4)
Point *C*: (26, 0)
Point *D*: (0, 0)

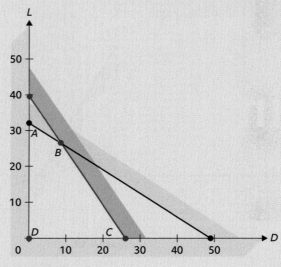

Figure 4.21

Note that for the purposes of calculating the maximum point, the co-ordinates of point *B* have been rounded down to (8, 26). This accounts for the fact that the number of chairs that can be made must be expressed as a whole number.

The objective function is maximized when *x* = 8 and *y* = 26 (point *B*), giving a total profit of £1532.00.

Chapter 5

Finance and growth

Topics covered

5.1 Introduction	118
5.2 Arithmetic progressions	119
5.3 Geometric progressions	123
5.4 Practical applications: simple and compound interest	129
5.5 Practical applications: investment appraisal	132
5.6 A further practical application: economic growth	140

LEARNING OUTCOMES

By the end of this chapter, you should understand:

1. The meaning of an 'arithmetic progression' and how to calculate terms

2. How to calculate the total or partial value of an arithmetic progression

3. The meaning of a 'geometric progression' and its calculation

4. How to apply a geometric progression to understand economic problems

5. How to calculate the summation of a geometric progression and simple application

6. The meaning of 'simple interest' and its calculation

7. Compound interest, how to calculate compound interest and solve compounding problems

8. The meaning and calculation of 'present values'

9. The meaning, calculation and inference of 'net present values'

10. How to calculate and interpret an 'internal rate of return'

11. The meaning and calculation of an 'annuity'

12. How to apply the compounding principle to economic growth.

5.1 Introduction

This chapter explores ways in which mathematics can be used to help solve problems regarding finance and growth, and aims to help you acquire the knowledge, understanding and skills to be able to independently apply these mathematical techniques.

The meaning or significance of the term, 'finance and growth' may not be obvious. Put simply, finance refers to a wide range of economic activities which are concerned with the management of income and wealth. Income is defined as a stream of payments which are received in return for providing something: Apple Corporation, for example, received huge incomes from selling more than 14 million of its iPod personal music players in the last three months of 2005. Wealth on the other hand is a 'stock concept' and refers to the accumulation of valuables or assets over time, e.g., the Russian businessman Roman Abramovich has an estimated wealth of around £10 billion.[1]

But what relevance does mathematics have in this context? Most financial decisions require mathematical analysis to ensure the best outcome. For example, we would expect mathematics to help a private sector business choose which investment project it should select over a number of competing alternatives. In the public sector, the government needs to plan carefully to ensure it makes adequate provision for future spending such as education, health and pensions. At the individual level, households need to make judgements about where to put any savings or, indeed, whether they should save at all. Although these examples are very different, they all share a common theme: using mathematics to achieve a financial outcome.

The links between finance and growth are clear: frequently, business and individuals have to make decisions which involve how economic variables – the economy, unemployment, inflation, consumer spending, savings, etc. – will change over time. That is, these decisions often need to take a view on the future growth of something.

To be able to draw conclusions and inferences about how something might change in the future – for example the value of a share portfolio or savings account – we often need to try and understand how things have changed or behaved in the past.

For example, a firm forecasting future sales revenues will want to look at a range of factors including likely demand, sales of rival or substitute products, population changes and so on. In other words, economists and business leaders often need to try and work out if a sequence or pattern exists. If we can work out what this pattern or *progression* is we might be able to use it to make judgements about what might happen in the future.

---

[1] Source: *The Times* Rich List.

A *progression* is a sequence of numbers which increase reduce by a common factor. There are two types of progression: an *arithmetic progression* and a *geometric progression*.

An *arithmetic progression* exists when a sequence of numbers are linked by a fixed or common *addition*. For example, the sequence 3, 5, 7, 9, 11, . . . is an arithmetic progression with a *common difference* of +2.

A *geometric progression* exists when each number in a sequence is *multiplied* by a constant in order to obtain the next figure. For example, the sequence '1, 2, 4, 8, 16, 32, 64, . . .' is the start of a geometric progression with the fixed constant or *common ratio* being +2.

Student note

5.2 Arithmetic progressions

An arithmetic progression is a sequence of numbers which is based on the addition of a *common difference*.

Consider the following sequence:

1, 3, 5, 7, 9, 11, . . .

We can see quite quickly that the common difference here is +2. The first term is 1 and we get to the second term in the sequence – which is 3 – simply by adding 2. The third term then is the second term plus 2, i.e., $3 + 2 = 5$, and so on.

An arithmetic progression could involve a decreasing sequence of numbers where the common difference is a negative figure. For example,

5, 2, −1, −4, −7

is also an arithmetic progression but here each number is 3 *less* than the previous figure. The common difference which moves us from one term to the next is −3.

Calculating a term in an arithmetic progression

Once we can identify what the common difference is, we can work out the value of any number in our sequence or progression. The long-handed way of doing this is to write out the sequence until we arrive at the term we are interested in. This method would involve a great deal of time – and ink! – if we needed to find a term which is far down in the sequence.

For example, if we wanted to find out the 127th term in the sequence 3, 8, 13, 18, 23, 28 we would probably not want to write out the whole series until we reached the 127th term. A far quicker way is to use a formula.

Let:

U_n = the value of the nth term

d = the common difference

U_1 = the first term in the sequence

$U_n = U_1 + (n - 1) \times d$

Example
Using the data above, we have:

3, 8, 13, 18, 23, 28, . . .

$U_1 = 3$

$d = +5$

$U_n = U_{127}$

Using the equation above,

$U_{127} = 3 + (126 \times 5) = 3 + 630 = 633$

So, the 127th term in the sequence 3, 8, 13, 18, 23, 28, . . . is 633.

Quick problem 1

An economist is researching the impact of a computerized scheme on the number of taxpayers who complete their tax returns on time over a number of years. He finds the following sequence:

120 000, 160 000, 200 000, 240 000, . . .

(a) If this sequence is an arithmetic progressions, what is the expected number of taxpayers who complete their tax return on time in the seventh year?

(b) If he subsequently discovers that he has made a mistake and, in fact, the common difference is +35 000 per year, what is the expected number of taxpayers who complete their tax return on time in the seventh year?

✔ **Learning outcome 1**

Calculating the sum of terms in an arithmetic progression

It is also useful to be able to calculate the sum of an arithmetic progression. This means working out the *total* of all of the numbers in an arithmetic progression up to a certain point.

Example
A business researcher discovers that an investment produces profits as follows:

£4000, £6500, £9000, £11 500, . . .

Table 5.1

Year	Profits (£)
1	4 000
2	6 500
3	9 000
4	11 500
5	14 000
6	16 500
7	19 000
8	21 500
9	24 000
10	26 500
Total	152 500

She wants to know the total value of investment profits over a ten year period. Again, we could use a slow and cumbersome method and work out the profits for each year in this arithmetic progression up to year 10 and then add the numbers together. If we did this we would get the stream of profits shown in Table 5.1.

Instead, we could use a formula.

Let:

d = the common difference

U_1 = the first term in the sequence

S_n = the sum of terms in the sequence up to the nth term

$$S_n = \frac{n}{2}(2U_1 + (n-1)d)$$

In our example,

$d = £2500$

$U_1 = £4000$

$n = 10$

Our summation formula is:

$$S_n = \frac{n}{2}(2U_1 + (n-1)d)$$

So:

$$S_{10} = \frac{10}{2}(2 \times 4000 + (10-1)2500)$$

$$= 5(8000 + (9 \times 2500))$$

$$S_{10} = £152\ 500$$

After 10 years the total cumulative profits would be expected to be £152 500.

The benefits of using the formula are obvious if we consider having to work out the summation of a large number of terms

Quick Problem 2

An economist believes that the size of an regional economy (as measured by GDP) can be accurately measured using an arithmetic progression.

He discovers that GDP over the past five years is as follows:

Year 1: $ 250 million

Year 2: $ 267.5 million

Year 3: $ 285 million

Year 4: $ 302.5 million

Year 5: $ 320 million

Task One

Assuming that the arithmetic progression is correct and a robust guide to the future, calculate the size of the regional economy in year 17 only, using a formula.

Task Two

At the end of year 17 what will the cumulative vale of the regional economy output be, i.e., S_{17}.

Task Three

Using the S_n formula, calculate the cumulative value of the regional economy for years 16 and years 17 inclusive.

Task Four (extension)

Write a simple expression which calculates the cumulative value of the regional economy between years 16 and 17 inclusive.

✔ **Learning outcome 2**

Student note

If we have an *arithmetic progression* then:

Calculation of a particular term (U_n)
This can be found by:

Let:

U_n = the value of the nth term

d = the common difference

U_1 = the first term in the arithmetic progression

Then:

$$U_n = U_1 + (n-1) \times d$$

Calculation of the total sum of terms in a sequence (S_n)
This can be found by:

Let:

d = the common difference

U_1 = the first term in the arithmetic progression

S_n = the sum of terms in the sequence up to the nth term

$$S_n = \frac{n}{2}(2U_1 + (n-1)d)$$

5.3 Geometric progressions

Geometric progressions are very similar to arithmetic progressions in that they both describe a common pattern or replication. The crucial distinction though is that a geometric progression is based on a *common multiplication* rather than a common addition we see with the arithmetic progression.

Geometric progressions can be a more useful mathematical tool because they tend to be more common in business and economics. The following are all applied or practical examples of geometric progressions:

- Calculation of compound interest on a savings account
- A pharmaceutical company modelling bacterial growth
- Measuring or modelling how the gross domestic product of an economy might increase
- Assessing the monthly repayments which a manufacturing firm would need to make on a large purchase of machinery
- Quantifying the environmental impact of rapid economic growth.

Consider the following sequence of values which represent the value of an investor's stocks and shares over a period of time:

£1000, £2000, £4000, £8000, £16 000

Here, each term is calculated by multiplying the previous term by 2. The fixed constant or multiplicative figure is also known as the *common ratio* (remember, the equivalent term for the arithmetic progression was the *common difference*).

We can often see the common ratio by inspecting the series of numbers. We can also look at dividing 'adjacent terms' – that is, terms which are next to one another – to see if they have a common ratio. For example, in the sequence in Table 5.2 it is not easy to see what the common

Table 5.2 Example of identifying the common ratio

Sequence	Common ratio
2.2, 2.42, 2.662, 2.9282, 3.221 02	$\frac{2.42}{2.2} = 1.1, \frac{2.662}{2.42} = 1.1, \frac{2.9282}{2.662} = 1.1$

ratio is but a simple division of adjacent terms makes this much clearer. Three adjacent terms in the sequence are divided by the preceding number. In each case, the common divider or common ratio is 1.1.

Quick problem 3

Task One
Calculate the common ratio for each series. You might find it helpful to look at dividing adjacent pairs to help you quickly identify the common ratio.

Sequence	Common ratio
(a) 3, 6, 12, 24, 48, 96, 192	
(b) 4, 16, 64, 256, 1024, 4096, 16 384	
(c) 2.2, 7.26, 23.958, 79.0614, 260.9026, 860.9786, 2841.23	
(d) +5, −4, +3.2, −2.56, +2.048, −1.6384, +1.310 72, −1.048 58, +0.8388 61	

Task Two
Look at the last sequence in Task One.
   What did you notice about the size or value of the terms as the series progressed and the signs of the terms?
   Why did this happen?

✔ **Learning outcome 3**

Calculating the value of a term in a geometric progression

There are many situations when an economist would want to work out the value of a particular term in a geometric progression. Typical examples would include:

■ Measuring the value of a savings pot after a period of time

■ Calculating the future size of an economy

■ Assessing future government expenditure by examining the likely size of the population

■ Judging the eroding effects of inflation on a workers' pension.

The value of a term in a geometric progression can be found using a simple formula.

Let:

U_n = the value of the nth term in a geometric progression.

d = the common ratio

U_1 = the first term in the geometric progression

Then:

$$U_n = U_1 \times d^{n-1}$$

Student note

Example

A worker invests a lump sum of £50 000 in bank account and expects to draw upon it when she is 60, i.e., after 10 years have elapsed. The bank have guaranteed she will earn 4 per cent each year on her savings. What will the value of her savings be when she comes to draw upon it? (See Table 5.3.)

This can be verified using the formula above. We have:

U_0 = £50 000

Hence:

U_1 = £50 000 $\times$ (1.04) = £52 000

$D = 1.04$

$U_n = U_{10}$

U_{10} = £52 000 $\times$ 1.04$^{10-1}$

U_{10} = £74 012.21

Table 5.3

Beginning of the year	Capital	Interest during the year ($r = 4\%$)
1	£50 000.00	£2000.00
2	£52 000.00	£2080.00
3	£54 080.00	£2163.20
4	£56 243.20	£2249.73
5	£58 492.93	£2339.72
6	£60 832.65	£2433.31
7	£63 265.95	£2530.64
8	£65 796.59	£2631.86
9	£68 428.45	£2737.14
10	£71 165.59	£2846.62
11	£74 012.21	

Quick problem 4

An economist is working as part of a small team investigating the economic effects of climate change. He investigates future global economic growth having first identified that total world GDP for 2005 was $44.4 trillion.[2] He believes that the world economy will grow at 4.5 per cent per year each year.

Task One
Assuming the economist is correct in his initial data, calculate the total value of the world economy in 2025.

Task Two
A government think tank recommends a raft of measures which would slow down climate change but would reduce annual global economic growth to 3 per cent.

(i)   Recalculate the total value of the world economy in 2025 in the assumption that these measures are introduced.

(ii) Express the new estimate as a percentage of the original estimate and briefly interpret the likely impact of the measures on global economic growth.

Task Three (extension)
Another economist suggests that by 2025 total global GDP will be £124 trillion by 2025. If this forecast is correct, what is the average annual growth rate over the period 2005 – 2025?

✔**Learning outcome 4**

Calculating the sum of terms in a geometric progression

It is useful to be able to calculate the total value or sum of a geometric progression e.g. measuring the total value of a savings account or pension over time. To do this we need to first understand the formula which calculates the sum of a geometric progression.

We can calculate the value or sum of terms in a geometric progression by using the following formula.

Let:

d = the common ratio in the geometric progression

U_1 = the first term in the geometric progression

S_n = the sum of terms in the geometric sequence up to the nth term

$$S_n = U_1\left(\frac{d^n - 1}{d - 1}\right), d \neq 1$$

Student note

---

[2] Source: World Development Indicators database, April 2006.

Example

An economy has a GDP of $40 billion and is expected to grow at 9 per cent per year every year. What will be the total and accumulated value of all economic activity over the first seven years?

The economy is following a geometric progression: it increases by 9 per cent each year and so the common ratio is 0.09. Using the formula above:

$d = 1.09$

$U_1 = \$40 \text{ billion}$

$$S_n = U_1\left(\frac{d^n - 1}{d - 1}\right), d \neq 1$$

$$= \$40 \text{ billion} \times \left(\frac{1.09^7 - 1}{1.09 - 1}\right)$$

$$= \$40 \text{ billion} \times \left(\frac{0.828\ 039\ 12}{0.09}\right)$$

$$= \$40 \text{ billion} \times 9.2 = \$368 \text{ billion}.$$

We can double check this using the long-hand method too (see Table 5.4).

Table 5.4

	GDP ($ bn)
Year 1	40.000
Year 2	43.600
Year 3	47.524
Year 4	51.801
Year 5	56.463
Year 6	61.545
Year 7	67.084
Total	368.017

Quick problem 5

Task One
Calculate S_{10} for the following geometric progression: 2, 6, 18, 54.

Task Two
Calculate S_7 for the following geometric progression: 100, 50, 25, 12.5.

Task Three
Calculate S_{17} or the following geometric progression: 7, 10.5, 15.75, 23.625.

Task Four (extension)
A nuclear power plant hires an economist to advise on the costs of running the plant and disposing of waste. Every five years the powerplant has to apply for a 'Processing Permit' which costs

▶

£75 for every kilo of radioactive waste that the powerplant has made. The nuclear materials are not stable – they decay at a certain rate – and the quicker they decay so the less radioactive they are and the lower the Processing Permit.

The powerplant expects to produce 250 million kilos of radioactive waste in year 1. Assuming this decays by one half each year:

(a)   What will the quantity of radioactive waste produced in year 1 be after five years?

(b)   What will the Processing Permit be in year 5 for the waste created in year 1?

✔**Learning outcome 5**

An arithmetic progression or a geometric progression?

Sometimes it might not be immediately obvious whether the series you are examining is an arithmetic progression or a geometric progression. One quick way to tell is follow the simple flowchart in Figure 5.1.

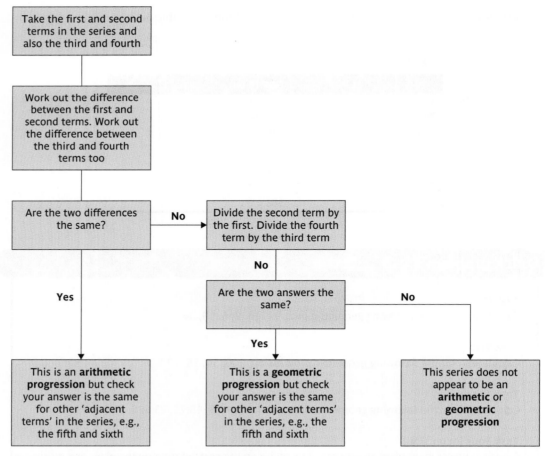

Figure 5.1 A simple flowchart for identifying whether a sequence is an arithmetic or a geometric progression

5.4 Practical applications: simple and compound interest

A common application of sequences and progression is the calculation of simple and compound interest. Interest can be seen in two ways. First, it can be viewed as the charge by a lender to a borrower for the use of his or her money, e.g., a homeowner raises a mortgage and over 25 years they repay the sum they borrowed ('the principal') plus interest to pay for the mortgage service. Second, interest can be described as the reward to investors for loaning their money to a third party, e.g., somebody who deposits a sum of money in a bank account would expect to receive a return or interest for so doing.

Student note

Simple interest
Simple interest is worked out as a flat percentage rate on a sum of money and is based purely on the original sum.

Simple interest received = (interest rate × £ principal sum invested)

For example, if I invest £5000 in a bank account and expect to receive simple interest of 5 per cent after five years.

$$\text{Simple interest received} = \left(\frac{5}{100} \times £5000 \right) = £250$$

The total sum I would receive after five years would then be the principal plus the interest i.e. £5000 + £250 = £5250. Note that we converted the interest as a percentage (5 per cent) into a decimal (0.05) by dividing by 100.

Quick problem 6

Complete Table 5.5 for each investor on the basis of simple interest:

Table 5.5

	Investor A	Investor B	Investor C	Investor D
Principal invested	£10 000		£30 000	£125 000
Rate of interest payable after five years	3%	4%	5%	
Total interest receivable after five years		£320		£16 000

✔ **Learning outcome 6**

Compound interest is a slightly more complex but much more common method of earning interest. Many savings accounts pay a rate of interest to savers every year. If the savers do not withdraw any of their money from the savings account then the next time the bank comes to calculate interest it would be on the new and higher amount in the account – that is, the interest

Table 5.6

End of year	Value of the savings	Interest earned
0	£1000	0
1	(£1000 × 1.1) = £1100.00	£100.00
2	(£1000 × 1.1^2) = £1210.00	£210.00
3	(£1000 × 1.1^3) = £1331.00	£331.00
4	(£1000 × 1.1^4) = £1464.10	£464.10
5	(£1000 × 1.1^5) = £1610.51	£610.51

would be calculated on the principal plus the amount of interest which had already been added to the account after the first year. Compound interest then calculates interest taking into account both the original principal and accumulated interest.

The link between compound interest and geometric progressions

You may have already made the link with the earlier concept of geometric progressions.

A sum of £1000 which earns 10 per cent interest each year can be expressed as shown in Table 5.6.

The common ratio in this geometric progression is 1.1.

Student note

Compound interest

Compound interest then calculates interest taking into account both the original principal and accumulated interest.

The value of savings after n years (V_n) using compound interest can be calculated by:

$V_n = (\text{principal}) \times (\text{interest rate})^n$

Remember, the principal is the original amount of money that was inverted.

Example

A stockbroker invests £50 000 in a bank account and is guaranteed a 3 per cent return each year.

Task One

What is the value of his savings after seven years?

Task Two

How many years will he need to invest his money to ensure he has £100 000 in his savings account?

Task Three

The stockbroker opts for a new savings scheme. He invests £25 000 in a new account on 1 January and he adds a further £10 000 on each 31 December. He is guaranteed 2.5 per cent interest on his savings deposits. He makes no withdrawals.

What is the value of his savings account at the end of year 7?

Solution to Task One

$$V_n = (\text{principal}) \times (\text{interest rate})^n$$

$$= £50\ 000 \times (1.03)^7$$

$$= £61\ 493.69$$

Solution to Task Two

$$V_n = (\text{principal}) \times (\text{interest rate})^n$$

$$\Rightarrow 1\ 000\ 000 = 50\ 000 \times 1.03^n$$

$$1.03^n = 2$$

$$n \times \ln 1.03 = \ln 2$$

$$n = \left(\frac{\ln 2}{\ln 1.03} \right)$$

$$n = 23.45 \text{ years} \approx 23 \text{ years } 6 \text{ months}$$

(*Note*: you might want to review Chapter 1 regarding logarithms.)

So, the investor could expect his investment to reach £100 000 after 23 years and six months.

Solution to Task Three

For this task, a simple spreadsheet is probably the best way to structure your solution (Table 5.7).

In January of year 1 we see £25 000 is deposited and this accrues £625 of interest at the end of the year. A further £10 000 is invested at the end of the year.

We can see that the value of his savings at the end of year 7 is worth £105 191.45 and this includes the £10 000.00 which is deposited on 31 December in year 7.

Table 5.7

	Jan year 1	Jan year 2	Jan year 3	Jan year 4	Jan year 5	Jan year 6	Jan year 7
Principal	£25 000.00	£35 625.00	£46 515.63	£57 678.52	£69 120.48	£80 848.49	£92 869.70
Interest at end of year	£625.00	£890.63	£1 162.89	£1 441.96	£1 728.01	£2 021.21	£2 321.74
Further investment	£10 000.00	£10 000.00	£10 000.00	£10 000.00	£10 000.00	£10 000.00	£10 000.00
Total savings	£35 625.00	£46 515.63	£57 678.52	£69 120.48	£80 848.49	£92 869.70	£105 191.45

Quick problem 7

Task One
A nephew inherits £8300 from his Auntie. He wants to invest the money so that he will £10 000 as quickly as possible. If he invests in a bank account paying 6.2 per cent each year, how long will it take him to reach his £10 000 target?

✔ **Learning outcome 7**

5.5 Practical applications: investment appraisal

Investment appraisal refers to a management process of evaluating an investment opportunity. It can be used in a wide variety of contexts including:

- Government agencies planning for the provision of future transfer payments such as unemployment benefits or income support schemes
- An individual deciding which savings account to select
- A worker approaching retirement choosing whether to opt for a larger lump sum and a reduced monthly income stream
- A corporation judging whether it would be economic to purchase a large item of capital machinery
- An investment company evaluating how to invest clients' money over a range of competing investment products, e.g., stocks, shares bonds, etc.

All of these examples share a common theme: they all involve making investment decisions today by trying to make reasoned judgements about the future. It is this process of making sensible and analytical financial assessments which captures the fundamental idea of investment appraisal.

Student note

Investment appraisal involves a number of key ideas or terms:

Present values
The present worth of a future amount of money taking into account the time value of money.

Net present values
The net present value calculates the present value of a future sum of money.

The internal rate of return
The internal rate of return compares the rate of return offered by an investment project against the interest rate offered by a simple savings account.

Discounting
Discounting refers to the process of finding the present worth of a future amount of money.

Annuities
Annuities are a financial product which pay an individual a sum of money each year for a given number of years in return for an upfront cash payment.

Present values

Many investment strategies such as endowments policies or some fixed term investments provide an individual or firm receiving a fixed sum of money at some point in the future. On the face of it, the decision is quite straightforward: you simply decide whether or not the sum of money you would receive under the scheme offers you an appropriate return. But in reality the decision is more complex because to make a proper assessment you would need to analyse what that fixed sum of money in the future would be worth to you today.

We can use a formula to perform this calculation and this should look familiar from our previous discussion on geometric progressions (see above):

Let:

F denote 'The future value of the investment after n years'

P denote 'The value of the initial investment or principal'

i denote the rate of interest also referred to as 'the discount rate'

n denote the number of years of investing

Then:

$$F = P\left(1 + \frac{i}{100}\right)^n$$

and to then find out what that future value (F) is worth today (P) we need to rearrange and make P the subject. We then get:

$$P = \frac{F}{\left(1 + \dfrac{i}{100}\right)^n}$$

or $\quad P = F\left(1 + \dfrac{i}{100}\right)^{-n}$

where we simply multiply instead of dividing by making the index negative. (See Chapter 1 for a recap on using powers.)

Example

Jean Cheesman is worried about her retirement pension and approaches a bank who offer her a fixed return of 7 per cent per year on any deposit she makes with them. Jean invests £5000 but wants to know what she should expect to receive in eight years' time when she retires.

Using the above formula,

$$F = P\left(1 + \frac{i}{100}\right)^n$$

where:

$P = £5000$

$i = 7\%$

$$F = 5000\left(1 + \frac{7}{100}\right)^8 = 5000(1.07)^8$$

$$F = £8590.03$$

So Jean should expect to have £8590.03 in her savings account after eight years.

Jean is disappointed: she wants to have £10 000 in eight years time so she can celebrate her retirement with a cruise around the world. She needs to know how much she needs to deposit with the bank today to ensure she has the full £10 000 in eight years' time. Put another way, what is the discounted value of the £10 000?

Using the above formula,

$$F = P\left(1 + \frac{i}{100}\right)^n$$

Rearranging to make *P* the subject:

$$P = F\left(1 + \frac{i}{100}\right)^{-n}$$

$$P = 10\,000\left(1 + \frac{0.07}{100}\right)^{-8}$$

$$P = £5820.09$$

So Jean needs to invest £5820.09 today to ensure she has £10 000 in eight years' time given that the bank is offering 7 per cent per year.

We can check this calculation using a long-hand calculation:

Year 0	£5 820.09
Year 1	£6 227.50
Year 2	£6 663.42
Year 3	£7 129.86
Year 4	£7 628.95
Year 5	£8 162.98
Year 6	£8 734.39
Year 7	£9 345.79
Year 8	£10 000.00

Quick problem 8

Task One
Calculate the present value of £4500 in six years' time if the compound interest rate is 4 per cent.

Task Two
What must the principal investment be if £90 000 is received in 10 years' time and the compound rate of interest is 3.2 per cent.

Task Three

An investor faces two choices: she can invest in either Product A or Product B.

Product A: This investment product would require an investor depositing £4000 in a bank account and receiving £5000 in three years' time.

Product B: This investment would pay £7000 in nine years' time in return for a £5000 deposit.

Which product offers the highest compound interest rate?
(Tip: rearrange the present value formula to make '*i*' the subject.)

Task Four (extension)

How might inflation affect the present value of an investment? How could inflation be taken into account?

✔ **Learning outcome 8**

Net present value (NPV)

Net present value is a simple extension of the material we have covered above on present values. Net present values are typically used to analyse whether a potential investment is likely to be profitable or not; that is, will the revenues which the investment is expected to generate be at least as big as the investment costs. Usually in business and economics the word 'net' means that a subtraction has taken place, and in this context the subtraction refers to the cost of the investment project.

The NPV of a project can be calculated by calculating the present value of an investment and then subtracting the cost of the investment.

$$\text{Net present value} = F\left(1 + \frac{i}{100}\right)^{-n} - C$$

where:

F denotes 'The future value of the investment after n years'

P denotes 'The value of the initial investment or principal'

i denotes the rate of interest also referred to as 'the discount rate'

n denotes the number of years of investing

C denotes the cost of the investment

Interpretion of the results is shown in Table 5.8.

Table 5.8

	NPV < 0	NPV = 0	NPV > 0
Interpretation of NPV figure	The project is not expected to be profitable.	The project will just break even: projected discounted revenues will equal the investment cost.	The project is expected to earn a profit.

Student note

Example

The Dorf Motor Company is exploring ways to improve revenue and is considering purchasing a new robotic welding system to improve the quality of its vehicles. The robotic welding system would cost £3 million and is expected to produce an additional £4 million of revenue after three years. The discount rate is 6 per cent.

$$\text{Net present value} = F\left(1 + \frac{i}{100}\right)^{-n} - C$$

$$\text{Net present value} = £4 \text{ million}\left(1 + \frac{6}{100}\right)^{-3} - £3 \text{ million}$$

Net present value = +£0.358 477 132 million
or +£358 477.13

The investment is expected to produce a positive present value of £358 477 and the Dorf car company should proceed.

In effect, this calculation is testing whether the Dorf car company should spend the £3 million and recoup £4 million in three years' time or whether instead it should simply put £3 million in a bank account paying interest of 6 per cent per year.

Quick problem 9

Task One

Consider the following investment opportunities for a large manufacturing company. The discount rate is 5 per cent.

Investment A: costs £150 000 and pledges to pay £175 000 after six years.

Investment B: costs £180 000 and pledges to pay £201 000 after seven years.

Investment C: costs £165 000 and pledges to pay £170 000 after two years.

Which investment would you recommend and why?

Task Two

A third investment D is considered. This costs £150 000 and pays a return of £190 000 after 10 years.
　　What discount rate is needed for this investment to:

(i)　Have a NPV of £10 000?

(ii)　Break even? (*Note:* 'Break even' means that the NPV is zero.)

Task Three

What other factors might the company want to consider before making its final investment decision?

✔ **Learning outcome 9**

The internal rate of return (IRR)

The internal rate of return offers another method of evaluating the profitability of an investment project. This method compares the rate of return offered by an investment project against the rate of return offered by simply investing in a savings account.

We can rearrange our present value formula to make 'i' the subject as follows.
   Let:

F denote 'The future value of the investment after n years'

P denote 'The value of the initial investment or principal'

i denote the rate of interest also referred to as 'the discount rate'

n denote the number of years of investing

Then:

$$F = P\left(1 + \frac{i}{100}\right)^n$$

and so,

$$i = \left(\sqrt[n]{\frac{F}{P}}\right) - 1$$

We can then compare the rate of return offered by our project (i) against what we believe to be the interest rate available elsewhere and simply choose whichever project promises the highest interest rate.

Student note

Example
A stockbroker wants to increase his business and decides to offer 'guaranteed returns'. She offers potential investors £30 000 in six years' time in return for a £20 000 investment. She is aware that the market interest rate is 8 per cent.
   Using the internal rate of return, assess her offer.

$$i = \left(\sqrt[n]{\frac{F}{P}}\right) - 1$$

$$i = \left(\sqrt[6]{\frac{30\ 000}{20\ 000}}\right) - 1$$

$$i = 0.0699 \quad \text{or} \quad 6.99\%$$

Interpretation: the stockbroker may find it difficult to boost demand with her proposal. Her offer implies a return of 6.99 per cent while investors could earn 8 per cent per year simply by putting their money elsewhere.

Quick problem 10

Task One
A worker has their annual appraisal and receives a bonus of £6000. His firm offers to invest his bonus in the company and guarantees to pay him £10 000 in five years' time. He researches other investment opportunities and believes he could secure 5 per cent elsewhere. Should he accept the firm's offer?

Task Two
The company reviews its offer and now guarantees the worker the sum of £7841.76 for the same deal. He believes that the rate he could secure elsewhere has risen to 5.5 per cent.
    Should he accept the revised offer?

✔ **Learning outcome 10**

Annuities

Annuities are a popular financial product and are designed to provide a stream of income over a period of time. Typically, an investor pays a single lump sum of cash and in return receives a interest payment and a regular payment. Where the investor opts for a regular payment which is larger than the interest they receive, they must be tapping into some of the original investment – or principal – with the effect that the annuity eventually becomes exhausted.

It is already obvious that annuities can be very appealing for investors wishing to make arrangements for their retirement: they can plan with some certainty regarding their monthly or annual income.

Investors considering purchasing an annuity will want to consider a range of issues such as risk and certainty, and so on. They will also want to consider:

■ The present value of an annuity
■ How long the annuity can be expected to last before the original principal is exhausted.

Student note

Annuities offer a stream of income plus interest in return for a lump sum investment.

Present value of an annuity
Over time we can see that the present value of an annuity is really a geometric progression.
    We work out the present value of each payment as:

$$PV = F(1 + i/100)^{-1}$$

If we want to work out the total value of the annuity we then need to add or sum all of the payments. That is, we want to calculate the sum of a geometric progression.

We can apply our earlier knowledge and understanding to calculate that:

The total present value of annuity (TPVA) $= F\left(\dfrac{i^n - 1}{i - 1}\right)$

where:

F denotes 'The value of the regular annuity payment'

TPVA denotes 'The total present value of the annuity'

i denotes the rate of interest also referred to as 'the discount rate'

n denotes the number of years of investing

Worked example

An annuity offers an annual income of £5000 for eight years. The interest rate is 6.5 per cent compounded annually.

   What is the present value of the annuity?

After one year, the investor receives £5000
The present value of this payment is $£5000(1.065)^{-1} = £4694.84$.

After two years, the investor receives a further £5000.
The present value of this second payment is $£5000(1.065)^{-2} = £4408.30$.

The total present value of annuity (TPVA) $= F\left(\dfrac{i^n - 1}{i - 1}\right)$

where:

$F = £5000(1.065)^{-1}$ (*Note:* this is the present value of the first annual payment.)
$i = (1.065)^{-1}$
$n = 8$

The total present value of annuity (TPVA) $= £5000(1.065)^{-1}\left(\dfrac{(1.065^{-1})^8 - 1}{1.065^{-1} - 1}\right)$

The total present value of annuity (TPVA) $= £5000(1.065)^{-1}\left(\dfrac{(1.065^{-8}) - 1}{1.065^{-1} - 1}\right)$

TPVA $= £30\,443.75$

Interpretation: An investor would need to invest £30 443.75 in order to receive an annual payment of £5000 for eight years' assuming the annual compound interest rate is 6.5 per cent.

Quick problem 11

Task One

An annuity product guarantees to pay £7500 each year for 12 years. The interest rate is 9 per cent compounded on an annual basis.

What is the present value?

Task Two

A worker approaching retirement considers a range of products which offer to provide a regular annual income. He is attracted to one particular scheme which guarantees an annual income of £10 000 for 10 years with the interest rate being 7.1 per cent.

The scheme would require him paying a sum of £120 000 to the investment company.

Advise him whether he should accept the offer or not.

Task Three

The same worker considers an alternative investment annuity. This product offers: £3000 each year with the interest rate being 4 per cent in return for a £35 000 payment.

What is the minimum number of whole years this annuity should be paid for it to be worthwhile for the investor?

✔ **Learning outcome 11**

5.6 A further practical application: economic growth

Economists are frequently interested in understanding how key economic variables such as consumption, inflation and income change over time. Often economists will want to calculate the average annual growth rates and use this to make judgements or inferences about what might happen in the future. It is often not easy to identify growth trends simply by looking at raw data. This information can help agencies plan public service provision.

Consider the data in Figure 5.2, taken from the Office of National Statistics, which graphs gross domestic product (GDP) over a period of time. Gross domestic product is a measure of total or aggregate economic activity in an economy over a period of time. The term 'market prices' simply means that the value of the economic activities have been added together using the prevailing prices at the time, i.e., GDP at market prices includes any inflation that exists.

Although we can see that GDP is on an upward trend over the given time period, it is not clear what the growth rate might be. We could not state easily by how much the economy has expanded or what the equivalent rate of average annual rate of economic growth might be.

A simple percentage calculation can be undertaken as follows:

Annual GDP growth rate

$$= \left(\frac{(\text{GDP at the end of the year} - \text{GDP at the beginning of the year})}{\text{GDP beginning of the year}} \right) \times 100\%$$

Table 5.9 calculates the annual GDP growth rate for each year using the above data for the period 2001 to 2007.

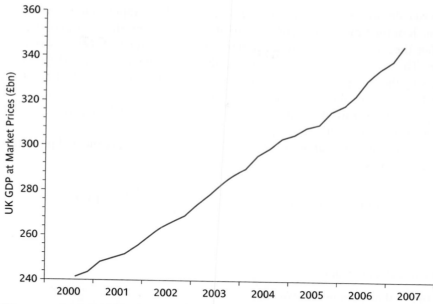

Figure 5.2 UK GDP at market prices (£million)
Source: Office for National Statistics

Table 5.9

	GDP at market prices (£bn)	Annual GDP Growth
Q1 01	247 905	
Q2 01	249 597	
Q3 01	251 028	
Q4 01	254 767	
Q1 02	259 054	4.50
Q2 02	262 774	
Q3 02	265 836	
Q4 02	268 129	
Q1 03	272 953	5.37
Q2 03	277 119	
Q3 03	281 996	
Q4 03	286 177	
Q1 04	288 912	5.85
Q2 04	295 066	
Q3 04	297 941	
Q4 04	302 377	
Q1 05	303 996	5.22
Q2 05	307 306	
Q3 05	308 515	
Q4 05	314 159	
Q1 06	316 789	4.21
Q2 06	321 453	
Q3 06	328 388	
Q4 06	332 992	
Q1 07	336 652	6.27

The third column provides a useful insight into what has happened to UK GDP. We can tell that for much of the time period GDP at market prices has typically increased by around 5 per cent. In 2006 the annual growth rate was still positive at just over 4 per cent but less than in previous years. This reduced growth rate could signify a global downturn or perhaps a deflationary fiscal policy by the UK government. The point here is that the growth calculations allow us to start to make inferences about what has been going on.

We might want to know more about the growth rate over the whole period, e.g., what is the overall average annual growth rate.

One way is to simply repeat our earlier calculation using the start and end points for GDP at market prices. That is,

$$\text{Total GDP growth rate over the time period} = \left(\frac{(\text{GDP}_{t+1} - \text{GDP}_t)}{\text{GDP}_t} \right) \times 100\%$$

where:

GDP_t = the initial GDP value

GDP_{t+1} = the final or closing value of GDP

$$\text{Total GDP growth rate over the time period} = \left(\frac{(336\ 652 - 247\ 905)}{247\ 905} \right) \times 100\%$$

$$= 35.8\%$$

We could divide this figure by the number of years to arrive at the annual average GDP growth rate. We will use the full six years' of data and ignore the last data observation for 2007 Q1.

Initial GDP value = 247 905

Last GDP value = 332 992 (remember we have ignored the last value in Table 5.9 so we have six full years' of observations)

Total GDP growth = (332 992 − 247 905)/247 905 = 34.3

$$\text{Annual average GDP growth rate} = \left(\frac{\text{Total GDP growth}}{\text{Number of years}} \right)$$

$$= 34.33\%/6 \text{ years} = 5.7\% \text{ per year}$$

The problem with this approach is that it does not take into account the concept of compounding and because of this it will tend to overstate the real average annual growth rate. In the same way as we differentiated between simple and compound interest, so we need to incorporate exactly the same notion to make the distinction between simple and compound growth. Therefore, to work out the average annual compounded growth rate we need to refer to our earlier formula.

$$\text{Average annual compounded growth rate } (g) = \sqrt[n]{\left(\frac{\text{GDP}_{t+1}}{\text{GDP}_t} \right)} - 1$$

where n = the number of years between GDP_{t+1} and GDP_t

For our example then we get:

$$g = \sqrt[6]{\left(\frac{332\ 992}{247\ 905}\right)} - 1 = 0.054\ 867\ 736 \text{ or } 5.04\% \text{ per year on a compounded basis.}$$

We can check the accuracy of this result. Rearranging:

$$GDP_{t+1} = 247\ 905 \times (1.050\ 408)^6 = 332\ 992 \text{ (which we know is the final value)}$$

Quick problem 12

Consider the data (Table 5.10) on the economy of China. This states the real value (i.e., with inflation removed) of GDP per capita in China from 1986 to 2000 (inclusive).

Assume the figures relate to the first day in each calendar year, i.e., the real GDP per capita for 1986 is 1 January 1986.

Table 5.10

Year	Real GDP per capita ($ in current prices)
1986	1231.736 862
1987	1344.609 442
1988	1419.553 566
1989	1400.499 078
1990	1568.282 772
1991	1788.926 969
1992	2031.611 566
1993	2306.039 113
1994	2551.965 096
1995	2759.921 255
1996	2972.606 456
1997	3141.065 904
1998	3317.788 097
1999	3483.390 775
2000	3843.665 599

Source: Penn World Data

Task One

Looking at the data explain why it is difficult to infer what the growth rate in real GDP per capita over the period.

Task Two

(a) Calculate the annual growth rate for 1985 to 2000 using the formula for compounding growth.

(b) Comment on this figure.

Task Three

(a) Why might the Chinese government be interested to know the figure you found in (a)? How might they use these data?

(b) Why might other countries be interested to know the figure you calculated for Task Two?

✔ **Learning outcome 12**

Answers to quick problems

Quick problem 1

(a)
Let:

U_n = the value of the nth term.

d = the common difference

U_1 = the first term in the sequence

$$U_n = U_1 + (n - 1) \times d$$

We want to find out U_7

$d = +40\ 000$

$U_1 = 120\ 000$

$$U_n = U_1 + (n - 1) \times d$$

$$U_7 = 120\ 000 + (6 \times 40\ 000)$$

$$U_7 = 120\ 000 + 240\ 000 = 360\ 000$$

(b)
We want to find out U_7

$d = +35\ 000$

$U_1 = 120\ 000$

$$U_n = U_1 + (n - 1) \times d$$

$$U_7 = 120\ 000 + (6 \times 35\ 000)$$

$$U_7 = 120\ 000 + 210\ 000 = 330\ 000$$

Quick problem 2

Task One

$$U_n = U_1 + (n - 1) \times d$$

$$
\begin{aligned}
U_{17} &= \$250\text{ million} + (16 \times \$17.5\text{ million}) \\
&= \$250\text{ million} + (16 \times \$17.5\text{ million}) \\
&= \$250\text{ million} + \$280\text{ million} \\
&= \$530\text{ million}
\end{aligned}
$$

Task Two

$$S_n = \frac{n}{2}(2U_1 + (n-1)d)$$

$$S_{17} = \frac{17}{2}(2 \times \$250 \text{ million} + (17-1)\$17.5 \text{ million})$$

$$S_{17} = \$6630 \text{ million or } \$6.63 \text{ billion}$$

Task Three
We want $S_{17} - S_{15}$

$S_{17} = \$6630$ million
$S_{15} = \$5587.5$ million

$$S_{17} - S_{15} = \$6630 \text{ million} - \$5587.5 \text{ million}$$
$$= \$1042.5 \text{ million or } 1.0425 \text{ billion}$$

Task Four (extension)

$$S_n = \frac{n}{2}(2U_1 + (n-1)d)$$

$$S_{17} - S_{15} = \frac{17}{2}(2U_1 + (16)d) - \frac{15}{2}(2U_1 + (14)d)$$

$$= 8.5(2U_1 + (16)d) - 7.5(2U_1 + (14)d)$$
$$= 17U_1 + 136d - 15U_1 - 105d$$

$$S_{17} - S_{15} = 2U_1 + 31d$$

Quick problem 3

Task One

Sequence	Common ratio
(a) 3, 6, 12, 24, 48, 96, 192	2
(b) 4, 16, 64, 256, 1024, 4096, 16 384	4
(c) 2.2, 7.26, 23.958, 79.0614, 260.9026, 860.9786, 2841.23	3.3
(d) +5, −4, +3.2, −2.56, +2.048, −1.6384, +1.310 72, −1.048 58, +0.838 861	−0.8

Task Two
In the last sequence, the common ratio is negative and less than 1. This produces two effects. First, because the common ratio is less than 1, each term is smaller than the preceding one. Second, because the common ratio is negative the progression switches from positive and negative and back to positive again (since every other term involves the multiplication of two negative numbers which produces a positive figure).

Quick problem 4

Task One

Let:

d = the common ratio in the geometric progression

U_1 = the first term in the geometric progression

U_n = the value of the nth term in the geometric progression

We have:

$d = 1.045$

$U_1 = \$44.4$ trillion

$U_n = U_{20}$, i.e., 20 years or 20 terms

$U_n = U_1 \times d^n$

$U_{20} = \$44.4 \times 1.045^{20}$
$\quad = \$107.08$ trillion

Task Two

(i) U_{20} based on $d = 1.03 = \$44.4 \times 1.03^{20} = \$80.19$ trillion

(ii) The revised estimate of the global economy is $\left(\dfrac{\$80.19 \text{ trillion}}{\$107.08 \text{ trillion}} \right) \times 100\% = 74.89\% \approx 75\%$

This means that the proposed measures, by reducing annual global growth from 4.5 per cent to 3 per cent per year, could be expected to reduce global economic activity by around 25 per cent.

Task Three

Let:

d = the common ratio in the geometric progression

U_1 = the first term in the geometric progression

U_n = the value of the nth term in the geometric progression

We know that:

$U_1 = \$44.4$ trillion

$U_n = U_{20}$, i.e., 20 years or 20 terms

$U_n = U_1 \times d^n$

$U_{20} = \$44.4 \text{ trillion} \times d^{20}$
$\quad = \$124$ trillion

We need to find 'd'.

$124 = 44.4 \times d^{20}$

Dividing both sides by 44.4:

$2.79 = d^{20}$

$d = \sqrt[20]{2.79}$

$d = 1.052\ 64$

i.e., the world economy would grow each year by 5.26 per cent.

Quick problem 5

Task One

$S_{10} = 59\ 048$

Task Two

$S_7 = 198.44$

Task Three

$S_{17} = 13\ 779.66$

Task Four

(i) The geometric progression is 250, 125, 62.5, with a common ratio of 0.5.
We need to find:

$$U_5 = U_1 \times d^n$$
$$= 250 \times 0.5^5$$
$$= 7.8125 \text{ million kilos}$$

The 250 million kilos of waste will have become 7.8125 million kilos after five years have elapsed.

(ii) The Processing Permit costs £75 for each kilo.
The Processing Permit cost will be £75 × 7.8125 million kilos = £585.94 million.

Quick problem 6

Table 5.11

	Investor A	Investor B	Investor C	Investor D
Principal invested	£10 000	£8000	£30 000	£125 000
Rate of interest payable after five years	3%	4%	5%	12.8%
Total interest receivable after five years	£300	£320	£1500	£16 000

Quick problem 7

Task One

$$n = \left[\frac{\ln\left(\dfrac{10\,000}{8300}\right)}{\ln 1.062}\right] = 3.1 \text{ (to 1 dp)}.$$

The bank account will reach £10 000 in a little over three years and one month.

Quick problem 8

Task One

$P = £4500(1.04)^{-6} = £3556.42$

Task Two

$P = 90\,000(1.032)^{-10}$

$P = £65\,681.87$

Task Three
Rearranging for i, we get:

$$i = \left(\sqrt[n]{\frac{F}{P}}\right) - 1$$

Product A:

$$i = \left(\sqrt[3]{\frac{5000}{4000}}\right) - 1$$

$i = 0.0772$
or, as a percentage, $i = 7.72\%$

Product B:

$$i = \left(\sqrt[9]{\frac{7000}{5000}}\right) - 1$$

$i = 0.0381$
or, as a percentage, $i = 3.81\%$

Product A implies a higher annual rate of compound interest.

Task Four
Inflation is the rate of increase in the general price level of all goods and services in an economy over a period of time. Inflation leads to an erosion in the value of money and this includes savings and investments. One way to factor in inflation to investment appraisals is to use the real rate of interest. The real rate of interest is calculated as the nominal annual rate of interest (the rate which the bank pays you) minus the annual rate of inflation.

Quick problem 9

Task One

Table 5.12

	Investment A	Investment B	Investment C
Initial cost	£150 000.00	£180 000.00	£165 000.00
Present Value	£130 587.69	£142 846.95	£154 195.01
NPV	−£19 412.31	−£37 153.05	+£10 804.99

Only Investment C offers a positive NPV. Investments A and B would not be economic: the manufacturer would be better off simply investing the money needed to cover the initial costs in a bank account and receive 6 per cent per year.

Task Two

(i)

$$\text{Net present value} = F\left(1 + \frac{i}{100}\right)^{-n} - C$$

$$+10\,000 = 190\,000(1 + i)^{-10} - 150\,000$$

$$i = -\left(\sqrt[10]{\frac{160\,000}{190\,000}}\right) - 1 = 0.0173, \quad \text{i.e., } 1.73\%$$

(ii) Break even implies NPV = 0

$$\text{Net present value} = F\left(1 + \frac{i}{100}\right)^{-n} - C$$

$$0 = 190\,000(1 + i)^{-10} - 150\,000$$

$$i = -\left(\sqrt[10]{\frac{150\,000}{190\,000}}\right) - 1 = 0.023\,920\,49, \text{ i.e., } 2.39\%$$

Task Three

Any individual or firm making an investment decision will want to take into account a number of key factors including:

- Future rates of inflation
- The risk associated a particular project or strategy, e.g., how secure is the likely return?
- The effects which taxation might have on the final discounted return
- Any benefit from not committing to a project for a period of time and waiting to see which other and potentially more profitable opportunities arise.

Quick Problem 10

Task One

$$i = \left(\sqrt[n]{\frac{F}{P}}\right) - 1$$

$$i = \left(\sqrt[5]{\frac{10\,000}{6000}}\right) - 1$$

$i = 0.010\,756\,6$ or 10.8%

Interpretation: the firm is offering an IRR of 10.8 per cent which is much higher than the 5 per cent prevailing in the market. He should accept the offer.

Task Two

$$i = \left(\sqrt[5]{\frac{7841.76}{6000}}\right) - 1$$

$i = 0.054\,97$ or 5.5%

Interpretation: Looking purely at the IRR, the worker should be indifferent to the scheme since he would receive an identical rate of return if he invested elsewhere. However, he might want to look at other factors such as reputation and risk before making his final choice.

Quick problem 11

Task One

The total present value of annuity (TPVA) = $£7500(1.09)^{-1}\left(\dfrac{(1.09^{-1})^{12} - 1}{1.09^{-1} - 1}\right)$

The total present value of annuity (TPVA) = £53 705.44

Task Two

The total present value of annuity (TPVA) = $£10\,000(1.071)^{-1}\left(\dfrac{(1.071^{-1})^{10} - 1}{1.071^{-1} - 1)}\right)$

The total present value of annuity (TPVA) = £69 912.30

He should not accept the offer: in effect he would be paying £120 000 for a product which would offer him £69 912.30

Task Three

We need to find 'n' such that:

$$£35\ 000 = £3000(1.04)^{-1}\left(\frac{(1.04^{-1})^n - 1}{1.04^{-1} - 1}\right)$$

$$\left[\left(\frac{35\ 000 \times 1.04}{3000}\right) \times (1.04^{-1} - 1)\right] = 1.04^{-n} - 1$$

$$[(12.133\ 3) \times (-0.038\ 46) = 1.04^{-n} - 1$$

$$-0.46 + 1 = 1.04^{-n}$$

$$+0.53 = 1.04^{-n}$$

$$n = -\left(\frac{\ln 0.53}{\ln 1.04}\right) = 16.19\ \text{years}$$

Interpretation: The investor needs to ensure that the annuity will be paid for a minimum of 17 years for it to be worthwhile.

Quick problem 12

Task One

The figures are detailed and it is not possible to easily see what the rate of growth is although it is clearly positive. This problem is magnified by the need to compound the growth rates: this cannot be done through visual inspection of the figures and the formula must be applied for us to see what is really happening to annual economic growth.

Task Two

(a)

$$\text{Annual compound growth in real GDP per capita (G)} = \sqrt[n]{\left(\frac{\text{Real GDP per capita}_{t+1}}{\text{Real GDP per capita}_t}\right)} - 1$$

$$= \left(\sqrt[15]{\frac{3843.665\ 599}{1231.736\ 862}}\right) - 1$$

$$= 0.0788\ \text{or}\ 7.88\%\ \text{per annum}$$

(b) This is a high figure and confirms that the Chinese economy grew strongly over the period 1985–2000. The real output per person rose by nearly 8 per cent every year.

Task Three

(a) The Chinese government would be interested in this statistic for many reasons. An economy which is expanding rapidly could put pressure on natural resources, e.g., water, minerals, etc. There could be increased pressure on the demand for infrastructure, e.g., access to roads, railways, airports and telecommunications. The government might expect rising real GDP per capita to lead to rising real incomes for its citizens. This could lead to rising imports of foreign goods and services. The government might then use this to plan for future public services, e.g., a programme of roadbuilding.

(b) Other countries are likely to be interested in the growth of the Chinese economy. This growth might mean that the demand for foreign goods rises and this in turn could drive incomes, output and employment in countries which supply China. Foreign countries might notice that the world price of some factors of production increases as China 'sucks in' huge additional supplies of iron, steel, copper, timber, etc. to fuel its manufacturing. There is some evidence, for example, in recent years that China's huge construction boom has led to increases in the world price of steel. This linkage or inter-connection can mean that strong demand for products in one part of the world can shape the prices that firms and consumers end up paying on the other side of the globe.

Chapter 6

Non-linear equations and principles of differentiation

Topics covered

6.1 Introduction	*154*
6.2 Functions with more than one independent variable	*154*
6.3 Factorization	*160*
6.4 The quadratic formula	*163*
6.5 Economics applications of quadratic equations	*168*
6.6 Basic principles of differentiation	*173*
6.7 The simple derivative	*173*
6.8 The sum rule and the difference rule	*180*
6.9 The product rule	*182*
6.10 The quotient rule	*185*
6.11 The chain rule	*186*

LEARNING OUTCOMES

By the end of this chapter, you should understand:

1. The different types of non-linear equations

2. How to factorize a simple quadratic equation

3. How to use the quadratic formula

4. The application of quadratic equations in economics

5. Basic principles of differentiation.

6.1 Introduction

In the previous chapters we have looked at linear supply and demand relationships. These examples were useful in explaining some basic relationships in economics. However, it is necessary also to consider non-linear equations as these are often a more realistic representation of scenarios that we find in the study of economics. Supply, demand, cost, profit, and revenue functions can, and often are, non-linear and the following chapter introduces the different types of non-linear equation that you need to understand. The chapter then focuses on the quadratic equation – the most common non-linear relationship used in economics.

The second part of the chapter presents the basic rules of differentiation and how to solve for a number of different types of derivative. Subsequent sections also consider some simple applications of derivatives in economics. Further, and more complex, applications are presented in Chapter 7.

6.2 Functions with more than one independent variable

So far, we have focused on functions with only one independent variable and which take the general form $f(x) = ax + b$. These are known as linear functions and result in a graph that is a straight line. Examples of linear functions have been presented and applied to the field of economics throughout Chapters 2 and 3.

This concept can now be extended so that the function includes more than one independent variable, taking the general form $y = f(x, z, \ldots)$. In this case the function contains the dependent variable, y, and then a number of independent variables which are included in the brackets.

Examples of functions with more than one independent variable are presented below. Note that the shape of the graph changes depending on how many independent variables are included in the function.

Quadratic functions

A general quadratic equation is presented as $f(x) = ax^2 + bx + c$. Note that if $a = 0$ then the term ax^2 will also equal zero and the function will revert to a linear function which is presented as a straight line, i.e., $f(x) = bx + c$.

A linear function is specifically identified by the x term having a power of 1. If the x term has a power of 2 and $a \neq 0$ then the function is called quadratic and its graph is a parabola.

The graph of the quadratic function can either open upwards or downwards. If $a < 0$ then it opens downwards as illustrated in Figure 6.1(a). If $a > 0$ then the parabola opens upwards as illustrated in Figure 6.1(b). The position of the parabola on the graph relates to the coefficients of the x^2 and x terms.

(a)

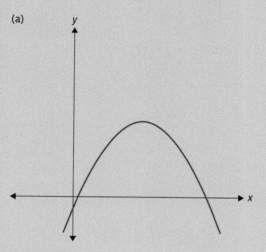

(b)

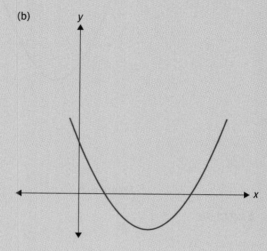

Figure 6.1

Example

$y = x^2 + 4x + 3$

Find co-ordinates when x takes the values $-3, -1$ and 0.

Co-ordinates:

$(-3, 0)$

$(-1, 0)$

$(0, 3)$

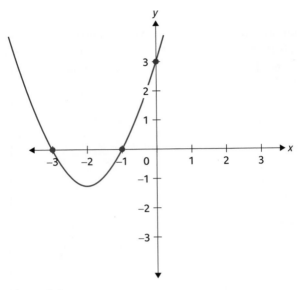

Figure 6.2

Example

$y = -x^2 + 6x - 5$

Find co-ordinates when x takes the values 5, 1 and 0.

Co-ordinates:

$(5, 0)$

$(1, 0)$

$(0, -5)$

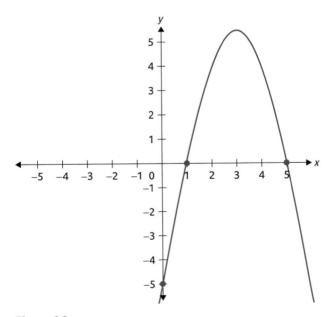

Figure 6.3

Functions with two independent variables are often used in economic models relating to the concepts of demand, price and income. Specific applications and examples are presented in section 6.8 to help you understand the relationship between quadratic function and economic analysis.

Cubic functions

A cubic function is simply an extension of the quadratic function in the sense that it includes a term raised to the power of 3 (called 'cubed'). The general form of a cubic function is presented as $f(x) = ax^3 + bx^2 + cx + d$ where $a \neq 0$ and $b \neq 0$. If $a = 0$ then the function reverts to a quadratic equation and if a and b are both equal to zero then the function becomes linear.

The exact shape of a cubic function is dependent on the sign associated with the coefficients of the x^3 and x^2 terms. Examples of cubic functions are presented in Figures 6.4 and 6.5.

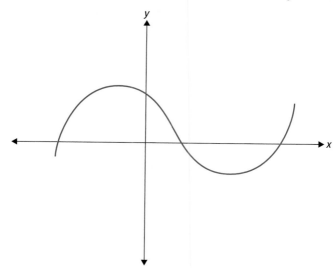

Figure 6.4

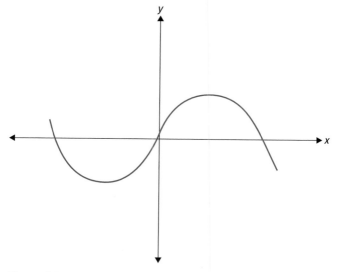

Figure 6.5

Student note

To summarize, the type of function is determined by the highest power of the independent variable. It will be useful to be familiar with the following:

$$f(x) = 8x - 12$$

In this case the power of x (the unknown variable) is 1 which tells us that the function is linear (a straight line).

$$f(x) = 3x^2 + 8x - 12$$

In this case the power of the first term ($3x^2$) is 2 (called 'squared') which tells us that this is a quadratic function.

$$f(x) = 4x^3 + 3x^2 + 8x - 12$$

In this case the power of the first term ($4x^3$) is 3 (called 'cubed') which tells us that this is a cubic function.

$$f(x) = a_n x^n + a_{n-1} x^{n-1} + \ldots + a_0$$

is the general form of a polynomial.

Graphing a quadratic function

The process of graphing a quadratic equation simply involves inputting different values of x into the equation and then solving for y. As long as you select a fairly broad range of values for x you are more than likely to be able to sketch the general shape of the function by inputting three or four x values. An example of this process is presented below.

Example
Sketch the graph of the following quadratic function:

$$f(x) = 2x^2 - 85x + 200$$

Always begin by inputting the value of $x = 0$ as this will give you the point at which the equation crosses the y-axis. Other points can be chosen at random.

When $x = 0$, $y = 200$.

When $x = 1$, $y = 2 - 85 + 200 = 117$. When considered in conjunction with the above point you can see that at $x = 1$ the graph of the quadratic function is downward sloping.

When $x = 3$, $y = 18 - 255 + 200 = -37$. This indicates that the quadratic function crosses the x axis (although we do not know exactly where).

When $x = 50$, $y = 5000 - 4250 + 200 = 950$. This shows that the point $(50, 950)$ is on the upward sloping portion of the graph.

Student note

Sketching a graph of a quadratic equation is fine if you simply want to know the shape of the function or if the function actually has a solution. However, this process is not very useful in the study of economics. Much more information is gained by solving for the quadratic and the key points that make up the associated graph, i.e., the exact points at which the quadratic crosses the x and y axes and/or the minimum and maximum points. In order to solve for these values you need to feel confident with the concepts of factorisation and the quadratic formula. These are presented in the following sections.

These points can now be plotted on a graph (Figure 6.6). Co-ordinates: (0, 200), (1, 117), (3, −37), (50, 950).

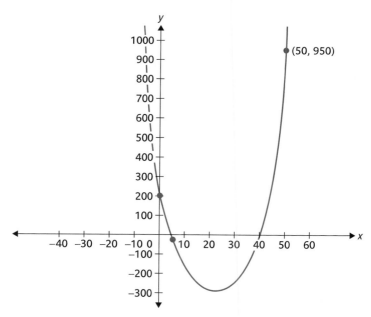

Figure 6.6

(a) $f(x) = 3x^2 - 4x + 20$

(b) $f(x) = 5x^2 + 20x - 80$

(c) $y = 6x^2 - 9x - 30$

✔ Learning outcome 1

6.3 Factorization

First, why do we want to factorize the quadratic function? The answer is that we want to find the value(s) for x that make the function equal to zero because these are the points at which the function crosses the horizontal axis. When quadratic equations are used in the study of economics these intersection points give us valuable information about price, quantity, revenue and costs. This will be illustrated further in the latter part of this chapter which looks at applications of quadratic equations to the field of economics.

There are two ways to solve for a quadratic function: by factorization or the quadratic formula. Both of these methods are explained in detail below. It is useful at this point to note that factorization is only really useful when you are faced with a simple quadratic equation, i.e., one where the factors can easily be determined. As soon as either of these characteristics change, it is faster and easier for you to apply the quadratic formula. Let us first look at the process of factorization and consider when this is a useful tool.

Factorization of a quadratic function involves reverting the quadratic function back to its original two bracketed expressions. The process of expressing a quadratic function in the form of two brackets is called *factorizing the quadratic expression.*

An expression such as $(x+3)(x+4)$ can be expanded to give the quadratic equation $x^2 + 7x + 12$. Factorization then refers to the process of reverting $x^2 + 7x + 12$ back to the two associated brackets $(x+3)$ and $(x+4)$.

To do this you need to work through the following steps:

$$f(x) = x^2 + 7x + 12$$

Set the function equal to zero:

$$x^2 + 7x + 12 = 0$$

Draw two sets of brackets:

$$(\quad)(\quad)$$

The first terms in each bracket will multiply together to give the first term in the quadratic equation. In this case the first term in both brackets is x because x times x gives x^2 which is the first term of the equation.

$(x\quad)(x\quad)$

The second term in each bracket is worked out as follows.

The two numbers should add together to give the coefficient of the x term divided by the coefficient on the x^2 term (in this case 7/1) and should multiply together to give the constant term divided by the coefficient on the x^2 term (in this case 12/1).

Often the solution to this problem is an obvious one. However it can also be considered as a sequence of equations:

$$a + b = 7$$

$$ab = 12$$

writing it this way often makes the solution more obvious.

The only combination of numbers that satisfy these two criteria are 3 and 4 so these are the two terms that are put in the brackets:

$(x\quad 3)(x\quad 4)$

Note that in this case it does not matter which number you put in which bracket as the answer will be the same. This is the case when all the terms in the original function are positive. When one or all of the terms in the original function are negative then you need to consider more closely the order of the second terms in the brackets. Also note that as the coefficient of x and the constant are both positive numbers that the terms in the brackets are also positive. Therefore the two brackets can be written as:

$$(x + 3)(x + 4) = 0$$

Therefore, in order for the whole expression to be equal to zero, x will either equal -3 or -4. If x is equal to either of these values then one of the brackets will equal zero which will result in the whole expression being equal to zero.

This is the easiest form of factorization and, with a little practice, you will be able to work out the factors just by looking at the equation. However, as soon as the equations become more complex, or you notice that there are no obvious combinations that add and multiply together to give the values you need, then you are best to move swiftly on to the application of the quadratic equation.

There are other examples of this process that are worth reviewing at this stage. Different combinations of signs (positives and negatives) will change the way that you construct the corresponding brackets. For example, suppose we start with the following quadratic equation:

$$x^2 - 12x + 35 = 0$$

In this case the first term in each bracket will be x. The second term in each bracket will depend on you finding two numbers that add up to -12 (remember you have to incorporate the associated sign in your calculations!) and that multiply together to give you 35.

First, list all the factors of 35. These are (1×35) and (5×7). Only 5 and 7 can give you a value of 12 (when added) and 35 (when multiplied) so these must be the numbers you are looking for. Now consider the signs. The terms must multiply together to give $+35$ which means that both terms must either be positive or negative. The terms also have to add up to -12. Therefore both terms must be negative in order to achieve both -12 and $+35$ with the same pair of numbers. So the factors associated with this quadratic equation are:

$$(x-5)(x-7) = 0$$

and the values of x that make this expression equal to zero are $x = +5$ and $x = +7$.

A third scenario is illustrated with the following quadratic equation:

$$x^2 + 14x - 32$$

The first term in each bracket will be x. Note that in this case the coefficient of x is positive but the constant term is negative. Therefore you need two numbers that add up to $+14$ and that multiply together to give -32. As in the previous case we need to consider the different combinations of numbers that have a product of -32. These are:

$(-1, 32)$
$(-32, 1)$
$(-16, 2)$
$(-2, 16)$
$(-8, 4)$
$(-4, 8)$

Considering each of these combinations you can see that the only one that also adds up to $+14$ is $(-2, 16)$. So the factors of your quadratic equation are:

$$(x-2)(x+16) = 0$$

and the values of x that make this expression equal to zero are $x = 2$ and $x = -16$.

Finally, you may be given an equation in the following form:

$$x^2 - 6x - 27$$

The first term in each bracket will be x. Note that in this case the coefficient of x and the constant term are both negative. Therefore you need two numbers that add up to -6 and that multiply together to give -27. As in the previous case we need to consider the different combinations of numbers that have a product of -27. These are:

$(-27, 1)$
$(-1, 27)$
$(-3, 9)$
$(-9, 3)$

Considering each of these combinations you can see that the only one that also adds up to -6 is $(-9, 3)$. So the factors of your quadratic equation are:

$$(x-9)(x+3) = 0$$

and the values of x that make this expression equal to zero are $x = 9$ and $x = -3$.

These examples cover the main types of quadratic equation that, with practice, are easier and faster to do by factorization than by using the quadratic formula. The following section shows you how to use the quadratic formula for more complex equations.

Finding the values of x that make the whole equation equal to zero gives you the points where the function crosses the x axis, i.e., the two values for x where y (or $f(x)$) is equal to zero. By substituting in a value of $x = 0$ you will also find the associated value for y which is the point at which the quadratic function crosses the y axis. Apart from the maximum/minimum point which we will consider later, these three points provide key information when quadratic equations are used in economics.

Quick problem 2

Solve the following quadratic equations using factorization:

(a) $x^2 - 11x + 30 = 0$

(b) $x^2 + x - 42 = 0$

(c) $x^2 - 4x - 12 = 0$

(d) $x^2 + 10x + 24 = 0$

✔ **Learning outcome 2**

6.4 The quadratic formula

The quadratic formula is a much more straightforward way of solving for quadratic equations. Remember that the general form of a quadratic equation is:

$$ax^2 + bx + c = 0$$

Based on this general equation you can use the following formula to solve for the values of x that make this equation true.

Quadratic formula

$$x = \frac{-b \pm \sqrt{b^2 - 4ac}}{2a}$$

The values for a, b and c are taken directly from the general equation above. An example of this formula is presented below.

Example
Given the equation $y = 3x^2 - 24x + 42$, find the values of x that make this equation equal to zero. In this case $a = 3$, $b = -24$ and $c = 42$.

Student note

The quadratic formula is simple to use as long as you plug in the correct values for a, b and c. Always remember:

1. The values for a and b do *not* include the x^2 and x terms, just the coefficients.

2. It is essential to include the sign when plugging the values for a, b and c into the formula. For example, given the equation $3x^2 - 24x + 42$ the value of a is $+3$ and the value of c is $+42$ but the value of b is -24. It is essential to plug -24 (rather than 24) into the formula in order to calculate the correct answer.

The formula can now be written as:

$$x = \frac{-b \pm \sqrt{b^2 - 4ac}}{2a} = \frac{-(-24) \pm \sqrt{-24^2 - ((4)(3)(42))}}{2(3)} = \frac{24 \pm \sqrt{576 - 504}}{6}$$

$$= \frac{24 \pm \sqrt{72}}{6} = \frac{24 \pm 8.49}{6} = 5.42 \text{ or } 2.59$$

Student note

The formula now provides two solutions to the problem. Note the $\pm$ sign in the formula. To achieve the first solution you add $24 + 8.49$ and divide by 6, and to achieve the second solution you subtract $24 - 8.49$ and divide by 6.

Also remember that the denominator applies to the whole of the numerator. This means that you do the calculation on the top of the equation before dividing the solution by the bottom of the equation. A common mistake is to divide 8.49 by 6 and then either add or subtract the solution to the number to the left of the $\pm$ sign.

Remember that you cannot solve for a quadratic equation unless you have set the equation equal to zero. Always gather the terms together on one side of the equation so that you can identify the correct values for a, b and c.

You can now apply the quadratic formula given that $a = 2$, $b = 3$ and $c = -50$.

$$P = \frac{-b \pm \sqrt{b^2 - 4ac}}{2a} = \frac{-3 \pm \sqrt{3^2 - ((4)(2)(-50))}}{2(2)} = \frac{-3 \pm \sqrt{9 + 400}}{4}$$

$$= \frac{-3 \pm \sqrt{409}}{4} = \frac{-3 \pm 20.22}{4} = -5.81 \text{ or } 4.31$$

$P = 4.31$ or $P = -5.81$

We disregard the negative price and accept that the firm will need to charge £4.31 per unit in order to sell 150 units of the good.

Example

A firm has a total cost schedule of $TC = 10 - 3q + 12q^2$. Assuming that the quantity sold is greater than 2 units ($q > 2$), at what output level will $TC = £200$?

In this case $TC = 10 - 3q + 12q^2$ and $TC = 200$. Therefore:

$$10 - 3q + 12q^2 = 200$$

which can be rearranged to give:

$$12q^2 - 3q - 190 = 0$$

Therefore, $a = 12$, $b = -3$ and $c = -190$. You can now plug these values into the quadratic formula:

$$q = \frac{-b \pm \sqrt{b^2 - 4ac}}{2a} = \frac{-(-3) \pm \sqrt{3^2 - ((4)(12)(-190))}}{2(12)} = \frac{3 \pm \sqrt{9 + 9120}}{24}$$

$$= \frac{3 \pm \sqrt{9129}}{24} = \frac{3 \pm 95.55}{24} = -3.86 \text{ or } 4.11$$

$q = 4.11$ or $q = -3.86$

Again, we disregard the negative solution as the quantity cannot be negative. This gives us the solution that total cost will be £200 when quantity is 4.11 units. Note that this also satisfies our original constraint that $q > 2$.

Example

Finally we will consider a situation in which we are given a linear demand function but asked to calculate the level of output necessary to achieve a specific amount of total revenue.

Student note

It may be useful to refer back to Chapter 3 for a list of relevant economic relationships. For example, the table explains that total revenue is equal to price x quantity ($TR = p \times q$) which is important to this example.

A firm has the demand function $p = 90 - q$. At what output level will total revenue be equal to £750?

This type of question involves an additional step in that you have to calculate the total revenue function before you are able to solve the problem.

Total revenue is equal to price × quantity. In this case price, p, is equal to $90 - q$. So we need to multiply this equation through by q:

$TR = p \times q$

$p = 90 - q$

$TR = p \times q = (90 - q) \times q$

$TR = 90q - q^2$

In this example TR is also equal to £750 which means:

$750 = 90q - q^2$

To solve for this quadratic equation we must rearrange it and set it equal to zero:

$q^2 - 90q + 750 = 0$

In this case $a = 1$, $b = -90$ and $c = 750$.

Applying the quadratic formula gives:

$$= \frac{-b \pm \sqrt{b^2 - 4ac}}{2a} = \frac{-(-90) \pm \sqrt{(-90)^2 - ((4)(1)(750))}}{2(1)} = \frac{90 \pm \sqrt{8100 - 3000}}{2}$$

$$= \frac{90 \pm \sqrt{5100}}{2} = \frac{90 \pm 71.41}{2} = 9.30 \text{ or } 80.71$$

$q = 80.71$ or $q = 9.30$

This tells us that total revenue will be equal to £750 when quantity is either 80.71 or 9.30.

Quick problem 5

A firm has a total cost schedule of $TC = 15 - 4q + 22q^2$. Assuming that the quantity sold is greater than 2 units ($q > 2$), at what output level will $TC = £450$?

✔ **Learning outcome 4**

6.6 Basic principles of differentiation

In previous chapters it has been noted that the slope of a function is an important concept in the study of economics. For example, it is important for a firm to know whether the demand for a good is relatively elastic (a fairly flat line) or more inelastic (a fairly steep line). Likewise it is relevant to a firm to have information about the slope of its cost curve. Differentiation is the operation that enables you to calculate the slope of a curve at any point. The basic rules of differentiation are explained and demonstrated in the final part of this chapter.

Chapter 7 then focuses on the application of these rules in the study of economics through the calculation and manipulation of marginal functions. This is one of the most important and useful mathematical concepts that you will learn at this stage and you will find that the basic rules of differentiation covered in Chapters 6 and 7 will reappear in almost every topic and application that you tackle from this point on.

6.7 The simple derivative

In Chapter 2 we considered linear functions and learned how to calculate the slope of a line. Specifically the slope of a line was defined as the change in the value of y as a result of a one unit increase in the value of x. We can now expand this definition and state that the general form of the slope, or gradient, of a line is the change in y divided by the corresponding change in x as measured between two defined points on a line.

The change in y is normally denoted as Δy and the change in x is denoted as Δx. The slope of the line can therefore be expressed as:

Slope $= \Delta y / \Delta x$

where the change is defined as the difference between two specified points on the given line.

Example

Given the co-ordinates (3, 5) and (6, 4) find the slope of the line passing through these two points.

Remember from Chapter 2 that the co-ordinates are expressed as (x, y). When you have two sets of co-ordinates you should label one of them (x_1, y_1) and the other (x_2, y_2). It does not matter which set of co-ordinates are assigned (x_1, y_1) and (x_2, y_2) as long as you do not mix the co-ordinates up. In this case we will assign the labels as follows:

$(3, 5)$ and $(6, 4)$
(x_1, y_1) (x_2, y_2)

$\text{Slope} = \Delta y/\Delta x = (y_2 - y_1)/(x_2 - x_1)$
$\text{Slope} = (4 - 5)/(6 - 3) = -1/3$

This tells us that the line is downward sloping and has a slope of $-1/3$.

This situation is illustrated in Figure 6.12.

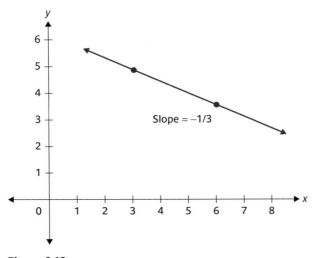

Figure 6.12

So far this explanation has been a recap of the information that was covered in Chapter 2. However, now that we have worked through various types of non-linear equations we can introduce the concept of differentiation and its use in the study of economics.

The above formula shows you how to find the slope of a straight line between two points. We can now consider the calculation of a slope for a non-linear function, such as one of the quadratic functions that we solved earlier in this chapter. Consider the graph (Figure 6.13) of the quadratic function:

$y = 3x^2 - 24x + 42$

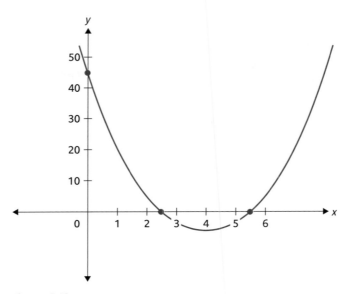

Figure 6.13

The slope of this line is different at each point along the curve. A quadratic function (or any other function that is nonlinear) has many slopes and we therefore need to select a specific point along the curve and work out the slope at that point. We do this by drawing a straight line that is tangent to the curved line at a specified point. We can then work out the slope of the straight line which will in turn tell us the slope of the non-linear function at that point. Every point along the non-linear function has a tangency line with its own slope. This situation is illustrated in Figure 6.14.

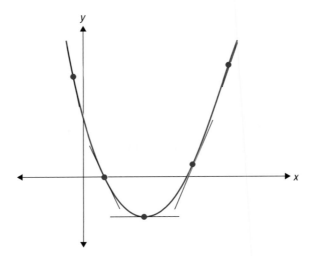

Figure 6.14

Student note

Note that the slope of the tangency line gives you key information about the function. For instance if the slope of the tangency line is positive then this tells you that you have chosen a point that is on the upward sloping part of the curve, while a tangency line that has a negative slope represents a point on the downward sloping section of the curve.

Consider the function $f(x) = 2x^2 - 42x + 30$. Inputting values for x would then give you the value of the function at a specific point and $f'(x)$ ('f prime x') which is the *derivative* of $f(x)$ denotes the slope of the function at that point.

So $f'(x)$ is the derivative of $f(x)$ which means that for each point along the x axis you can calculate the slope ($f'(x)$) at that point. An alternative notation for the derivative of a function is presented as:

dy/dx

but be careful to remember that this does not mean that you divide a y value by an x value. This notation is simply a way of illustrating that you are going to work out the derivative of y in terms of x. This brings us neatly to an explanation of the simple derivative.

You will need to remember the following rule:

If $f(x) = x^n$, then $f'(x) = nx^{n-1}$.

Or

If $y = x^n$, then $dy/dx = nx^{n-1}$.

This says that to take the derivative of x^n you bring the power, n, down to the front of the function, leave the x where it is and subtract 1 from the power.

It does not matter whether you use $f'(x)$ or dy/dx to denote the derivative. Generally if you use $y = x^3$ to identify the cubed function then you would use dy/dx to identify the derivative of that function. On the other hand if you use $f(x) = x^3$ to identify the cubed function then you would use $f'(x)$ to describe the derivative of that function.

This simple operation can now be used to find the slope of a non-linear function at any point.

Example

Sketch the function $f(x) = x^2$ and then find the slope of the function at points $x = -2$, $x = 1$ and $x = 2$.

To sketch the graph of $f(x) = x^2$ we input a selection of numbers into the function and then join the points on the graph (Figure 6.15).

When $x = -2$, $f(x) = 4$

When $x = 0$, $f(x) = 0$

When $x = 2$, $f(x) = 4$

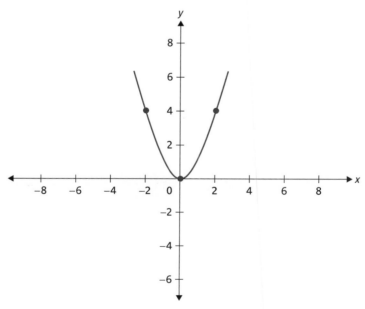

Figure 6.15

Now we want to find the slope of the function at various points. As the function is quadratic the graph is a curved line which means that the slope at any given point is different from the slope at other points along the same curve. By finding the derivative of the function and then plugging in values for x we can find the slope of the function at these points.

If $f(x) = x^2$, then $f'(x) = 2x$.

(Note that to find the derivative we brought the power of 2 down to the front of the function and then subtracted 1 from the power.)

Now we plug different values into the derivative to find the slope of the line at that point:

The slope of the function at $x = -2$ is $f'(x) = 2(-2) = -4$

The slope of the function at $x = 1$ is $f'(x) = 2(1) = 2$

The slope of the function at $x = 2$ is $f'(x) = 2(2) = 4$

These points are illustrated in Figure 6.16.

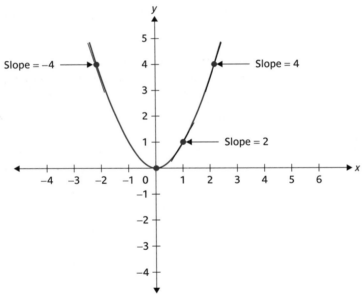

Figure 6.16

Quick problem 6

(a) Sketch the function $f(x) = x^2$ and then find the slope of the function at points $x = -4$, $x = 0$ and $x = 6$.

(b) Sketch the function $f(x) = x^3$ and then find the slope of the function at points $x = -1$, $x = 0$ and $x = 2$.

✔ **Learning outcome 5**

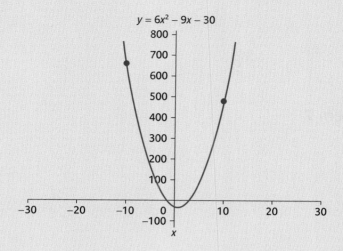

$$y = 6x^2 - 9x - 30$$

Figure 6.20

Quick problem 2

(a) $(x - 6)(x - 5)$

(b) $(x - 6)(x + 7)$

(c) $(x - 6)(x + 2)$

(d) $(x + 6)(x + 4)$

Quick problem 3

(a) $x = -1.87$ or $x = 4.27$

(b) $x = 2.49$ or $x = -3.78$

(c) $x = 0.36$ or $x = -8.36$

Quick problem 4

(a) $P = 2.5, Q = 8.5$

(b) $P = 0.89, Q = 7.44$

Quick problem 5

$Q = 4.53$

Quick problem 6

(a) $f'(x) = 2x$

   Slope $= -8$

   Slope $= 0$

   Slope $= 12$

(b) $f'(x) = 3x^2$

  Slope = 3
  Slope = 0
  Slope = 12

Quick problem 7

(a) $y' = 0$

(b) $y' = 5$

(c) $y' = -0.7$

(d) $f'(x) = -18x^{-4}$

(e) $f'(x) = 108x^{11}$

(f) $f'(x) = x^{-2}$

Quick problem 8

(a) $y' = 5$

(b) $y' = -0.7$

(c) $y' = 18x^2$

(d) $y' = -2$

(e) $f'(x) = 8x^{-3} - 36x^3 + 24x^{-7}$

(f) $f'(x) = -6x^2 - 6x - 20x^{-5}$

(g) $f'(x) = -12x^{-2} + 6x + 36x^{-10}$

(h) $f'(x) = -4x^{-3} - 4x - 5$

Quick problem 9

(a) $384x^3 - 360x^2$

(b) $90x^2 + 160x$

(c) $-20 + 144x^{-3} - 30x^{-2}$

Quick problem 10

(a) $\dfrac{-27x^6 + 486x^2}{(x^4 + 6)^2}$

(b) $216x^5/81x^4$

(c) 4

Quick problem 11

(a) $36x^3$

(b) $144x^2(12x^3)^3$

(c) $(8x^3 - 5x^2)^4(120x^2 - 50x)$

Chapter **7**

Marginal concepts and optimization

Topics covered

7.1 Introduction 192
7.2 Marginal functions 192
7.3 Demand, total revenue and marginal revenue 193
7.4 Total and marginal cost 197
7.5 Production 198
7.6 Consumption and savings 202
7.7 Second-order derivatives 203
7.8 Optimization 205
7.9 The use of optimization in economics 210

LEARNING OUTCOMES

By the end of this chapter, you should understand:

1. How to calculate marginal functions

2. How to calculate second-order derivatives

3. Optimization

4. The application of marginal functions, second-order derivatives and optimization in economics.

7.1 Introduction

In Chapter 6, the basic rules of differentiation were introduced along with the techniques of calculating derivatives using basic differentiation, the sum rule, the difference rule, the product rule, the quotient rule and the chain rule. However, it is not immediately obvious how differentiation is used in economics. This issue is dealt with in this chapter where differentiation is used in the understanding and calculation of revenue, cost, production, consumption and savings.

7.2 Marginal functions

In Chapter 3 we considered the total revenue function and identified the fact that total revenue (TR) is the product of price and quantity (PQ). Therefore if we are given a demand equation which is written as:

$$P = 50 - 3Q$$

then the total revenue function can be calculated by multiplying the demand equation through by Q:

If $P = 50 - 3Q$, then $TR = PQ = (50 - 3Q)Q$

$$TR = 50Q - 3Q^2$$

Total revenue is expressed in terms of Q and as total revenue is a quadratic equation (see Chapter 6) we can use the quadratic formula to solve for the value of Q corresponding to different values of total revenue. Such calculations do not require the use of differentiation.

However we are often interested in the effect on total revenue of a change in the value of Q. In this case we use differentiation to calculate a *marginal function*.

Table 7.1 comprises the most commonly used total and marginal functions along with the corresponding notation.

Table 7.1

Function	Marginal function	Notation
Total revenue (TR)	Marginal revenue (MR)	$MR = d(TR)/dQ$
Total cost (TC)	Marginal cost (MC)	$MC = d(MC)/dQ$
Production (Q)	Marginal product of labour (MP_L) Marginal product of capital (MP_K)	$MP_L = dQ/dL$ $MP_K = dQ/dK$
Consumption (C)	Marginal propensity to consume (MPC)	$MPC = dC/dY$
Savings (S)	Marginal propensity to save (MPS)	$MPS = dS/dY$

7.3 Demand, total revenue and marginal revenue

Marginal Revenue is defined as the effect on total revenue of a one unit change in Q. Referring to Table 7.1, marginal revenue is the derivative of total revenue with respect to quantity demanded.

Example

$TR = 300Q - 4Q^2$

$MR = d(TR)/dQ = 300 - 8Q$

If the value of Q is 37 then $MR = 300 - 8(37) = 300 - 296 = 4$.

What does this mean?

The derivative of any function is the slope of that function at a specific point. As we learned in Chapter 6 a non-linear total revenue function is illustrated as a curved line (hence the term 'non-linear'). As the graph of the function is a curved line, the slope changes at each point along the curve. The slope at any given point on the total revenue function is given by the marginal revenue. Therefore, if you take the derivative of the total revenue function and then plug in a value for Q, you will find the slope of the total revenue function at that point.

In the example above the total revenue function was:

$TR = 300Q - 4Q^2$

and the associated marginal revenue function was:

$MR = d(TR)/dQ = 300 - 8Q$

At a value of $Q = 37$, marginal revenue is equal to 4 which is the slope of the total revenue function when $Q = 37$.

At a value of $Q = 38$, marginal revenue is equal to -4 which is the slope of the total revenue function at that point.

Using the example above we can illustrate the total revenue function on a graph and then show the slope of that function at various points. This is illustrated in Figure 7.1.

Note that the total revenue function has a 'turning point'; the point where the function changes from being upward sloping to downward sloping. This is the point at which total revenue is maximized. Now look at the the value of marginal revenue at this point. When $Q = 37.5$, $MR = 0$ and total revenue is maximized. This is because at the maximum level of total revenue the line that is tangent to the total revenue curve is completely horizontal which means it has a slope of zero. As marginal revenue is the slope of the total revenue curve, it means that when total revenue is at its maximum value, the slope, or marginal revenue, will equal zero.

This will also be the case when you have a quadratic function that is 'u' shaped as illustrated in Figure 7.2. The slope of the marginal function will be zero when the total function is at a minimum point.

This confirms that whenever you are dealing with total and marginal functions, if the marginal function equals zero, then the total function is either at a maximum or minimum point.

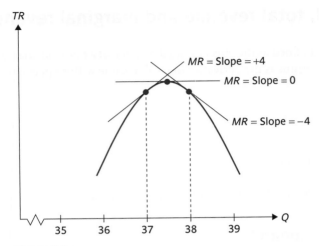

Figure 7.1

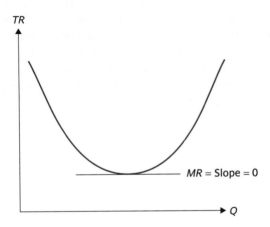

Figure 7.2

Example

If total revenue is given as:

$$TR = 30Q - 5Q^2:$$

(a) Determine the marginal revenue function
(b) Calculate the slope of the total revenue function when $Q = 2$, $Q = 3$ and $Q = 4$
(c) Illustrate the total revenue and the slope of the total revenue function on a graph.

Solution

(a) $MR = \mathrm{d}(TR)/\mathrm{d}Q = 30 - 10Q$
(b) When $Q = 2$, $MR = 10$
    When $Q = 3$, $MR = 0$
    When $Q = 4$, $MR = -10$
(c) See Figure 7.3.

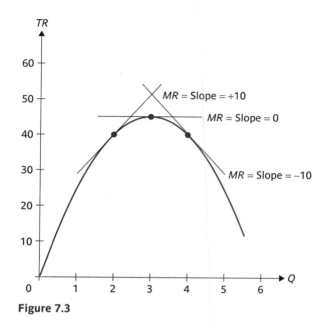

Figure 7.3

Note that the slope of the line is positive when $Q = 2$, and negative when $Q = 4$. When $Q = 3$, marginal revenue is equal to zero and the tangency line is perfectly horizontal. At this point total revenue is maximized.

Illustrating demand, total revenue and marginal revenue

You should now understand the relationship between demand, total revenue and marginal revenue. It is therefore useful to show these three expressions graphically so that the link between them can be clarified.

The demand function and the marginal revenue function are both linear so are typically represented together on one graph. It is worth noting that the marginal revenue function always has an intercept (on the vertical/price axis) that is the same as that of the demand function, and that the marginal revenue curve intersects the horizontal axis exactly halfway between the origin and the intersection of the demand curve and the horizontal axis.

The total revenue curve is then illustrated on the bottom graph and is a curved line that typically takes the shape of an upside down 'u'. The two points at which the total revenue curve intersects with the horizontal axis are the values of Q for which total revenue is equal to zero. The top of the total revenue curve is the point at which total revenue is maximized.

The meaning of the demand curve is clear – it simply shows the relationship between the price and quantity of a good. The meaning of the marginal revenue curve is less obvious. As the marginal revenue is the slope of the total revenue at any given value for Q, you can break the marginal revenue curve down into three sections. As illustrated in Figure 7.4, the section above the horizontal axis represents the portion of the total revenue curve that has a positive slope; when marginal revenue is positive, the slope of the total revenue curve is positive (labelled as A). The section of the marginal revenue curve that is situated below the horizontal axis represents the portion of the total revenue curve that has a negative slope (labelled B). The point at which marginal revenue intersects with the horizontal axis is the point at which $MR = 0$. This is the

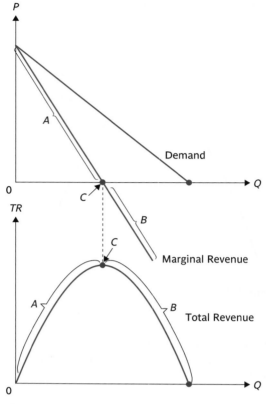

Figure 7.4

point where the slope of the total revenue curve is equal to zero and this occurs when total revenue is at its maximum point. This is labelled on the graph as point *C*.

Student note

Average revenue is defined as total revenue divided by quantity:

$AR = TR/Q$

As total revenue is equal to *PQ*, $TR/Q = P$ which means that the demand curve is also the average revenue curve.

Quick problem 1

(a) For the total revenue function $TR = 500Q - 2Q^2$, find the value of marginal revenue when $Q = 80$.

(b) For the total revenue function $TR = 25Q - 4Q^2$, find the value of marginal revenue when $Q = 4$, $Q = 5$, $Q = 6$.

(c) For the demand schedule $P = 40 - 0.5Q$, find total revenue and marginal revenue. Find the value of marginal revenue when $Q = 3$ and $Q = 7$.

(d) For the demand schedule $P = 100 - 0.25Q$, find the total revenue and marginal revenue functions and calculate the value of marginal revenue when $Q = 25$ and $Q = 50$.

✔ **Learning outcome 1**

7.4 Total and marginal cost

Marginal cost (MC) is defined in the same way as marginal revenue; it is the derivative of total cost (TC) in terms of quantity and is denoted as:

$$MC = dTC/dQ$$

Note that average cost (AC) is denoted as:

$$AC = TC/Q$$

This means that if we are given an expression for average cost we can calculate total cost and marginal cost.

It is also important to be able to calculate the change in total cost as a result of an increase or decrease in output. The change in total cost is equal to the marginal cost multiplied by the change in output. This expression is denoted as:

$$\Delta TC = MC \times \Delta Q$$

Using this expression will give you the change in total cost as a result of a change in output which is an important calculation when firms are making decisions about how much of a particular good to produce.

Example
Given the average cost function:

$$AC = 4Q + 8 + 12/Q$$

find an expression for marginal cost. If current output is 10 units, calculate the effect on total cost of an increase in production of five units.

As we have an expression for average cost we need to find an associated expression for total cost and then differentiate to obtain an expression for marginal cost.

$$TC = AC(Q) = 4Q^2 + 8Q + 12$$

$$MC = 8Q + 8$$

If the current output is 10 units:

$$TC = 4(10^2) + 8(10) + 12 = 400 + 80 + 12 = 492$$

$$MC = 8(10) + 8 = 88$$

If output now increases by five units, to 15 units, the change in total cost can be calculated as follows:

$$\Delta TC = MC \times \Delta Q$$

Where MC is evaluated at the halfway point between 10 and 15, i.e., 12.5:

$$MC = 8(12.5) + 8 = 108$$

$$\Delta TC = 108 \times 5 = 540$$

Hence total cost, TC, is now $492 + 540 = 1032$:

$$4(15^2) + 8(15) + 12 = 4(225) + 88 + 12 = 900 + 120 + 12 = 1032$$

A common calculation used in economics that relates to total and marginal costs is called optimization which will be presented later in this chapter.

Quick problem 2

Given the average cost function:

$$AC = 2Q - 5 + 7Q^{-1}$$

find an expression for marginal cost. If current output is 20 units, calculate the effect on total cost of an increase in production of 15 units.

✔ **Learning outcome 1**

Answers to quick problems

Quick problem 1

(a) 180

(b) $MR = 25 - 8Q$; When $Q = 4$, slope $= -7$; when $Q = 5$, slope $= -15$; when $Q = 6$, slope $= -23$.

(c) $MR = 40 - Q$; when $Q = 3$, $MR = 37$; When $Q = 7$, $MR = 33$.

(d) $MR = 100 - 0.5Q$; when $Q = 25$, $MR = 87.5$; when $Q = 50$, $MR = 75$.

Quick problem 2

$TC = 2Q^2 - 5Q + 7$

$MC = 4Q - 5$

When $Q = 20$, $TC = 707$, $MC = 75$

$MC = 4(27.5) - 5 = 105$

$\Delta TC = 1650$

$TC = 2357$

Quick problem 3

(a) $Q = 100.98$

(b) Increasing returns to scale.

Quick problem 4

$MPC = 0.08Y + 0.3$

When $Y = 45$, $MPC = 3.9$

Quick problem 5

(a) $y' = 72x^2 - 36x^8 + 36x^{11}$; $y'' = 144x - 288x^7 + 396x^{10}$

(b) $y' = 90x^2 + 160x$; $y'' = 180x + 160$

(c) $y' = 13.5x$, $y'' = 13.5$

Quick problem 6

(a) $y' = 18x + 54 = 0$; $y'' = 18$; $x = -3$ is a minimum

(b) $y' = -20x - 20$; $y'' = -20$; $x = -1$ is a maximum

(c) $y' = 10x + 75$; $y'' = 10$; $x = -7.5$ is a minimum

Quick problem 7

(a) $y' = 9x^2 - 54x - 20$; critical values $x = 6.35$ and $x = -0.35$.

(b) $y'' = 18x - 54$; when $x = 6.35$, $y'' = 60.3$. As this is positive the function is concave and $x = 6.35$ is a minimum. When $x = -0.35$, $y'' = -6.3$. As this is negative the function is convex and $x = 0.35$ is a maximum.

(c) $x = 3$

(d) $f(0.39) = £45.88$; $f(3) = -£60$.
$f(6.35) = -405.56$; $f(-0.35) = -45.56$; $f(3) = -180$.

Quick problem 8

(a) $x = 35$

(b) $\pi'' = -225$ which is a maximum point.

(c) Maximum profit $= £94\,262.5$

Quick problem 9

$t = 18$. Therefore a tax of £18 would maximize the tax revenue for the government.

Chapter **8**

Partial differentiation

Topics covered

8.1	Introduction	*216*
8.2	Functions of two variables	*216*
8.3	Partial derivatives	*217*
8.4	Second-order partial derivatives	*219*
8.5	Changes to independent and dependent variables	*221*
8.6	Partial elasticity	*223*
8.7	Partial differentiation and marginal functions	*225*
8.8	Unconstrained optimization	*231*
8.9	Constrained optimization	*237*
8.10	Lagrange multipliers	*240*

LEARNING OUTCOMES

By the end of this chapter, you should understand:

1. How to evaluate functions of two or more variables

2. How to partially differentiate a function

3. How partial differentiation is used in elasticity

4. How partial differentiation is used in marginal functions

5. How partial differentiation is used to solve unconstrained optimization problems

6. How partial differentiation is used to solve constrained optimization problems

7. How and when to use Lagrange multipliers.

8.1 Introduction

In Chapter 4 we considered the fact that the quantity of a particular good that a consumer decides to purchase depends on more than just the price of that good; it also depends on the price of the alternative goods (complementary and substitutable), the income of the consumer and costs to the producers. Likewise, the quantity produced of each good depends on inputs such as land, labour and capital.

This chapter focuses on using partial differentiation to retrieve information about different functions which have more than one variable and then using that information to better understand the different economic relationships that we deal with on a day-to-day basis.

8.2 Functions of two variables

A function of two variables is an operation that takes the two incoming variables, x and y, and combines them with a unique mathematical operation in order to produce the solution, denoted as z. An example of a simple function in two variables is:

$$f(x, y) = 2xy - 5x$$

which can also be presented as:

$$z = 2xy - 5x$$

We evaluate the function by plugging in different combinations of x and y. For instance if $x = 3$ and $y = 1$:

$$f(3, 1) = 2(3)(1) - 5(3) = -9$$

Alternatively, if $x = 2$ and $y = 8$:

$$f(2, 8) = 2(2)(8) - 5(2) = 22$$

Note that the x and y are the *independent variables* while z is the *dependent variable* (because its value is dependent on the values of the inputs).

Student note

It is useful though to consider the notation used when the function has two or more variables.

When the function has only two variables then it is most common to denote the function either as $f(x, y)$ or as z.

When the function has more than two variables then it is most common to label each of the inputs as $x_1, x_2, x_3, x_4, \ldots x_n$ and then to denote the function as $f(x_1, x_2, x_3 \ldots x_n)$ including as many inputs as you want.

Example

Evaluate the function $f(x, y) = 36xy - 4x + 8y$ when $x = 3$ and $y = 5$

$$f(3, 5) = 36(3)(5) - 4(3) + 8(5) = 568$$

A function with more than two variables can be evaluated as follows.

Example

$$f(x_1, x_2, x_3, x_4) = 3x_1x_3 + 5x_4x_1 - 2x_2 - x_3x_4$$

Evaluate the function if $x_1 = 3$, $x_2 = 5$, $x_3 = 1$ and $x_4 = 2$

$$f(3, 5, 1, 2) = 3(3)(1) + 5(2)(3) - 2(5) - (1)(2) = 27$$

Example

Evaluate the function $f(x, y) = 8x^2y^3 - xy^2 + 4x$ when $x = 2$ and $y = 4$.

$$f(2, 4) = 8(2)^2(4)^3 - (2)(4)^2 + 4(2) = 2048 - 32 + 8 = 2024$$

Quick problem 1

Evaluate the following functions:

$f(x, y) = 12x^2 - 3xy + 5y^2$ when $x = 4$ and $y = 6$

$f(x, y) = 5x^3 + 2x^3y^2 - 10y^3$ when $x = 5$ and $y = 3$

$f(x_1, x_2) = 7x_1^3 - 5x_1x_2 - 6x_2$ when $x_1 = -1$ and $x_2 = 8$

$f(x_1, x_2, x_3) = 6x_1x_2^3 + 3x_2^4x_3^3 - 4x_1x_3^2 + 5x^3$ when $x_1 = 5$, $x_2 = 4$ and $x_3 = 3$

$f(x_1, x_2, x_3) = 5x_1^2x_2^2x_3 - 7x_2^3x_3^3 + 2x_1^4x_3^2$ when $x_1 = 3$, $x_2 = 5$ and $x_3 = 6$

✔ **Learning outcome 1**

8.3 Partial derivatives

Partial differentiation involves taking the first-order derivative of a function in terms of one of the variables included in the function. Previously we worked through problems that involved taking the first- and second-order derivatives of functions that had one variable. However, when a function has more than one variable there is a first-order derivative associated with each of these variables. The process of finding each of the first-order (and second-order) derivatives of a function with more than one variable is called partial differentiation. This appears to be a difficult concept, however there are no new rules to learn – taking a partial derivative is the same as taking a regular derivative, you just need to be a little careful to ensure that you do not mix up the terms, or take the derivative of the wrong variable! You should also note that when you take a partial derivative the other variables are held constant.

The partial derivative of f with respect to x is denoted as:

$$\frac{\partial f}{\partial x} \text{ or } f_x$$

The partial derivative is calculated by differentiating the function with respect to x while holding y constant. You can then take another partial derivative by differentiating the original function with respect to y while holding x constant. This derivative is denoted as $\partial f/\partial y$ or f_y. This process is shown in the following example.

Example

Find all the partial derivatives of the following function $f(x, y) = 9x^3 + 3x^2y^2 + 4y$.

$$f_x = 27x^2 + 6xy^2$$

Note that in the first term the power of 3 was brought down to the front of the expression and multiplied by the coefficient, 9, to give a total of 27. In the second term the power associated with x, 2, was brought down to the front of that expression and multiplied by the coefficient, 3, but the term y^2 remained constant. The final expression, $4y$, is not included in the derivative because there is no x term in the expression, so it is treated as a constant term. As the derivative of a constant is equal to zero this term does not appear in the derivative of the function in terms of x.

$$f_y = 6x^2y + 4$$

Note that the first term is left out because it is solely an x term and we are taking the derivative in terms of y. As the derivative of a constant is zero, this term is left out of the first-order derivative in terms of y. In the second term we brought the power associated with y, 2, down to the front of the expression and multiplied it by the coefficient to give a new coefficient of 6. We then subtracted one from the power of y but left the whole x term constant, and we differentiated the final term to get 4.

Student note

Considering the two examples above it is important to understand a few characteristics of a function. The coefficient at the front of each expression 'belongs' to all parts of the expression, not just the first part. So, for example, in the function $f(x, y) = 9x^3 + 3x^2y^2 + 4y$, 9 belongs to x^3 but in the second expression 3 belongs to both the x^2 and the y^2.

Therefore when you are partially differentiating the second term in terms of x you would multiply the power of x, 2, by the coefficient to get $6xy^2$. Similarly, when you are differentiating this same expression in terms of y you would multiply the power of y, 2, by the coefficient of the whole term, 3, to give $6x^2y$.

A common mistake made by students when finding partial derivatives is to keep the existing coefficient separate from the new coefficient created by taking a derivative. For example students often present the partial derivative of the second term as $3x^22y$. While this is not technically wrong you should always present terms in the simplest possible form which requires you to combine the two coefficients and present the term as $6x^2y$.

Example

Find all the partial derivatives associated with the following function:

$$f(x, y) = 3x^4y - 12x^2y^2 + 8xy^3 - 4x + 2y$$
$$f_x = 12xy^2 + 24xy^2 + 8y^3 - 4$$
$$f_y = 3x^4 - 24x^2y + 24xy^2 + 2$$

Example

Find all of the first-order partial derivatives associated with the function:

$$f(x_1, x_2, x_3) = 4x_1^2x_2^3x_3^5 - 5x_1x_2^2x_3^4 + 6x_2x_3^3 - 7x_3^2$$
$$f_{x1} = 8x_1x_2^3x_3^5 - 5x_2^2x_3^4$$
$$f_{x2} = 12x_1^2x_2^2x_3^5 - 10x_1x_2x_3^4 + 6x_3^3$$
$$f_{x3} = 20x_1^2x_2^3x_3^4 - 20x_1x_2^2x_3^3 + 18x_2x_3^2 - 14x_3$$

Quick problem 2

Find all the partial derivatives associated with the following functions:

$$f(x, y) = 4x^2 + 8xy^2 - 6x^4y - 6y + 18$$
$$f(x, y) = x^5y^5 - x^2y^2 - xy - 3$$
$$f(x_1, x_2) = 5x_1^3 - 2x_2^2 - 4x_1^4x_2^2 - x_2$$
$$f(x_1, x_2, x_3) = 7x_1^3x_2^4x_3^2 + x_2^4x_3 + 3x_3 + x_3^3$$

✔ **Learning outcome 2**

8.4 Second-order partial derivatives

Just as we took the second-order derivatives of functions with one variable, we can also take the second-order derivative of a function with more than one variable. In this case we can only concentrate on one variable at any given time. This means that for a function that has two variables there are four combinations of second-order derivatives:

f_{xx} which means taking the first-order derivative in terms of x and then the second-order derivative in terms of x

f_{yy} which means taking the first-order derivative in terms of y and then the second-order derivative in terms of y

f_{xy} which means taking the first-order derivative in terms of x and then the second-order derivative in terms of y

f_{yx} which means taking the first-order derivative in terms of y and then the second-order derivative in terms of x.

There is nothing complicated about this process as it simply involves taking the derivative of a function which we have already been doing in the previous sections. The only problem is remembering which variables remain constant for any given operation.

Example

Find all the partial derivatives of the following function $f(x, y) = 9x^3 + 3x^2y^2 + 4y$.

First-order partial derivatives:

$$f_x = 27x^2 + 6xy^2$$

$$f_y = 6x^2y + 4$$

Second-order partial derivatives:

$$f_{xx} = 54x + 6y^2$$

This is the derivative in terms of x of the first-order derivative (also taken in terms of x).

$$f_{yy} = 6x^2$$

This is the derivative of the function in terms of y of the first-order derivative (also taken in terms of y).

$$f_{xy} = 12xy$$

This is the derivative of the function in terms y of the first-order derivative which was taken in terms of x.

$$f_{yx} = 12xy$$

This is the derivative of the function in terms of x of the first-order derivative which was taken in terms of y.

It is useful to note that one characteristic of the second-order derivative is that $f_{xy} = f_{yx}$. This says that for second-order partial derivatives it does not matter which order you do the differentiation, the final expression will be the same.

Note also that although the examples of second-order derivatives in this section focus only on functions with two variables working through an example with more than two variables would be a very similar exercise. As long as you are clear about which variables you are using to find each of the different second-order derivatives the process should be relatively simple. Using the example from the previous section we can find an expression for all of the second-order partial derivatives associated with that function.

Example

Find the second-order partial derivatives associated with the function

$$f(x_1, x_2, x_3) = 4x_1^2x_2^3x_3^5 - 5x_1x_2^2x_3^4 + 6x_2x_3^3 - 7x_3^2.$$

The first-order partial derivatives were given in this example in the previous section:

$$f_{x1} = 8x_1x_2^3x_3^5 - 5x_2^2x_3^4$$

$$f_{x2} = 12x_1^2x_2^2x_3^5 - 10x_1x_2x_3^4 + 6x_3^3$$

$$f_{x3} = 20x_1^2x_2^3x_3^4 - 20x_1x_2^2x_3^3 + 18x_2x_3^2 - 14x_3$$

The second-order partial derivatives are calculated as follows:

$$f_{x1x1} = 8x_2^3x_3^5$$

$$f_{x1x2} = 24x_1x_2^2x_3^5 - 10x_2x_3^4$$

$$f_{x1x3} = 40x_1x_2^3x_3^4 - 20x_2^2x_3^3$$

$$f_{x2x1} = 24x_1x_2^2x_3^5 - 10x_2x_3^4$$

$$f_{x2x2} = 24x_1^2x_2x_3^5 - 10x_1x_3^4$$

$$f_{x2x3} = 60x_1^2x_2^2x_3^4 - 40x_1x_2^1x_3^3 + 18x_3^2$$

$$f_{x3x1} = 40x_1x_2^3x_3^4 - 20x_2^2x_3^3$$

$$f_{x3x2} = 60x_1^2x_2^2x_3^4 - 40x_1x_2x_3^3 + 18x_3^2$$

$$f_{x3x3} = 80x_1^2x_2^3x_3^3 - 60x_1x_2^2x_3^2 + 36x_2x_3 - 14$$

Notice that the second-order partial derivatives that combine the same variables result in the same answer. For example $f_{x1x3} = f_{x3x1}$ and $f_{x2x1} = f_{x1x2}$ which confirms that the order in which the derivatives are worked out does not matter.

Quick problem 3

Find all the first- and second-order partial derivatives associated with the following functions:

$$f(x, y) = 3x^2y^7 - 5x^4y^4 - x$$

$$f(x_1, x_2) = 12x_1^4 - 3x_2^3 - 4x_1^5x_2$$

$$f(x_1, x_2, x_3) = 8x_1^3x_2^4x_3^4 - 5x_1x_2^3x_3^3 + 8x_2x_3 - 6x_3$$

✔ Learning outcome 2

8.5 Changes to independent and dependent variables

The derivative of a function, $y = f(x)$, is the rate of change of y with respect to x. This means that if x changes by a small amount then the associated change in y will be:

$$\Delta y = \frac{\partial y}{\partial x}(\Delta x)$$

When a function has two variables (rather than one) a change in one of the independent variables will cause a change in the dependent variable, assuming the other independent variable remains fixed. This situation is denoted as:

$\Delta z = \partial z / \partial x \, (\Delta x)$

$\Delta z = \partial z / \partial y \, (\Delta y)$

However if a function has two variables and both of these change simultaneously then the change in z would be denoted as:

$\Delta z = dz / dx \, (\Delta x) + dz / dy \, (\Delta y)$.

This is called the *small increments formula* and its use is shown in the following example.

Example
Given the function $z = 4x^3y^2 + 3x^2y$ find the first-order partial derivatives and evaluate these derivatives when $x = 4$ and $y = 2$.

$$\frac{\partial z}{\partial x} = 12x^2y^2 + 6xy$$

$$\frac{\partial z}{\partial y} = 8x^3y + 3x^2$$

When $x = 4$ and $y = 2$:

$$\frac{\partial z}{\partial x} = 816$$

$$\frac{\partial z}{\partial y} = 1072$$

When $x = 4$ and $y = 2$,

$$z = 4 \times (4^3) \times (2^2) + 3 \times (4^2) \times (2) = 1120$$

Calculate the change in z when x increases from 4 to 4.001 and y decreases from 2 to 1.999 simultaneously.

The change in x is 0.001 and the change in y is -0.001 so the small increments formula can be used to calculate the overall change in z:

$dz / dx \, (0.001) + dz / dy \, (-0.001) = -0.256$

$816(0.001) + 1072(-0.001) = -0.256$

Therefore the overall change in z is approximately -0.256.

Re-evaluating z at $x = 4.001$ and $y = 1.999$ we obtain:

$$z = 4(4.001^3)(1.999^2) + 3(4.001^2)(1.999) = 1119.744$$

a change of -0.256.

Quick problem 4

Given the function $z = 7x^4y - 2x^4y^2$ find the first-order partial derivatives and evaluate these derivatives when $x = 4$ and $y = 2$. Calculate the change in z associated with an increase in x to 4.001 and a decrease in y to 1.999.

✔ **Learning outcome 2**

8.6 Partial elasticity

In Chapter 7 we used the first derivative to measure the responsiveness of the quantity demanded to a change in the price. Thus we were able to calculate the elasticity for functions of one independent variable. With knowledge of partial differentiation we can now work out partial elasticities for functions of more than one independent variable.

To illustrate the concept of partial elasticity we will assume that Q_1, the quantity demanded of good 1 is a function of the price of good 1, denoted as P_1, the price of good 2, denoted as P_2, and the consumers income denoted as Y. The demand function is presented as:

$$Q_1 = f(P_1, P_2, Y)$$

Elasticity can then be used to measure the responsiveness of demand to a change in any one of these three variables. Outlined below are details of how to calculate *own price elasticity of demand*, *cross price elasticity of demand* and *income elasticity of demand*.

Own price elasticity of demand simply means calculating the responsiveness of demand to a change in the price of a specified good. The formula for this calculation is presented as:

$$E_p = \text{percentage change in } Q_1/\text{percentage change in } P_1$$

where the price of the alternative good, P_2, and the consumer's income, Y, are held constant.

The above formula can also be presented as:

$$E_{p1} = -P_1/Q_1 \times \partial Q_1/\partial P_1$$

Note that partial elasticity notation is used because Q_1 is a function of three variables, P_1, P_2 and Y and in this calculation we are only looking at the responsiveness of demand to one of these three variables, a change in P_1.

We can similarly calculate cross price elasticity of demand and income elasticity of demand.

Cross price elasticity of demand is defined as:

E_{p2} = percentage change in Q_1/percentage change in P_2

where P_1 and Y are held constant.

As was the case above, the cross price elasticity of demand can be expressed as:

$$E_{p2} = P_2/Q_1 \times \partial Q_1/\partial P_2$$

The cross price elasticity of demand may be positive or negative depending on whether the alternative good is substitutable or complementary. If P_2 is substitutable then Q_1 would increase as P_2 increased (consumers would buy more of P_2 as good one became more expensive as the two goods act as substitutes) and $\partial Q/\partial P_2$ would be positive and E_{p2} would be positive. Alternatively, if the two goods are complementary then Q_1 would decrease as P_2 increases and $\partial Q_1/\partial P_2$ will be negative so E_{p2} will also be negative.

The income elasticity of demand is presented as:

E_y = percentage change in Q_1/percentage change in Y

which can also be written as:

$$E_y = Y/Q_1 \times \partial Q_1/\partial Y$$

As in the case of cross price elasticity of demand, income elasticity of demand can be positive or negative depending on whether the good is normal, luxury or inferior. If the good is normal or a luxury good then demand increases as income increases and E_y will be positive. If the good is inferior then demand decreases as income increases and E_y will be negative.

Student note

There are many interesting examples of goods that will lead to positive and negative income elasticities of demand. For example, during the war many families on tight budgets ate large quantities of foods that were nutritious but inexpensive, i.e., cabbage, potatoes, rice, etc. In the years following the war as many family incomes increased these foods were substituted with others that would provide greater nutritional value and variety. In this case the original food items can be considered inferior goods because as incomes increased, so the demand for these goods decreased. In this case the income elasticity of demand was negative.

However this is not to say that these goods are considered inferior to all consumers. Whether a good is inferior or superior is strongly related to personal preference so while one consumer could calculate a personal income elasticity of demand that is positive, another consumer might calculate a personal income elasticity of demand that is negative using the same levels of income but having different tastes.

Example

$$Q_1 = 60 - 3P_1 + 2P_2 + 0.25Y$$

where $P_1 = 5$, $P_2 = 10$ and $Y = 800$.
    Calculate:

(a) Own price elasticity of demand
(b) Cross price elasticity of demand
(c) Income elasticity of demand

First, substitute the above values into the demand equation:

$$Q_1 = 60 - 3(5) + 2(10) + 0.25(800)$$

$$Q_1 = 60 - 15 + 20 + 200$$

$$Q_1 = 265$$

(a) $E_{p1} = -5/265 \times (-3) = 0.057$
(b) $E_{p2} = 10/265 \times (2) = 0.075$
      E_{p2} is positive which means that the two goods are substitutes.
(c) $E_y = 800/265 \times (0.25) = 0.755$
      The positive value of E_y confirms that the good is superior; as income increases so does the demand for good 1.

Quick problem 5

Given the demand function $Q_1 = 150 - 5P_1 + 15P_2 + 0.2Y$, where $P_1 = 5$, $P_2 = 10$ and $Y = 800$, calculate:

(a) Own price elasticity of demand
(b) Cross price elasticity of demand
(c) Income elasticity of demand

✔ **Learning outcome 3**

8.7 Partial differentiation and marginal functions

Utility functions

So far we have dealt mainly with the behaviour of producers looking at issues such as profit maximization and cost minimization. In this section we are going to consider issues related specifically to the consumer.
    Two main areas of concern for consumers are the maximization of income and leisure time. Consumers also need to decide how many items of each good they want to purchase, and what

their preferences are regarding the different goods available. To measure these preferences and choices we attach a level of utility to each set of options, where utility is representative of levels of satisfaction.

Consider the situation in which there are two goods, X_1 and X_2, and consumers purchase T_1 items of X_1 and T_2 items of X_2. Utility, U, is then a function of T_1 and T_2 and can be presented as:

$$U = U(T_1, T_2)$$

If the consumer buys 10 units of X_1 and 20 units of X_2 then their utility function will be written as:

$$U = U(10, 20)$$

If, instead, the consumer buys 15 units of X_1 and 10 units of X_2 then their utility function will be written as:

$$U = U(15, 10)$$

If total utilities were assigned to these functions such that $U = U(10, 20) = 50$ and $U = U(15, 10) = 65$, then this tells us that the consumer derives greater satisfaction from buying 15 units of X_1 and 10 units of X_2 than from the purchase of 10 units of x_1 and 20 units of x_2.

Consumers are ultimately concerned with the maximization of their utility and, as outlined in Chapter 7, a utility function is maximized by working with the derivative of that function. In this case the consumer's utility is a function of two variables, T_1 and T_2, which means that we have to calculate partial derivatives in order to maximize the utility function.

The general form of these partial derivatives is presented as $\partial U/\partial T_1$ and $\partial U/\partial T_2$ and we can use these to calculate marginal utility which is the rate of change of utility with respect to a change in either T_1 or T_2.

If T_1 changes by a small amount but T_2 is held constant then the change in utility can be calculated as:

$$\Delta \text{ in Utility} = (\partial U/\partial T_1)(\Delta T_1)$$

Similarly a change in utility caused by a change in T_2 while T_1 is held constant will use the formula above but replace T_1 with T_2.

However, if T_1 and T_2 both changed then the net change in utility would be calculated as:

$$\Delta \text{ in Utility} = (\partial U/\partial T_1)(\Delta T_1) + (\partial U/\partial T_2)(\Delta T_2)$$

Example
A consumer's total utility function is determined to be:

$$U = T_1^{1/3} T_2^{2/3}$$

Determine the value of the marginal utilities when $T_1 = 50$ and $T_2 = 125$.

$$\partial U/\partial T_1 = 1/3 T_1^{-2/3} T_2^{2/3}$$
$$\partial U/\partial T_2 = 2/3 T_1^{1/3} T_2^{-1/3}$$

Therefore when $T_1 = 50$ and $T_2 = 125$

$\partial U/\partial T_1 = 1/3(50)^{-2/3}(125)^{2/3} = 0.61$

$\partial U/\partial T_2 = 2/3(50)^{1/3}(125)^{-1/3} = 0.49$

Now estimate the change in utility when T_1 decreases from 50 to 49.5 and T_2 increases from 125 to 125.5.

Using the small increments formula:

The change in utility $= 0.61(-0.5) + 0.49(0.5) = -0.06$

This can be verified by substituting the new values for T_1 and T_2 into the formula for U.

The conclusion from this calculation is that a small decrease in the number of units of T_1 purchased and a small increase in the number of units of T_2 purchased will provide the consumer with a decrease in their overall utility.

The law of diminishing marginal utility

Taking the second-order derivative of a utility function enables you to check if the marginal utility is increasing or decreasing in response to changes in T_1 and/or T_2. A negative second-order derivative means that the marginal utility of T_1 decreases as T_1 increases; as the consumption of T_1 increases each additional unit of T_1 that is purchased gives slightly less utility than the previous unit.

Using the example above:

$$\partial^2 U/\partial T_1^2 = -\frac{2}{9}T_1^{-5/3}T_2^{2/3}$$

$$\partial^2 U/\partial T_2^2 = -\frac{2}{9}T_1^{1/3}T_2^{-4/3}$$

As both second-order derivatives are negative this tells us that the marginal utility of the consumer decreases slightly with each unit of T_1 and T_2 that is purchased.

Utility is graphed as an indifference curve where each curve shows all the different combinations of X_1 and X_2 that give the consumer the same level of utility. This situation is illustrated in Figure 8.1.

The curves in Figure 8.1 represent the different levels of utility, or satisfaction, that a consumer gets from different bundles of goods. The curve closest to the origin provides the lowest level of utility while those further away from the origin provide the consumer with greater levels of satisfaction. Different points along the same indifference curve give the same level of utility to the consumer. For example the consumer is indifferent between points A and B where A is a bundle of goods that consists of 10 units of X_1 and 5 units of X_2, while point B represents a bundle of goods that consists of 5 units of X_1 and 10 units of X_2. Both of these bundles of goods, and all those that similarly fall on that indifference curve will provide the consumer with the same level of utility. However a bundle that contains, say, 8 units of X_1 and 8 units of X_2, point C on Figure 8.1, would give the consumer a higher level of utility and so is located on an indifference curve that

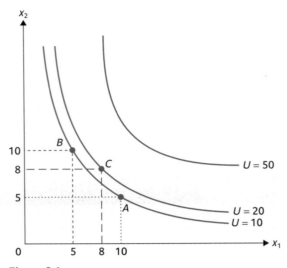

Figure 8.1

is further away from the origin. Ultimately the consumer wants a bundle of goods that gives them the highest possible level of utility. They are constrained by their budget constraint which in economics is combined with these indifference curves to determine which utility indifference the consumer can achieve given their income constraint.

Indifference curves are downward sloping. An increase or decrease of the purchase of one good to make up for the increase or the decrease of another good to maintain the same level of utility is called the marginal rate of substitution. Therefore the marginal rate of substitution is the slope of the utility curve or indifference curve and is denote as:

$$MRS = \frac{-dx_2}{dx_1} = \frac{\partial U}{\partial x_1} \Big/ \frac{\partial U}{\partial x_2}$$

Example
Given the utility function

$$U = x_1^{1/4} x_2^{3/4}$$

Calculate the marginal rate of substitution in terms of x_1 and x_2 when $x_1 = 100$ and $x_2 = 200$.

$$MRS = \frac{\partial U}{\partial x_1} \Big/ \frac{\partial U}{\partial x_2}$$

$$MRS = \frac{x_1^{-3/4} x_2^{3/4}}{4} \Big/ \frac{3x_1^{1/4} x_2^{-1/4}}{4}$$

$$MRS = \frac{1}{3} \frac{x_2}{x_1} = \frac{x_2}{3x_1}$$

If:

$x_1 = 100$ and $x_2 = 200$

then

$$MRS = \frac{1}{3}\left(\frac{200}{100}\right) = \frac{2}{3}$$

Quick problem 6

(a) Given the utility function

$$U = x_1^{2/3}x_2^{2/3}$$

calculate the marginal rate of substitution in terms of x_1 and x_2 when $x_1 = 55$ and $x_2 = 125$.

(b) Given the utility function

$$U = x_1^{4/5}x_2^{1/2}$$

calculate the marginal rate of substitution in terms of x_1 and x_2 when $x_1 = 80$ and $x_2 = 75$.

✔ **Learning outcome 4**

Production functions

Output, Q, depends on capital, K, and labour, L. A typical production function can therefore be represented as:

$$Q = f(K, L)$$

A producer wants to maximize production and so calculates all the combinations of capital and labour available to produce the highest possible level of output. The different combinations of capital and labour that give the same level of output are illustrated on a line called an isoquant.

Student note

On the production side, an isoquant illustrates the different combinations of inputs that will produce a set amount of output. This is illustrated in Figure 8.2.

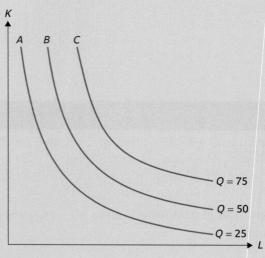

Figure 8.2

Isoquant A shows all the combinations of inputs K and L that can produce 25 units of good X. Isoquant B shows all the combinations of inputs K and L that can produce 50 units of good X. Isoquants that are situated further away from the origin show the combination of inputs that will produce higher levels of output, and those closer to the origin are those which show lower levels of production.

The distance between the isoquants is measureable and significant as each isoquant represents a specific level of production.

In terms of marginal productivity the production function is analysed in the same way as the utility function with partial derivatives being denoted as dQ/dK and dQ/dL. These partial derivatives give the rate of change of output with respect to capital and labour.

This concept is used to measure the effect on output of a small change in one, or both of the inputs. For example, a small change in capital, while keeping labour constant, results in a change in output of:

Change in output, $\Delta Q = (\partial Q/\partial K)(\Delta K)$

Likewise a change in labour while keeping capital constant would result in a change in output of:

$\Delta Q = (\partial Q/\partial L)(\Delta L)$

If K and L both change together then the net change in output is:

$\Delta Q = (\partial Q/\partial K)(\Delta K) + (\partial Q/\partial L)(\Delta L.)$

This is called the *marginal product of capital/labour* and simply indicates the change in output that results from a small change in one, or both, of the inputs. These marginal products are denoted as MP_K and MP_L respectively.

If the amount of capital is reduced, the amount of labour is then increased in order to maintain the production level. The substitution of one for the other is called the *marginal rate of technical substitution* and is denoted as:

$$MRTS = -dK/dL = \partial Q/\partial L \, / \, \partial Q/\partial K = MP_L/MP_K$$

This is easily illustrated in the following example.

Example

Given the production function $Q = K^2 + 3L^2$, find an expression for the marginal product of capital, the marginal product of labour and the marginal rate of technical substitution.

$$MPK = \partial Q/\partial K = 2K$$

$$MPL = \partial Q/\partial L = 6L$$

$$MRTS = MP_L/MP_K = 6L/2K = 3L/K$$

Quick problem 7

(a) Given the production function $Q = K^3 + 9L$, find an expression for the marginal product of capital, the marginal product of labour and the marginal rate of technical substitution.

(b) Given the production function $Q = 6K^{0.5} + 0.25L^{1/3}$, find an expression for the marginal product of capital, the marginal product of labour and the marginal rate of technical substitution.

✔ **Learning outcome 4**

8.8 Unconstrained optimization

Unconstrained optimization is used to find the maximum and minimum points associated with a given function. The method used for finding these points for a function of two variables is very similar to that used for functions of one variable.

However, it is worth noting here that the nature of economic functions of several variables forces us to subdivide optimization problems into two types; constrained and unconstrained. The main difference between these two approaches is whether or not constraints need to be considered in order to find a solution to the problem. First, we'll review the concepts learned in Chapter 7 that consider the procedure for solving a function with one variable and then we'll expand this to more complex functions.

When a function only has one variable it can be written as:

$$Y = f(x)$$

To maximize this function we first solve for the derivative of the function in order to find an expression for the slope. By setting $f'(x)$ equal to zero we will then be able to identify the critical values; the points that either represented a maximum or minimum point.

We then need to determine whether the point actually is a maximum or a minimum. To do this we take the second derivative of the function ($f''(x)$) and consider the following rules:

If $f''(x) > 0$ then we have found a minimum point.

If $f''(x) < 0$ then we have found a maximum point.

Now we can expand this scenario to consider what we would have to do in order to solve for a function with two variables. Consider the function:

$$z = f(x, y)$$

The stationary points are found by taking the partial derivatives of the function and then setting each of these partial derivatives equal to zero.

$$\partial z / \partial x = fx = 0$$

$$\partial z / \partial y = fy = 0$$

By solving for these partial derivatives we will be able to determine whether a critical value represents a minimum, a maximum or a saddle point.

A point is a minimum if the following conditions are met: $f_{xx} > 0, f_{yy} > 0$ and $f_{xx}f_{yy} - f_{xy}^2 > 0$.

A point is a maximum if the following conditions are met: $f_{xx} < 0, f_{yy} < 0$ and $f_{xx}f_{yy} - f_{xy}^2 > 0$.

If $f_{xx}f_{yy} - f_{xy}^2 < 0$ then the point is known as a saddle point.

Student note

A saddle point is a point of a function (of one or more variables) which is both a stationary point and a point of inflection (Figure 8.3). Since it is a point of inflection, it is not a local extremum.

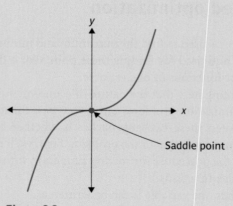

Saddle point

Figure 8.3

Example
Given

$$f(x, y) = 2x^3 - 4x + xy^2$$

find the critical values and determine whether these points are maxima or minima.

The first-order partial derivatives of the given function are:

$$f_x = 6x^2 - 4 + y^2$$

$$f_y = 2xy$$

To find the critical values we need to set the first-order partial derivatives equal to zero and solve for x and y.

Using the second equation:

If $x = 0$, then the whole derivative is equal to zero. Substituting this value for x into the first equation:

If $x = 0$,

$$f_x = -4 + y^2 = 0$$

$$y^2 = 4$$

$$y = 2 \text{ or } -2$$

Using the second equation again:

If $y = 0$, then the whole derivative is equal to zero. Substituting this value for y into the first equation:

If $y = 0$

$$f_y = 6x^2 - 4$$

$$6x^2 = 4$$

$$x^2 = 2/3$$

$$x = \sqrt{2/3} \text{ or } -\sqrt{2/3}$$

Therefore there are four critical values associated with the original function. These are $(0, 2), (0, -2), (\sqrt{2/3}, 0), (-\sqrt{2/3}, 0)$.

We can then classify these points (find out whether they are maximums or minimums) by looking at the second-order derivatives.

The second-order partial derivatives of the given function are:

$$f_{xx} = 12x$$

$$f_{yy} = 2x$$

$$f_{xy} = 2y$$

$$f_{yx} = 2y$$

We now need to evaluate the second-order derivatives using the critical values (stationary points) identified above.

At the point $(0, -2)$:

$$f_{xx}f_{yy} - f_{xy}^2 = 12(0)2(0) - (2(2))^2 = -16$$

As this value is less than 0 we have confirmed that we have found a saddle point.

At the point $((0, -2)$:

$$f_{xx}f_{yy} - f_{xy}^2 = 12(0)2(0) - (2(-2))^2 = -16 < 0$$

As this value is less than zero we have confirmed that the point $(0, -2)$ is a saddle point.

At the point $(\sqrt{2/3}, 0)$:

$$f_{xx} = 12(-\sqrt{2/3}) = -9.79 < 0$$
$$f_{yy} = 2(-\sqrt{2/3}) = -1.63 < 0$$
$$f_{xy} = 2(0) = 0$$
$$f_{xx}f_{yy} - f_{xy}^2 = 15.95 > 0$$

We can confirm that the point $(-\sqrt{2/3}, 0)$ is a maximum point.

At the point $(\sqrt{2/3}, 0)$:

$$f_{xx} = 12(\sqrt{2/3}) = 9.79 > 0$$
$$f_{yy} = 2(\sqrt{2/3}) = 1.63 > 0$$
$$f_{xy} = 2(0) = 0$$
$$f_{xx}f_{yy} - f_{xy}^2 = 15.95 > 0$$

We can confirm that the point $(1, 0)$ is a minimum point.

Quick problem 8

(a) Given

$$f(x, y) = 2x^3 - 16xy + xy^2$$

find the critical values and determine whether these points are maximums or minimums.

✔ **Learning outcome 5**

Application to economics

Given the function:

$$U(x_1, x_2) = x_1^{1/2} x_2^{1/4}$$

initially it would seem logical to select values for x_1 and x_2 in order to make utility, U, as large as possible. This would then maximize utility. However x_1 and x_2 cannot be increased without bounds. The bounds are the amount of money that an individual has to spend on the two goods. Suppose G_1 costs £4 and G_2 costs £5 and we allocate £200 for total spending. Then:

$$4x_1 + 5x_2 = 200$$

We need to consider this constraint when we attempt to maximize utility. In order to do this the original problem would now be written as:

Maximize $U(x_1, x_2) = x_1^{1/2} x_2^{1/4}$ subject to the constraint $4x_1 + 5x_2 = 200$

This constraint allows us to increase x_1 and x_2 to a realistic limit. This example describes a situation where we would need to introduce a constraint in order to solve a problem. We will return to the concept of constrained optimization in the next section. First, though, we will look at problems that do not require constraints. A common example would be problems relating to profit maximization.

Profit is equal to total revenue minus total cost ($\pi = TR - TC$). In this case the constraint is already built into the equation; we are trying to make total revenue as large as possible while trying to make total costs as small as possible. Thus the maximization of total revenue has already been constrained by the limits of cost minimization. We therefore don't need an additional constraint to find a solution to the problem. The following example illustrates a situation where the constraint is already built into the equation and so the solution to the problem represents one of unconstrained optimization.

Example

A perfectly competitive firm sells two goods y_1 and y_2 at £900 and £700 respectively. The total cost of producing these goods is:

$$TC = 3Q_1^2 + 4Q_1Q_2 + 2Q_2^2$$

where Q_1 and Q_2 denote output levels of x_1 and x_2 respectively.

Find the maximum profit and the values of Q_1 and Q_2 at which this maximum point is achieved.

Total revenue:

$$TR_1 = 900Q_1$$

$$TR_2 = 700Q_2$$

Therefore $TR = 900Q_1 + 700Q_2$.

Total costs:

$$TC = 3Q_1^2 + 4Q_1Q_2 + 2Q_2^2$$

Total profit:

$$\pi = TR - TC = 900Q_1 + 700Q_2 - 3Q_1^2 - 4Q_1Q_2 - 2Q_2^2$$

First- and second-order partial derivatives of the profit function:

$$\partial\pi/\partial Q_1 = 900 - 6Q_1 - 4Q_2$$
$$\partial\pi/\partial Q_2 = 700 - 4Q_1 - 4Q_2$$
$$\partial^2\pi/\partial Q_1^2 = -6$$
$$\partial^2\pi/\partial Q_2^2 = -4$$
$$\partial^2\pi/\partial Q_1 dQ_2 = -4$$

At a stationary point the first-order derivative is equal to zero. We therefore need to find the values of Q_1 and Q_2 that make the two first-order partial derivatives equal to zero. We can calculate these values by subtracting one first-order derivative from the other in order to eliminate one of the unknown variables and then solving for the remaining unknown.

$$900 - 6Q_1 - 4Q_2 = 0$$
$$700 - 4Q_1 - 4Q_2 = 0$$

Subtracting the second equation from the first we get:

$$200 - 2Q_1 = 0$$
$$2Q_1 = 200$$
$$Q_1 = 100$$

Substituting this value for Q_1 into either of the first order partial derivatives will give:

$$700 - 4(100) - 4Q_2 = 0$$
$$700 - 400 - 4Q_2 = 0$$
$$300 = 4Q_2$$
$$Q_2 = 75.$$

These calculations show that the profit function has one stationary point with co-ordinates (100, 75).

To show that this point really is a maximum point we must ensure that the following conditions hold:

$$\partial^2\pi/\partial Q_1^2 < 0$$

We know that this holds true as we have shown above that the second-order partial derivative of profit in terms of Q_1 is equal to -6.

$$\delta^2\pi/\delta Q_2^2 < 0$$

We know that this holds true as we have shown above that the second-order partial derivative of profit in terms of Q_2 is equal to -4.

$$(\partial^2\pi/\partial Q_1^2) \times (\partial^2\pi/\partial Q_2^2) - (\partial^2\pi/\partial Q_1\partial Q_2)^2 > 0$$

$$(-6)(-4) - (-4)^2 = 24 - 16 = 8 > 0$$

Therefore profit is maximized by producing $Q_1 = 100$ and $Q_2 = 75$.

The actual profit that would be made from producing 100 units of Q_1 and 75 units of Q_2 is:

$$\pi = 900(100) + 700(75) - 3(100)2 - 4(100)(75) - 2(75)^2 = 213\ 750$$

Quick problem 9

A firm is a perfectly competitive producer and sells two goods G_1 and G_2 at £300 and £700 respectively. The total cost of producing these goods is:

$$TC = Q_1^2 + 3Q_1Q_2 + 4Q_2^2$$

where Q_1 and Q_2 denote output levels of G_1 and G_2.

Find the maximum profit and the values of Q_1 and Q_2 at which this maximum point is achieved.

✔ **Learning outcome 5**

8.9 Constrained optimization

The previous section dealt with problems where the variables x and y could take on any values. This is acceptable for general problems but can produce unrealistic results for problems specifically related to economics. Common problems in economics relate to issues such as utility and income. In these situations we want to optimize a function subject to a constraint. Consider the following objective function:

$U = f(x, y)$ Utility function

To make this function realistic we need to acknowledge that it would be subject to an income constraint. Each consumer wants to reach the highest level of utility possible which we assume is achieved by obtaining the largest possible bundle of goods, i.e., the highest quantity of x and y. Therefore we need to add a constraint that takes account of income:

$P_xX + P_yY = M$

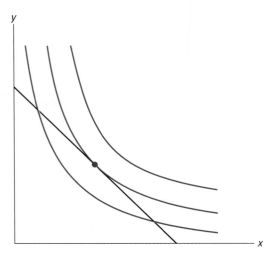

Figure 8.4

where P_x is the price of X and X represents the quantity of X, and P_y is the price of Y and Y represents the quantity of Y. The constraint states that the value of X and Y purchased must be equal to the total income of the consumer.

This defines the concept of indifference curves where a consumer wants to attain the highest possible bundle of goods but is constrained by their income. The maximum utility that can be achieved by the consumer is the point where the indifference curve is tangent to the budget constraint. This is illustrated in Figure 8.4.

A similar constraint would be placed on a firm that was hoping to maximize their output. The firm would like to produce as much of good X as possible, where X is produced using a fixed amount of capital, K, and labour, L, per unit. The production function for X is presented as:

$$Q = f(K, L)$$

The firm want the quantity of X produced to be as high as possible in order to reap the largest possible profit however they are constrained by the price of capital and the price of labour and their total income available to spend on these two inputs. The constraint would therefore be presented as:

$$P_K K + P_L L = M$$

This is known as the firm's cost constraint.

This specific example relates to the relationship between the cost constraint and the isoquant that was identified in section 8.7. As all the points on each isoquant yield a specific level of output the firm will produce the quantity, represented by the isoquant that is tangent to the cost constraint, or the isocost curve. This scenario is illustrated in Figure 8.5.

Note that points B and C also lie on the isocost curve and are therefore also viable options. However these two points lie on lower isoquants and therefore yield smaller amounts of output than the more profitable point A. In the case of point A the slope of the isoquant is equal to the slope of the isocost.

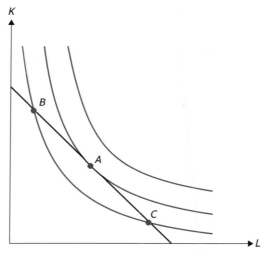

Figure 8.5

Note that a key difference between an indifference curve and an isoquant is that the distance between the former cannot be measured and therefore the exact position of the indifference curve is not very meaningful. What is meaningful is that greater utility is gained from the indifference curve that is the furthest away from the origin. In the case of the isoquant the distance between the curves is measurable so the position of the isoquant is important in that each identifies a specific quantity produced.

Student note

Quick problem 10

(a) Minimize the objective function $z = -3x^2 + 2y^2$ subject to the constraint $y = 3x - 2$.

(b) Maximize the objective function $z = 6x^2 - 4xy - 2y$ subject to the constraint $y = 5x$.

(c) A firm pays £2 per unit for labour and £2 per unit for capital. Maximize the production function $Q = 5KL + 5L^2$, and identify the levels of K and L used when the total input costs are £246.

✔ **Learning outcome 6**

8.10 Lagrange multipliers

In mathematical optimization problems *Lagrange multipliers* is a method for finding the local extrema of a function of several variables subject to one or more constraints. This method reduces a problem in n variables with k constraints to a solvable problem in $n + k$ variables with no constraints. The method introduces a new unknown scalar variable, the Lagrange multiplier, for each constraint and forms a linear combination involving the multipliers as coefficients. Using Lagrange multipliers is particularly useful when solving problems with more than two variables and non-linear constraints.

Consider the following objective function:

$$f(x, y)$$

subject to the constraint:

$$\phi(x, y) = M$$

where ϕ identifies a function of two variables and M is a constant.

Lagrange multipliers can be used to solve this problem. Consider the following steps:

1. Define a function from the information above:

    $$g(x, y, \lambda) = f(x, y) + \lambda[M - \phi(x, y)] \quad \text{Lagrangian function}$$

    where λ (lambda) is the Lagrange multiplier.

    The solution to this problem involves combining the original function and the identified constraint. This is done by rearranging the constraint $(M - \phi(x, y))$ and multiplying it by λ. Then we add this to the objective function.

2. Solve:

    $$\partial g / \partial x = 0$$

    $$\partial g / \partial y = 0$$

    $$\partial g / \partial \lambda = 0$$

    These are the three unknowns identified in the new function.

    First we calculate the three first order partial derivatives and set these equal to zero to produce simultaneous equations.

Example

Use Lagrange multipliers to find the optimal value of:

$$4x^2 - 2xy$$

subject to the constraint

$$x + 2y = 16$$

Step 1

Rearrange the above terms to follow the general form detailed above:

$$f(x, y) = 4x^2 - 2xy$$

$$\phi(x, y) = x + 2y$$

$$M = 16$$

So the Lagrangian function is presented as:

$$g(x, y, \lambda) = 4x^2 - 2xy + \lambda(16 - x - 2y)$$

Step 2

Calculate the three partial derivatives of *g* and set each equal to zero.

$$\partial g/\partial x = 8x - 2y - \lambda = 0 \tag{8.1}$$

$$\partial g/\partial y = -2x - 2\lambda = 0 \tag{8.2}$$

$$\partial g/\partial \lambda = 16 - x - 2y = 0 \tag{8.3}$$

Solving for the simultaneous equations gives:

$$\lambda = -1.6 \tag{8.1}$$

$$x = 1.6 \tag{8.2}$$

$$y = 7.2 \tag{8.3}$$

The optimal solution is therefore $(1.6, 7.2, -1.6)$ and the value of the objective function is

$$4(1.6)^2 - 2(1.6)(7.2)$$

$$= -12.8.$$

Objective Functions and constraints in Economics

Consider an example related to consumer utility. A consumer faces the utility function:

$$U(x_1, x_2) = 3x_1x_2 + 4x_1$$

The price of a unit of x_1 is £3 and the price of x_2 is £2. We will assume that the consumer's income is £275. Therefore the associated constraint is

$$3x_1 + 2x_2 = 275$$

Use Lagrange multipliers to find the maximum value of utility if the consumer's income is £275.

Step 1:

$$g(x_1, x_2, \lambda) = 3x_1x_2 + 4x_1 + \lambda(275 - 3x_1 - 2x_2)$$

Step 2:

$$\partial g/\partial x = 3x_2 + 4 - 3\lambda = 0$$
$$\partial g/\partial y = 3x_1 - 2\lambda = 0$$
$$\partial g/\partial \lambda = 275 - 3x_1 - 2x_2 = 0$$

Now consider an example related to a producer of two goods x and y who has a total cost function

$$TC = 9x + xy + 12y$$

where P_x and P_y denote the price of each good and the corresponding demand functions are

$$P_x = 20 - x + 2y$$
$$P_y = 25 + x - 5y$$

Objective function:

$$\pi = TR - TC$$
$$TC = 9x + xy + 12y$$
$$TR_x = P_x x = (20 - x + 2y)x = 20x - x^2 + 2xy$$
$$TR_y = P_y y = (25 + x - 5y)y = 25y + xy - 5y^2$$

$$TR = TR_x + TR_y = 20x - x^2 + 2xy + 25y + xy - 5y^2$$

$$TR = 20x - x^2 + 3xy + 25y - 5y^2$$

$$\pi = TR - TC$$
$$= 20x - x^2 + 3xy + 25y - 5y^2 - (9x + xy + 12y)$$
$$= 11x - x^2 + 2xy + 13y - 5y^2 \quad \text{(Objective function)}$$

This is subject to the constraint:

$$x + y = 25$$

Quick problem 11

A producer of two goods x and y has a total cost function

$TC = 6x + 3xy + 8y$

Where P_x and P_y denote the price of each good and the corresponding demand functions are:

$P_x = 10 - 2x + y$
$P_y = 18 + 4x - 9y$

Find the maximum profit if the firm is contracted to produce a total of 45 goods of either type.

✔ **Learning outcome 7**

Answers to quick problems

Quick problem 1

i) $f(x, y) = 444$

ii) $f(x, y) = 2605$

iii) $f(x_1, x_2) = 21$

iv) $f(x_1, x_2, x_3) = 23\ 101$

v) $f(x_1, x_2, x_3) = -176\ 418$

Quick problem 2

i) $f_x = 8x + 8y^2 - 24x^3y$

$f_y = 16xy - 6x^4 - 6$

ii) $f_x = 5x^4y^5 - 2xy^2 - y$

$f_y = 5x^5y^4 - 2x^2y - x$

iii) $f_{x1} = 15x_1^2 - 16x_1^3x_2^2$

$f_{x2} = -4x_2 - 8x_1^4x_2 - 1$

iv) $f_{x1} = 21x_1^2x_2^4x_3^2$

$f_{x2} = 28x_1^3x_2^3x_3^2 + 4x_2^3x_3$

$f_{x3} = 14x_1^3x_2^4x_3 + x_2^4 + 3 + 3x_3^2$

Quick problem 3

i) $f_{xx} = 6y^7 - 60x^2y^4$

$f_{yy} = 126x^2y^5 - 60x^4y^2$

$f_{xy} = f_{yx} = 42xy^6 - 80x^3y^3$

ii) $f_{x1} = 48x_1^3 - 20x_1^4x_2$

$f_{x2} = -9x_2^2 - 4x_1^5$

$f_{x1x1} = 144x_1^2 - 80x_1^3x_2$

$f_{x2x2} = -18x_2$

$f_{x2x1} = -20x_1^4$

iii) $f_{x1} = 24x_1^2x_2^4x_3^4 - 5x_2^3x_3^3$

$f_{x1x1} = 48x_1x_2^4x_3^4$

$f_{x2} = 32x_1^3x_2^3x_3^4 - 15x_1x_2^2x_3^3$

$f_{x2x2} = 96x_1^3x_2^2x_3^4 - 30x_1x_2x_3^3$

$f_{x3} = 32x_1^3x_2^4x_3^3 - 15x_1x_2^3x_3^2 + 8x_2 - 6$

$f_{x3x3} = 96x_1^3x_2^4x_3^2 - 30x_1x_2^3x_3$

$f_{x1x2} = 96x_1^2x_2^3x_3^4 - 15x_2^2x_3^3$

$f_{x1x3} = 96x_1^2x_2^4x_3^3 - 15x_2^3x_3^2$

$f_{x2x1} = 96x_1^2x_2^3x_3^4 - 15x_2^2x_3^3$

$f_{x2x3} = 128x_1^3x_2^3x_3^3 - 45x_1x_2^2x_3^2 + 8$

$f_{x3x1} = 96x_1^2x_2^4x_3^3 - 15x_2^3x_3^2$

$f_{x3x2} = 128x_1^3x_2^3x_3^3 - 45x_1x_2^2x_3^2 + 8$

Quick problem 4

$$\frac{\partial z}{\partial x} = 1536$$

$$\frac{\partial z}{\partial y} = -256$$

$$\Delta z = \left(\frac{\partial z}{\partial x} \times \Delta x \right) + \left(\frac{\partial z}{\partial y} \times \Delta y \right)$$

$$= (1536 \times 0.001) + (-256 \times (-0.001))$$

$$= 1.792$$

Quick problem 5

$Q_1 = 435$

$E_{p1} = 0.057$

$E_{p1} = +0.34$, i.e. substitute goods

$E_y = +0.37$, i.e. superior goods

Quick Problem 6

(a) $MRS = 2.27$

(b) $MRS = 1.5$

Quick Problem 7

a) $MRTS = \dfrac{3}{K^2}$

b) $MRTS = \dfrac{1}{36} \dfrac{K^{1/2}}{L^{2/3}}$

Quick Problem 8

(a) critical values are (0, 4), (0, −4), (1.63, 0), (−1.63, 0)

   (1.63, 0) is a minimum
   (−1.63, 0) is a maximum
   (0, 4) and (0, −4) are saddle points.

Quick problem 9

Maximum profit is £31,428.58 when $Q_1 = 42.87$ and $Q_2 = 71.42$

Quick problem 10

(a) The constrained function has a minimum value of -1.6 at $(0.8, 0.4)$.

(b) The constrained function has a maximum value of 1.78 at $(-0.36, -1.8)$.

(c) The constrained function has a maximum value of £23 639.04 at $(46.2, 76.8)$.

Quick problem 11

$f(x, y) = 4x - 2x^2 + 2xy + 10y - 9y^2$

$\phi(x, y) = x + y$

$M = 45$

$g(x, y, \lambda) = 4x - 2x^2 + 2xy + 10y - 9y^2 + \lambda(45 - x - y)$

$\dfrac{\partial g}{\partial x} = -4x + 2y + 4 - \lambda = 0$

$\dfrac{\partial g}{\partial y} = -18y + 2x + 10 - \lambda = 0$

$\dfrac{\partial g}{\partial \lambda} = 45 - x - y = 0$

$\Rightarrow x = 34.38, y = 10.62, \lambda = -112.3$

The Goal Seek Function in Excel can be used to identify the exact point where $MC = MR$. This is best achieved by creating a formula with the difference between MC and MR and finding the Q that gives a value of zero. This is equal to $Q = 1.847$ (to three decimal places). In economics, $MC = MR$ is known as the point of profit maximization.

Task Three
When $MC = MR$

$$3Q^3 + 2Q^2 - 2Q + 3 = 4Q^2 + 4Q + 4$$

so,

$$3Q^3 - 2Q^2 - 6Q - 1 = 0$$

Plugging in the solution, $Q = 1.85$ from above, we get:

$$3(1.847^3) - 2(1.847^2) - 6(1.847) - 1 = -0.002 \text{ (to three decimal places)}$$

Note if you create this series $(3Q^3 - 2Q^2 - 6Q - 1)$ in Excel you get the same result as the difference between MC and MR.

Quick problem 8

(a) 8
(b) 24
(c) 0.5

Quick problem 9

Consumer surplus $= [2.5Q_x^d - Q_x^d/8]_0^{Q^*} - p^*q^*$

Quick problem 10

$Q_x^s = 30 + 10p$

$p = \dfrac{Q_x^s}{10} - 3$

Producer surplus $= \displaystyle\int_0^{Q^*} \dfrac{Q_x^s}{10} - 3dQ_x^s - p^*q^*$

$$= \left[\dfrac{Q_x^s}{20} - 3Q_x^s \right]_0^{Q^*} - p^*q^*$$

Quick problem 11

Task One

D: 29 683.75

A: 7140

B: 552.5

C: 34.6

Task Two

$$p = 40 - 3Q_x^d$$

and the equilbirum price is £5.
If $p = £5$ then:

$$Q_x^d = \frac{35}{3} = 11.6$$

$$\text{Consumer surplus} = \int_0^{11.6} 40 - 3Q_x^d dQ_x^d - (11.66 \times 5)$$

$$= \left[40Q_x^d - \frac{3}{2}Q_x^{d^2} \right]_0^{11.66} - 58.3$$

$$= 466.4 - 203.9 - 58.3$$

$$= 204.2 \text{ units}$$

Task Three
Consumer surplus can be used as one indicator of consumer welfare. In its simplest form, we would expect consumers to have less consumer welfare in a monopoly situation since the monopolist could be argued to set higher prices and reap additional profits. The competition authorities might look at consumer surplus to identify if it has changed over time. A reduction in consumer surplus over time could indicate an increase in monopoly power and prompt further intervention by the competition authorities.

Quick problem 12

(a) 12.69

(b) 12.33

(c) +0.95

Chapter 10

Matrices

Topics covered

10.1	Introduction	276
10.2	Definitions, notation and operations	276
10.3	Vectors	279
10.4	Adding and subtracting matrices	280
10.5	Dealing with 'zero matrices'	282
10.6	Scalar multiplication of matrices	282
10.7	Multiplying matrices	284
10.8	Matrix inversion	287
10.9	Application of 2×2 matrices and inversions: solving economic equations	290
10.10	Inversions of 3×3 matrices	292
10.11	Application of 3×3 matrices and inversions: solving economic equations	296
10.12	Cramer's rule	300

LEARNING OUTCOMES

By the end of this chapter you should understand:

1. The meaning of the term, 'matrix' and basic matrix notation
2. How to transpose a matrix
3. The meaning of row and column matrices and vectors
4. How to add and subtract matrices
5. Scalar matrices
6. How to multiply matrices
7. The determinant of a matrix and how to invert a matrix
8. Using inversions of 2×2 matrices to solve economic equations
9. How to calculate inversions for 3×3 matrices
10. How to use inversions of 3×3 matrices to solve economic equations
11. How to use Cramer's rule to solve economic equations.

10.1 Introduction

A matrix is another name for a table which can include data or other information. For example, the daily exchange rates which are published in most newspapers, railway timetables and election results all use simple tables or matrices to record useful information. We can use the idea of presenting information using rows and columns in mathematics, but the basic premise remains the same: we are trying to represent information in a simple format.

There are some straightforward rules which you will need to learn about how to use matrices. These rules will allow you to manipulate mathematical expressions and, more importantly, provide a further tool which can be used to analyse and solve economic problems and issues.

10.2 Definitions, notation and operations

A matrix comprises of n rows and m columns. A 3×4 matrix would have three rows and four columns. This describes the order of the matrix. In Table 10.1 the order is 2×3.

We frequently ignore the column and row headings and simply concentrate on the data in the table or matrix.

For example, consider an electronics multinational, Global Electrics PLC. The firm sells two products: an MP3 player (product A) and a car navigation system (product B). It sells these products in three countries: the UK, the USA and South Africa. The sales data are summarized in Table 10.1.

Table 10.1 Number of units sold of products A and B

	UK	USA	South Africa
MP3 player (product A)	2 million	12 million	1 million
Car navigation system (product B)	1 million	3 million	2 million

We can reduce this table to a much simpler matrix of information, which we will call 'G' to stand for Global Electrics PLC.

$$G = \begin{pmatrix} 2 & 12 & 1 \\ 1 & 3 & 2 \end{pmatrix}$$

The brackets indicate that we have a matrix of information. Each item within the matrix is called an entry or an element or a cell.

In a sense, a matrix can be seen as a sort of mathematical map: it sets out information over a set of rows and columns and, in the same way that we can use a grid reference to pinpoint a location on a geographic map, so we can use a special set of referencing or notation to identify a particular entry in the matrix.

For example, G_{12} means 'go to matrix G and record what it is in row 1 and column 2'. In our matrix G, the answer is 12 million. If you are familiar with Excel, this is very similar to the LOOKUP function and the process is identical.

A *matrix* is a table or array of information. The *matrix order* summarizes the number of rows and columns.

We use square or rounded brackets to show that we have a matrix of data and we identify particular entries using the following notation.

Generally, x_{ab} identifies the element in row a, column b in matrix X. The matrix below summarizes how the elements would be written in matrix X of the order 3×4:

$$X = \begin{pmatrix} x_{11} & x_{12} & x_{13} & x_{14} \\ x_{21} & x_{22} & x_{23} & x_{24} \\ x_{31} & x_{32} & x_{33} & x_{34} \end{pmatrix}$$

Student note

Quick problem 1

Consider the two matrices below, A and B.

$$A = \begin{pmatrix} 2 & 4 & 8 \\ 3 & 6 & 9 \\ 7 & 4 & 2 \end{pmatrix} \qquad B = \begin{pmatrix} 1 & 9 & 6 & 0 \\ 3 & 11 & 8 & 1 \\ 5 & 2 & 0 & 10 \\ 7 & 4 & 2 & 9 \end{pmatrix}$$

Task One
Identify a_{22}, a_{33}, b_{11}, b_{42}.

Task Two
Write down the order of A and B.

Task Three
What problem would you face when trying to state b_{55}?

✔ **Learning outcome 1**

Transposing a matrix

Transposition really means 'switching around' and you might have come across this as a function within a spreadsheet program such as Excel. The switching means that all of the information in a row is placed in a column instead.

Student note

Transposition means replacing or switching around.

$$\text{If } A = \begin{pmatrix} a & b & c \\ d & e & f \\ g & h & i \end{pmatrix} \quad \text{then} \quad A^T = \begin{pmatrix} a & d & g \\ b & e & h \\ c & f & i \end{pmatrix}$$

and so on for whatever size or matrix order we have.
   The superscripted T indicates that a transposition has taken place.

Consider:

$$A = \begin{pmatrix} 2 & 4 & 8 \\ 3 & 6 & 9 \\ 7 & 4 & 2 \end{pmatrix}$$

The transposition of matrix A involves taking the first column and rewriting it as a row and so on. We show that a transposition has taken place by placing a superscript 'T' next to the matrix so:

$$\text{Transposition of } A = A^T = \begin{pmatrix} 2 & 3 & 7 \\ 4 & 6 & 4 \\ 8 & 9 & 2 \end{pmatrix}$$

Quick problem 2

Task One

$$\text{If } X = \begin{pmatrix} 12 & 11 & 3 & 7 \\ 3 & 2 & 1 & 1 \end{pmatrix}$$

state X^T.

Task Two
Consider the following matrices, Y and Z:

$$Y = \begin{pmatrix} 1 & 2 & 4 \\ 6 & 5 & 3 \\ 11 & 7 & 9 \end{pmatrix} \quad Z = \begin{pmatrix} 2 & 2 & 4 \\ 3 & 4 & 3 \\ 1 & 1 & 0 \end{pmatrix}$$

Which statements, if any, are correct? Explain your reasoning in each case.

Statement 1: $Y^T = Z^T$

Statement 2: $Z^T = \begin{pmatrix} 2 & 3 & 1 \\ 2 & 4 & 1 \\ 4 & 3 & 0 \end{pmatrix}$

Statement 3: $Y^T = \begin{pmatrix} 1 & 6 & 4 \\ 11 & 5 & 3 \\ 6 & 7 & 9 \end{pmatrix}$

✔ **Learning outcome 2**

10.3 Vectors

Vectors is a mathematical term which can be used to describe in a single line important information, e.g., speed and direction or an instruction to a computer on how to plot graphics. It has a wider use which we can apply in economics.

We can use a vector when information is contained in a single row or a single column.

For example, the matrix A = [2 1 3 0] would be a *single row vector* because all of the data are contained in a single row. Similarly, the matrix

$$B = \begin{pmatrix} 1 \\ 2 \\ 2 \\ 7 \end{pmatrix}$$

would also be considered to be a vector but this time it would be labelled a *column vector* since all of the data are placed in one column.

Vectors are usually denoted by underlining the letter of the matrix and for historical reasons the lower case is always used. So, for example we would illustrate the row vector of matrix A simply by **a**. Equally, the column vector shown by matrix B would be denoted by **b**.

We can avoid the rather cumbersome expression of column vectors by simply rewriting them as a transposition. Look again at matrix B and consider how much easier and neater it is to simply write $\mathbf{b} = [1\ 2\ 2\ 7]^T$ – remember the T superscript tells us a transposition has taken place – rather than having to write out the whole column and waste a great deal of paper.

Quick problem 3

Task One
Write down how you can identify if a matrix is a vector.

Task Two
Which, if any, of the following are row vectors and column vectors?

$$H = \begin{pmatrix} 0 \\ 0 \\ 0 \\ -1 \end{pmatrix} \qquad I = \begin{pmatrix} 1 & 0 \\ 0 & 1 \\ 1 & 2 \end{pmatrix} \qquad J = (2 \quad 2 \quad 2 \quad -2) \qquad K = \begin{pmatrix} 1 & 0 & 1 \\ 0 & 1 & 0 \\ 1 & 0 & 1 \end{pmatrix}^T \qquad L = (0)^T$$

✔ **Learning outcome 3**

10.4 Adding and subtracting matrices

So far we have used matrices to express a set of data. In economics, we often want to manipulate data to create new information. For example, we might want to add together household consumption in different regions to arrive at a figure for total national consumption. Equally, we might want to subtract elements of data, e.g., subtracting tax from gross income to work out a household's net income. Clearly, to complete these mathematical tasks we need to understand how to add and subtract matrices.

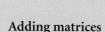

Student note

Matrices can be added or subtracted simply by adding or subtracting the matching entries.

In general, if we have two matrices A and B we can add them together to create a new matrix C as follows:

Adding matrices
If we have two matrices:

$$A = \begin{pmatrix} 2 & 3 \\ 7 & 4 \end{pmatrix} \quad \text{and} \quad B = \begin{pmatrix} 3 & 0 \\ 2 & 6 \end{pmatrix} \quad \text{then we can work out A + B by:}$$

$$A + B = \begin{pmatrix} 2 & 3 \\ 7 & 4 \end{pmatrix} + \begin{pmatrix} 3 & 0 \\ 2 & 6 \end{pmatrix} = \begin{pmatrix} 2+3 & 3+0 \\ 7+2 & 4+6 \end{pmatrix} = \begin{pmatrix} 5 & 3 \\ 9 & 10 \end{pmatrix}$$

So, in general:

$$A = \begin{pmatrix} a_{11} & \cdots & a_{1n} \\ \vdots & \ddots & \vdots \\ a_{m1} & \cdots & a_{mn} \end{pmatrix} \quad \text{and} \quad B = \begin{pmatrix} b_{11} & \cdots & b_{1n} \\ \vdots & \ddots & \vdots \\ b_{m1} & \cdots & b_{mn} \end{pmatrix} \quad \text{then}$$

$$A + B = C = \begin{pmatrix} a_{11} + b_{11} & \cdots & a_{1n} + b_{1n} \\ \vdots & \ddots & \vdots \\ a_{m1} + b_{m1} & \cdots & a_{mn} + b_{mn} \end{pmatrix}$$

Subtracting matrices

Subtracting matrices follows the same process: we subtract the second element from the first corresponding element. Using the same two matrices A and B as before:

$$A = \begin{pmatrix} 2 & 3 \\ 7 & 4 \end{pmatrix} \quad \text{and} \quad B = \begin{pmatrix} 3 & 0 \\ 2 & 6 \end{pmatrix}$$

$$A - B = \begin{pmatrix} 2 & 3 \\ 7 & 4 \end{pmatrix} - \begin{pmatrix} 3 & 0 \\ 2 & 6 \end{pmatrix} = \begin{pmatrix} 2-3 & 3-0 \\ 7-2 & 4-6 \end{pmatrix} = \begin{pmatrix} -1 & 3 \\ 5 & -2 \end{pmatrix}$$

So in general if:

$$A = \begin{pmatrix} a_{11} & \cdots & a_{1n} \\ \vdots & \ddots & \vdots \\ a_{m1} & \cdots & a_{mn} \end{pmatrix} \quad \text{and} \quad B = \begin{pmatrix} b_{11} & \cdots & b_{1n} \\ \vdots & \ddots & \vdots \\ b_{m1} & \cdots & b_{mn} \end{pmatrix} \quad \text{then}$$

then:

$$A - B = \begin{pmatrix} a_{11} - b_{11} & \cdots & a_{1n} - b_{1n} \\ \vdots & \ddots & \vdots \\ a_{m1} - b_{m1} & \cdots & a_{mn} - b_{mn} \end{pmatrix}$$

You will probably have already realised that you cannot add or subtract matrices which have a different order. For example, it would be impossible to add

$$\begin{pmatrix} 1 & 0 \\ 0 & 1 \end{pmatrix} \quad \text{and} \quad \begin{pmatrix} 2 & 4 & 6 \\ 1 & 2 & 0 \\ 3 & 3 & 2 \end{pmatrix}$$

because they do not share the same order: they do not have the same number of rows and columns.

Quick problem 4

Consider the following matrices

$$A = \begin{pmatrix} 1 & 0 \\ 0 & 1 \end{pmatrix} \qquad B = \begin{pmatrix} 2 & 3 \\ 4 & 4 \end{pmatrix} \qquad C = \begin{pmatrix} 4 & 4 & 5 \\ 5 & 3 & 2 \\ 6 & 7 & 12 \end{pmatrix}$$

$$D = \begin{pmatrix} 2 \\ 2 \end{pmatrix} \qquad E = \begin{pmatrix} 8 & 2 & 1 \\ 0 & 2 & 1 \\ 0 & 9 & 3 \end{pmatrix} \qquad F = (1 \quad 2) \qquad G = \begin{pmatrix} 2 \\ -1 \end{pmatrix}$$

Evaluate:

(a) $A + B$

(b) $B + C$

(c) $G - E$

(d) $C + E$

(e) $E - C$

(f) $G - D$

(g) $A + E$

✔ **Learning outcome 4**

10.5 Dealing with 'zero matrices'

Sometimes an addition or subtraction will lead to a zero answer.
    For example:

$$A - A = \begin{pmatrix} 1 & 0 \\ 0 & 1 \end{pmatrix} - \begin{pmatrix} 1 & 0 \\ 0 & 1 \end{pmatrix} = \begin{pmatrix} 0 & 0 \\ 0 & 0 \end{pmatrix}$$

$$E - E = \begin{pmatrix} 8 & 2 & 1 \\ 0 & 2 & 1 \\ 0 & 9 & 3 \end{pmatrix} - \begin{pmatrix} 8 & 2 & 1 \\ 0 & 2 & 1 \\ 0 & 9 & 3 \end{pmatrix} = \begin{pmatrix} 0 & 0 & 0 \\ 0 & 0 & 0 \\ 0 & 0 & 0 \end{pmatrix}$$

$$D - D = \begin{pmatrix} 2 \\ 2 \end{pmatrix} - \begin{pmatrix} 2 \\ 2 \end{pmatrix} = \begin{pmatrix} 0 \\ 0 \end{pmatrix}$$

In each case, the answer is a zero matrix and we can simplify and write **0**.

10.6 Scalar multiplication of matrices

Sometimes we want to multiply quantities by a factor. For example, a worker who earns £50 per day will need to multiply their daily wage rate by the number of days they work in a month to calculate their monthly earnings.

We can use this idea of scaling with matrices. In this context, 'scaling' means multiplying each element by a given number. The scaling number or 'scalar' can be positive or negative and it can be a fraction.

Example

If $A = \begin{pmatrix} 2 & 3 \\ 4 & 2 \end{pmatrix}$, calculate

(a) 3A (b) $\frac{1}{2}A$ (c) $-3A$

(a) $3A = \begin{pmatrix} 3 \times 2 & 3 \times 3 \\ 3 \times 4 & 3 \times 2 \end{pmatrix} = \begin{pmatrix} 6 & 9 \\ 12 & 6 \end{pmatrix}$

(b) $\frac{1}{2}A = \begin{pmatrix} \frac{1}{2} \times 2 & \frac{1}{2} \times 3 \\ \frac{1}{2} \times 4 & \frac{1}{2} \times 2 \end{pmatrix} = \begin{pmatrix} 1 & \frac{3}{2} \\ 2 & 1 \end{pmatrix}$

(c) $-3A = \begin{pmatrix} -3 \times 2 & -3 \times 3 \\ -3 \times 4 & -3 \times 2 \end{pmatrix} = \begin{pmatrix} -6 & -9 \\ -12 & -6 \end{pmatrix}$

Scaling a matrix means multiplying each element by a certain factor but remember that this can be a positive, negative, fractional or whole number.

If we have a matrix:

$$A = \begin{pmatrix} a_{11} & a_{12} \\ a_{21} & a_{22} \end{pmatrix}$$

and we want to find kA where k is the scalar then we multiple each element by k:

$$kA = \begin{pmatrix} k \times a_{11} & k \times a_{12} \\ k \times a_{21} & k \times a_{22} \end{pmatrix}$$

If:

$k > 1$ then each element in the matrix kA will be bigger than each element in A

$k = 1$ then each element in the matrix kA will identical to each element in A

$k < 1$ then each element in the matrix kA will smaller than each element in A

$k < 0$ then each element in the matrix kA will be negative

Student note

Quick problem 5

$$X = \begin{pmatrix} 1 & 0 \\ 0 & 1 \end{pmatrix} \quad Y = \begin{pmatrix} 2 \\ -2 \end{pmatrix} \quad Z = \begin{pmatrix} 3 & 7 & 6 \\ 4 & 7 & 3 \\ 5 & -2 & 7 \end{pmatrix}$$

Task One
Evaluate:

(a) 2X

(b) 3Y

(c) $\dfrac{1}{2}Z$

Task Two
Which statement, if any, is true?

Statement 1: $4X = 2(2X)$

Statement 2: $X - Y = 0$

Statement 3: $3Z = \begin{pmatrix} 9 & 21 & 18 \\ 12 & 14 & 6 \\ 15 & 6 & 21 \end{pmatrix}$

Statement 4: $5Y = \begin{pmatrix} 12 \\ 6 \end{pmatrix} - \begin{pmatrix} 2 \\ 16 \end{pmatrix}$

✔ **Learning outcome 5**

10.7 Multiplying matrices

In the previous section we considered how to scale a matrix by a given factor. The next step is to think about how we can multiply matrices together. Like many mathematical processes you will need to learn a certain technique for doing this but first we can think about why we might want to do this at all.

There are many practical examples including calculating a firm's revenue or turnover, the total dividend payment a shareholder should expect to receive or measuring the total output of an economy by multiplying the average output per workers in sectors of the economy by the total number of workers in each sector.

We will look at a firm's profits to illustrate matrix multiplication. Imagine a large mobile phone manufacturer examines the profits on three models of mobile phone that it produces: the A100, the A101 and the A102. The features, profits per phone and quantity sold are summarized in Table 10.2.

Table 10.2

	A100	A101	A102
Profit per mobile phone sold	£15.00	£18.00	£23.00
Main features:			
MP3 player	✗	✔	✔
Video messenging	✗	✗	✔
FM radio	✗	✔	✔
Bluetooth	✔	✔	✔

We are also give the following data on the worldwide quantity sold last year of each model:

A100: 100 million units sold

A101: 75 million units sold

A102: 130 million units sold

We can express the numerical data in simple matrices.

Let P denote the profit on each model of mobile phone A100, A101 and A102 respectively. That is,

$$P = (15 \quad 18 \quad 23)$$

Let Q denote the quantity of each model sold. That is,

$$Q = \begin{pmatrix} 100 \\ 75 \\ 130 \end{pmatrix}$$

If we want to work out total profits for each model, we need to multiply P by Q:

$$P \times Q = (15 \quad 18 \quad 23) \times \begin{pmatrix} 100 \\ 75 \\ 130 \end{pmatrix}$$

We need a quick technique to do this. In effect, we need to multiply the 15 by the 100, then multiply the 18 by the 75 and finally multiply the 23 by the 130. The scalar product we would arrive at would show the total profit attained in selling the three mobile phone models. That is, we need to calculate as follows:

$$P \times Q = (15 \quad 18 \quad 23) \times \begin{pmatrix} 100 \\ 75 \\ 130 \end{pmatrix}$$

Or, put another way

$$P \times Q = (15 \times 100) + (18 \times 75) + (23 \times 130) = (1500 + 1350 + 2990) = £5840$$

Student note

Matrices can be multiplied together if the number of rows in one matrix is the same as the number of columns in the other matrix.

We can multiply the two matrices together by taking the first row of the first matrix and placing it over the top of the first column of the second matrix. We then multiply the each pair of elements and add together.

For example if

$$A = \begin{pmatrix} a_{11} & a_{12} \\ a_{21} & a_{22} \end{pmatrix} \quad \text{and} \quad B = \begin{pmatrix} b_{11} & b_{12} \\ b_{21} & b_{22} \end{pmatrix}$$

and we want to calculate AB we take the first row of A and multiply each element against corresponding element of the first column of matrix B and add together.

So AB is then:

$$AB = \begin{pmatrix} (a_{11} \times b_{11}) + (a_{12} \times b_{21}) & (a_{11} \times b_{12}) + (a_{12} \times b_{22}) \\ (a_{21} \times b_{11}) + (a_{22} \times b_{21}) & (a_{21} \times b_{12}) + (a_{22} \times b_{22}) \end{pmatrix}$$

Example 1

Let: $A = \begin{pmatrix} 2 & 3 \\ 4 & 5 \end{pmatrix} \quad B = \begin{pmatrix} 2 & 1 \\ 1 & -1 \end{pmatrix}$

$$AB = \begin{pmatrix} (2 \times 2) + (3 \times 1) & (2 \times 1) + (3 \times (-1)) \\ (4 \times 2) + (5 \times 1) & (4 \times 1) + (5 \times (-1)) \end{pmatrix} = \begin{pmatrix} 7 & -1 \\ 13 & -1 \end{pmatrix}$$

Example 2

Let $C = (2 \quad 6 \quad 3) \quad \text{and} \quad D = \begin{pmatrix} 1 & 4 & 2 \\ 5 & 0 & 6 \\ -1 & 7 & 9 \end{pmatrix}$

$CD = ((2 \times 1) + (6 \times 5) + (3 \times (-1)) \quad (2 \times 4) + (6 \times 0) + (3 \times 7) \quad (2 \times 2) + (6 \times 6) + (3 \times 9))$

$CD = (2 + 30 - 3 \quad 8 + 0 + 21 \quad 4 + 36 + 27)$

$CD = (29 \quad 29 \quad 67)$

Example 3

$X = \begin{pmatrix} 1 & 2 & 3 & 4 \\ 5 & 6 & 7 & 8 \end{pmatrix} \quad Y = \begin{pmatrix} 1 & 2 \\ 3 & 7 \\ 0 & 3 \\ 5 & -2 \end{pmatrix}$

$$XY = \begin{pmatrix} (1 \times 1) + (2 \times 3) + (3 \times 0) + (4 \times 5) & (1 \times 2) + (2 \times 7) + (3 \times 3) + (4 \times (-2)) \\ (5 \times 1) + (6 \times 3) + (7 \times 0) + (8 \times 5) & (5 \times 2) + (6 \times 7) + (7 \times 3) + (8 \times (-2)) \end{pmatrix}$$

$$XY = \begin{pmatrix} 27 & 17 \\ 63 & 57 \end{pmatrix}$$

Quick problem 6

You are given the following economic data.

$$A = \begin{pmatrix} 1 & 0 \\ 0 & 1 \end{pmatrix} \qquad B = \begin{pmatrix} 1 \\ 2 \\ 3 \\ -2 \end{pmatrix} \qquad C = \begin{pmatrix} 2 & 1 & 5 \\ -1 & 3 & 0 \\ 6 & -2 & 4 \end{pmatrix}$$

$$D = \begin{pmatrix} 2 & -1 \\ -1 & 2 \end{pmatrix} \qquad E = (5 \quad 4 \quad 3 \quad 2) \qquad F = \begin{pmatrix} 1 & 2 & 3 \\ 2 & 1 & 3 \\ 4 & 1 & -2 \end{pmatrix}$$

Find the following. Identify which, if any, cannot be found and why this is the case.

(a) AD

(b) BE

(c) AF

(d) DC

✔ **Learning outcome 6**

10.8 Matrix inversion

The word 'inversion' simply means to turn something upside down. If, for example, we invert the number '4' we get '$1/4$': we have turned the number upside down or calculated its reciprocal and we did this by calculating 4^{-1} to arrive at $1/4$. In terms of matrices we can do something similar but we need to learn a special technique for doing this.

Consider the following, matrix A:

$$A = \begin{pmatrix} a & b \\ c & d \end{pmatrix}$$

and we want to find the inverse of A or A^{-1}.

We need to follow three separate steps:

Step 1: Swap elements a and d.

Step 2: Change the signs of elements b and c.

Step 3: Multiple the matrix we now have after steps 1 and 2 by

$$\frac{1}{(ad - bc)}.$$

The resulting answer gives us A^{-1}.

Example

If $A = \begin{pmatrix} 1 & -4 \\ 0 & 3 \end{pmatrix}$ then calculate A^{-1}.

Using our three-step method:

Step 1 gives us:

$\begin{pmatrix} 3 & -4 \\ 0 & 1 \end{pmatrix}$

Step 2 gives us:

$\begin{pmatrix} 3 & 4 \\ 0 & 1 \end{pmatrix}$

Step 3 gives us:

$\frac{1}{3} \times \begin{pmatrix} 3 & 4 \\ 0 & 1 \end{pmatrix} = \begin{pmatrix} 1 & 4/3 \\ 0 & 1/3 \end{pmatrix}$

So, if

$A = \begin{pmatrix} 1 & -4 \\ 0 & 3 \end{pmatrix}$

then

$A^{-1} = \begin{pmatrix} 1 & 4/3 \\ 0 & 1/3 \end{pmatrix}$

Note just as $4 \times {}^1/_4 = 1$ that $A \times A^{-1}$ equals $\begin{pmatrix} 1 & 0 \\ 0 & 1 \end{pmatrix}$ which is the identity matrix.

Student note

The Identity matrix

The matrix $\begin{pmatrix} 1 & 0 \\ 0 & 1 \end{pmatrix}$ in known as the identity matrix. This has a 1 for each element on the main

iagonal and 0 for all other elements. The identity matrix for a 3×3 matrix would be $\begin{pmatrix} 1 & 0 & 0 \\ 0 & 1 & 0 \\ 0 & 0 & 1 \end{pmatrix}$

$A \times A^{-1} = \begin{pmatrix} 1 & -4 \\ 0 & 1 \end{pmatrix} \times \begin{pmatrix} 1 & 4/3 \\ 0 & 1/3 \end{pmatrix} = \begin{pmatrix} 1 & 0 \\ 0 & 1 \end{pmatrix}$

In step 3, we used a special scalar

$$\frac{1}{(ad-bc)}$$

The term $(ad-bc)$ is known as *the determinant of the matrix*. In shorthand, we often write this as $det(A)$ to refer to the determinant of matrix A.

You can easily see that if $(ad-bc)$ or $det(A)$ is zero we cannot work the inversion because the scalar

$$\frac{1}{(ad-bc)}$$

would be infinity (remember: any number divided by zero cannot be worked out).

What does this mean in practice? It means that if:

$(ad-bc) = 0$ then the matrix is *a singular matrix, i.e., it cannot be inverted.*

$(ad-bc) \neq 0$ then the matrix is *a non-singular matrix, i.e., it can be inverted.*

It is worth checking whether $det(A) = 0$ before you start trying to invert it. If $det(A)$ is zero you know not to bother trying to invert the matrix: it cannot be done!

The identity matrix

You will have seen from the worked example a special matrix called the *identity matrix* which looks like this:

$\begin{pmatrix} 1 & 0 \\ 0 & 1 \end{pmatrix}$ for a 2×2 matrix and $\begin{pmatrix} 1 & 0 & 0 \\ 0 & 1 & 0 \\ 0 & 0 & 1 \end{pmatrix}$ for a 3×3 matrix

Student note

Quick problem 7

If:

$$A = \begin{pmatrix} -1 & -3 \\ 1 & 1 \end{pmatrix} \quad B = \begin{pmatrix} 6 & 3 \\ 2 & 1 \end{pmatrix}$$

$$C = \begin{pmatrix} 3 & -1 \\ -2 & 7 \end{pmatrix}$$

Task One

(a) Calculate $det(A)$, $det(B)$ and $det(C)$

(b) Which matrices are singular or non-singular?

Task Two

Using your answers from Task One, calculate A^{-1}, B^{-1}, C^{-1}.

✔ **Learning outcome 7**

10.9 Application of 2×2 matrices and inversions: solving economic equations

We can use this technique for solving economics problems. A common use is to solve problems involving prices of goods. For example, if we are told that:

$$aP_1 + bP_2 = e$$

$$cP_1 + dP_2 = f$$

how can we solve this to find the values of P_1 and P_2?

It is worth noting a general rule first before we start to solve problems. In this format we can see that we can form a matrix, A, with the values of a, b, c and d. We could multiply this by the P values P_1 and P_2 to get the values on the right-hand side of each equation e and f.

We can put this another way.

Let:

$$A = \begin{pmatrix} a & b \\ c & d \end{pmatrix} \qquad x = \begin{pmatrix} P_1 \\ P_2 \end{pmatrix} \quad \text{and} \quad z = \begin{pmatrix} e \\ f \end{pmatrix}$$

Then:

$$A \times x = z$$

$$Ax = z$$

You need to learn this can be rearranged to form:

$$x = A^{-1}z$$

where A^{-1} is the inverse of matrix A.

Example

This process can be useful when solving economic problems with equations. Consider the economic data below concerning two commodities, tea and coffee.

Let:

P_1 denote the equilibrium price of coffee

P_2 denote the equilibrium price of tea

An economist finds that:

$$4P_1 - P_2 = 1$$

$$-2P_1 + 3P_2 = 12$$

and he wants to find the values of P_1 and P_2.

We need to rewrite these two equations into matrix form. Using the structure above we can see that:

$$A = \begin{pmatrix} 4 & -1 \\ -2 & 3 \end{pmatrix}$$

$$x = \begin{pmatrix} P_1 \\ P_2 \end{pmatrix}$$

$$z = \begin{pmatrix} 1 \\ 12 \end{pmatrix}$$

We know that $x = A^{-1}z$

$$A^{-1} = \frac{1}{10} \begin{pmatrix} 3 & 1 \\ 2 & 4 \end{pmatrix}$$

$$x = \frac{1}{10} \begin{pmatrix} 3 & 1 \\ 2 & 4 \end{pmatrix} \times \begin{pmatrix} 1 \\ 12 \end{pmatrix}$$

Therefore,

$$x = \begin{pmatrix} 3/10 & 1/10 \\ 1/5 & 3/5 \end{pmatrix} \begin{pmatrix} 1 \\ 12 \end{pmatrix}$$

$$= \begin{pmatrix} 3/10 & 12/10 \\ 1/5 & 24/5 \end{pmatrix} = \begin{pmatrix} 3/2 \\ 5 \end{pmatrix}$$

Therefore, $P_1 = 1.5$ and $P_2 = 5$

The economist finds that the equilibrium price of coffee is 1.5 and the equilibrium price of tea is 5.

When using matrices to solve simple equations remember to reformulate the equations so they follow this structure:

$$A = \begin{pmatrix} a & b \\ c & d \end{pmatrix} \qquad x = \begin{pmatrix} P_1 \\ P_2 \end{pmatrix} \text{ and } z = \begin{pmatrix} e \\ f \end{pmatrix}$$

Then:

$$x = A^{-1}z$$

To get A^{-1} you'll need to follow the three-step process outlined at the beginning of section 10.8.

Student note

Quick problem 8

Task One
An economist believes that the equilibrium prices of two goods p_a and p_b are linked as follows.

$p_a - 3p_b = 3$

$5p_a - 9p_b = 11$

Assuming these data are correct, find the values of p_a and p_b using the matrix method.

Task Two
Look again at tour answers to Task One. What evidence is there that the economist might be using incorrect data?

Task Three
The economist finds new information which suggests the relationship between p_a and p_b has altered over time and can now be expressed as follows

$p_a + 3p_b = 1$

$2p_a - 4p_b = 1$

Do the values of p_a and p_b change? If so, what are they now?

✔ **Learning outcome 8**

10.10 Inversions of 3×3 matrices

We can expand this knowledge and understanding to larger matrices. Consider, for example, matrix A which has three rows and three columns.

$$A = \begin{pmatrix} a_1 & b_1 & c_1 \\ a_2 & b_2 & c_2 \\ a_3 & b_3 & c_3 \end{pmatrix}$$

To work out the inverse of this matrix we need to understand a new term: *cofactors*. Cofactors are a simple but powerful idea. If we remove the row and column which contains the element a_1 we are left with a 2×2 matrix. The *determinant* of this sub-matrix gives us the *minor of a_1*.

So, the minor of $a_1 = (b_2c_3 - c_2b_3)$.

Equally, the minor of $c_1 = (a_2b_3 - b_2a_3)$

The cofactor of each element is calculated by multiplying the minor by ± 1 using the following structure or pattern:

$$\begin{pmatrix} + & - & + \\ - & + & - \\ + & - & + \end{pmatrix}$$

We can create a new matrix by replacing each element of matrix A by its cofactor and *transposing* this to find the *adjoint of* A. This is sometimes written as *adj(A)*.

We need to then calculate the determinant of A. The determinant of A in a 3 × 3 matrix can be worked out by multiplying each member or element in a row or column by their respective cofactors and adding them together.

We can then calculate

$$A^{-1} = adj(A) \times \frac{1}{\det(A)}$$

In summary, to work out the inverse of a 3 × 3 matrix there are five steps:

Step 1: Work out the minors of each element in our matrix

Step 2: Calculate the matrix of cofactors

Step 3: Create the adjoint of A

Step 4: Calculate the det(A)

Step 5: Work out

$$adj(A) \times \frac{1}{\det(A)} \text{ arrive at } A^{-1}$$

Student note

Full example

We are given matrix A as follows and asked to calculate A^{-1}.

$$A = \begin{pmatrix} 1 & -2 & 3 \\ 2 & 1 & 0 \\ 1 & -1 & 1 \end{pmatrix}$$

Step 1: Work out the minors

The minors of each element in matrix A are as follows:

Minor of a_1 = determinant of the matrix $\begin{pmatrix} 1 & 0 \\ -1 & 1 \end{pmatrix} = (1 \times 1) - (0 \times 1) = 1$

Minor of a_2 = determinant of the matrix $\begin{pmatrix} -2 & 3 \\ -1 & 1 \end{pmatrix} = (-2 \times 1) - (3 \times (-1)) = 1$

Minor of a_3 = determinant of the matrix $\begin{pmatrix} -2 & 3 \\ 1 & 0 \end{pmatrix} = -3$

Minor of b_1 = determinant of the matrix $\begin{pmatrix} 2 & 0 \\ 1 & 1 \end{pmatrix} = 2$

Minor of b_2 = determinant of the matrix $\begin{pmatrix} 1 & 3 \\ 1 & 1 \end{pmatrix} = -2$

Minor of b_3 = determinant of the matrix $\begin{pmatrix} 1 & 3 \\ 2 & 0 \end{pmatrix} = -6$

Minor of c_1 = determinant of the matrix $\begin{pmatrix} 2 & 1 \\ 1 & -1 \end{pmatrix} = -3$

Minor of c_2 = determinant of the matrix $\begin{pmatrix} 1 & -2 \\ 1 & -1 \end{pmatrix} = 1$

Minor of c_3 = determinant of the matrix $\begin{pmatrix} 1 & -2 \\ 2 & 1 \end{pmatrix} = 5$

The matrix of minors is then:

$$\begin{pmatrix} 1 & 1 & -3 \\ 1 & -2 & 1 \\ -3 & -6 & 5 \end{pmatrix}$$

Step 2: Calculate the cofactors
We multiply the matrix of minors by

$$\begin{pmatrix} + & - & + \\ - & + & - \\ + & - & + \end{pmatrix}$$

Matrix of cofactors is then:

$$\begin{pmatrix} 1 & -2 & -3 \\ -1 & -2 & -1 \\ -3 & 6 & 5 \end{pmatrix}$$

Step 3: Create the adjoint of A by transposing the matrix of cofactors
From Step 2 we transpose this matrix to get:

$$\text{adj}(A) = \begin{pmatrix} 1 & -1 & -3 \\ -2 & -2 & 6 \\ -3 & -1 & 5 \end{pmatrix}$$

Step 4: Calculating the det(A)
The determinant of A is calculated by multiplying each member or element in any row or column by their respective cofactors and adding them together.

In other words take each element in Matrix A

$$\begin{pmatrix} 1 & -2 & 3 \\ 2 & 1 & 0 \\ 1 & -1 & 1 \end{pmatrix}$$

and multiply by the corresponding element in the matrix cofactors

$$\begin{pmatrix} 1 & -2 & -3 \\ -1 & -2 & -1 \\ -3 & 6 & 5 \end{pmatrix}$$

Looking at the first row we get: $(1 \times 1) + (-2 \times (-2)) + (3 \times (-3)) = 1 + 4 - 9 = -4$.

We get the same answer no matter which row or column we select. To prove this let us repeat this calculation of the determinant of A using the second row.

Looking at the second row we get: $(2 \times (-1)) + (1 \times (-2)) + (0 \times (-1)) = -4$.

Step 5: Multiplying adj(A) by $\dfrac{1}{\det(A)}$

Multiplying adj(A) by 1/det(A) we have:

$$A^{-1} = \text{adj}(A) \times \frac{1}{\det(A)}$$

$$A^{-1} = \begin{pmatrix} 1 & -1 & -3 \\ -2 & -2 & 6 \\ -3 & -1 & 5 \end{pmatrix} \times \left(-\frac{1}{4}\right)$$

or,

$$A^{-1} = -\frac{1}{4} \begin{pmatrix} 1 & -1 & -3 \\ -2 & -2 & 6 \\ -3 & -1 & 5 \end{pmatrix}$$

Brief example
If

$$A = \begin{pmatrix} -1 & 1 & 0 \\ 2 & -1 & 1 \\ 1 & 1 & 1 \end{pmatrix}$$

find A^{-1}.

Step 1
Minors are

$$\begin{pmatrix} -2 & 1 & 3 \\ 1 & -1 & -2 \\ 1 & -1 & -1 \end{pmatrix}$$

Step 2
Cofactors are

$$\begin{pmatrix} -2 & -1 & 3 \\ -1 & -1 & 2 \\ 1 & 1 & -1 \end{pmatrix}$$

Step 3

$$\text{adj}(A) = \begin{pmatrix} -2 & -1 & 1 \\ -1 & -1 & 1 \\ 3 & 2 & -1 \end{pmatrix}$$

Step 4

$$\det(A) = 1$$

Step 5

$$A^{-1} = \text{adj}(A) \times \frac{1}{\det(A)} = \begin{pmatrix} -2 & -1 & 1 \\ -1 & -1 & 1 \\ 3 & 2 & -1 \end{pmatrix} \times 1 = \begin{pmatrix} -2 & -1 & 1 \\ -1 & -1 & 1 \\ 3 & 2 & -1 \end{pmatrix}$$

Quick problem 9

Task One
Calculate the inverse of the following 3×3 matrices.

$$A = \begin{pmatrix} 2 & 1 & 1 \\ 1 & 1 & 2 \\ -1 & -2 & 3 \end{pmatrix}$$

$$B = \begin{pmatrix} 2 & 5 & 1 \\ -1 & 3 & 1 \\ -1 & 2 & 1 \end{pmatrix}$$

Task Two
What problem is there in trying to find D^{-1} where

$$D = \begin{pmatrix} 4 & 3 & 1 \\ 2 & -1 & 3 \\ 1 & 0 & 1 \end{pmatrix}$$

✔ **Learning outcome 9**

10.11 Application of 3×3 matrices and inversions: solving economic equations

In the same way as in section 10.9, we can apply our knowledge and understanding of matrix algebra to solve economic equations. We can use the same statement that $x = A^{-1}z$ where A^{-1} is the inverse of matrix A.

We have already seen how to use matrices to solve for an economic problem where two variables are linked. To do this we needed to invert a 2 × 2 matrix. We then looked at how to invert a 3 × 3 matrix. The next step is to use this leaning to solve for an economic problem where three variables are linked.

In the example below we follow this process of inverting a 3 × 3 matrix to work out the values of three economic variables. We do this by working through the 'five-step process' outlined in the previous section.

Consider the example below which follows closely the process we used in 10.9 to solve for two sets of pricing data. This time we have three economic variables: P_1, P_2 and P_3 representing the *profits* which a manufacturer earns from the production and sale of tea, coffee and cocoa respectively.

Example

Let:

p_1 denote the profits from the production and sale of tea

p_2 denote the profits from the production and sale of coffee

p_3 denote the profits from the production and sale of cocoa

We find that:

$$2p_1 - p_2 + p_3 = 5$$

$$p_1 - 3p_2 + 2p_3 = 2$$

$$2p_1 + p_2 + 4p_3 = -3$$

We create the matrix A:

$$A = \begin{pmatrix} 2 & -1 & 1 \\ 1 & -3 & 2 \\ 2 & 1 & 4 \end{pmatrix}$$

$$x = \begin{pmatrix} p_1 \\ p_2 \\ p_3 \end{pmatrix}$$

$$z = \begin{pmatrix} 5 \\ 2 \\ -3 \end{pmatrix}$$

We know that

$A \times x = z$

$Ax = z$

and that $x = A^{-1}z$ where A^{-1} is the inverse of matrix A.

Step 1
We calculate the minors to be:

$$\begin{pmatrix} -14 & 0 & 7 \\ -5 & 6 & 4 \\ 1 & 3 & -5 \end{pmatrix}$$

Step 2
We calculate the cofactors to be:

$$\begin{pmatrix} -14 & 0 & 1 \\ 5 & 6 & -4 \\ 1 & -3 & -5 \end{pmatrix}$$

Step 3
We work out adj(A) as:

$$\begin{pmatrix} -14 & 5 & 1 \\ 0 & 6 & -3 \\ 7 & -4 & -5 \end{pmatrix}$$

Step 4
We can see that det(A) can be calculated by taking the element of any row or column of A and multiplying each value by the cofactor obtained in step 2. Note using row 1:

$$2 \times (-14) + (-1) \times 0 + 1 \times 7 = -28 + 0 + 7 = -21$$

or using column 3:

$$1 \times 7 + 2 \times (-4) + 4 \times (-5) = 7 - 8 - 20 = -21$$

So the determinant of A is −21.

Step 5

$$A^{-1} = \frac{adj(A)}{det(A)} = -\frac{1}{21} \times \begin{pmatrix} -14 & 5 & 1 \\ 0 & 6 & -3 \\ 7 & -4 & -5 \end{pmatrix}$$

$x = A^{-1}z$

$$\Rightarrow \begin{pmatrix} p_1 \\ p_2 \\ p_3 \end{pmatrix} = -\frac{1}{21} \times \begin{pmatrix} -14 & 5 & 1 \\ 0 & 6 & -3 \\ 7 & -4 & -5 \end{pmatrix} \times \begin{pmatrix} 5 \\ 2 \\ -3 \end{pmatrix}$$

$$\begin{pmatrix} p_1 \\ p_2 \\ p_3 \end{pmatrix} = \begin{pmatrix} 2/3 & -5/21 & -1/21 \\ 0 & -2/7 & 1/7 \\ -1/3 & 4/21 & 5/21 \end{pmatrix} \begin{pmatrix} 5 \\ 2 \\ -3 \end{pmatrix}$$

$p_1 = 2^5/7$

$p_2 = -^1/7$

$p_3 = -^4/7$

Given the economic data we have been given, the manufacturer will make a profit of $2^5/7$ on tea but make a loss of $^1/7$ on coffee and a loss of $^4/7$ on cocoa.

We can verify that this is correct by substituting the values in the initial equations, as follows:

$2p_1 - p_2 + p_3 = 5$

$p_1 - 3p_2 + 2p_3 = 2$

$2p_1 + p_2 + 4p_3 = -3$

Quick problem 10

A multinational corporation produces a wide range of electronic products.

p_1 represents the profits from sales of a new DVD player

p_2 represents profits from the sales of a new plasma television

p_3 represents profits from the sales of an existing but popular hi-fi system.

Task One
The economics department believes that profits are linked as follows:

$p_1 + p_2 = 2$

$2p_2 - p_3 = -7$

$3p_1 + p_3 = 16$

Using a 3 × 3 matrix work out the profits of each product (p_1, p_2, and p_3).

Task Two
The economics department receives new data and believes that the relationship is now of the form:

$p_1 - 2p_2 + 3p_3 = -1$

$3p_1 + p_2 + p_3 = 2$

$2p_1 + p_2 - 3p_3 = -5$

Calculate the new values of p_1, p_2 and p_3 using a 3 × 3 matrix.

✔ **Learning outcome 10**

10.12 Cramer's rule

In previous sections we have looked at what matrices are and how they can be used to solve economic problems. We started by looking at 2 × 2 matrices and then by applying the idea of matrix inversion we were able to solve simple two variable problems. The next step involved extending this to a 3 × 3 matrix using the 'five-step technique'. We have built up a comprehensive set of tools for dealing with economic relationships involving two or three different variables.

We are now presented with a more general issue: can we find out a fundamental or general way of solving *any* matrix? At the moment we have confined our focus to only 2 × 2 and 3 × 3 matrices, but what if we have four or five economic variables? How could we solve these?

The practical need or significance of this might not be obvious. Economies are, in effect, very complex systems of variables such as consumption, investment, government spending, imports exports, taxation, interest rates and so on. Moreover, economic variables are commonly linked or related in some way: a household's consumption is usually linked to income, income is linked to factors such as wages, and the demand or consumption for goods and services produced in the first place. This sense of interconnectedness is captured in the simple circular flow of income model which is set out in most elementary economics textbooks.

If we think of an economy as a series of connections and relationships, it is perhaps easier to appreciate that economies can be expressed or articulated using mathematical expressions or functions. If economic variables are interconnected and linked, then we can also see that one way of thinking about an economy is a massive set of mathematical expressions. We can therefore use matrices to try and better understand what the values of economic variables are.

To move from 3 × 3 matrices to bigger systems we need a general rule or technique. One rule we will use is *Cramer's rule*, named after a Swiss mathematician who looked at large systems of mathematical relationships or equations.

Student note

Cramer's rule helps us to solve *any matrix with an equal number of rows and columns.*

First, we must a have a matrix with m rows and m columns.

Second, if we have a matrix A, a set of unknowns x and a set of knowns (see section 10.9) we need to recall that A × x = z and then Ax = z.

Third, Cramer's rule tells us that if we want to find a certain 'x variable' – let us call it x_i – then we can find it as follows:

$$x_i = \frac{\det(A_i)}{\det(A)}$$

So what is meant by A_i?

A_i can be found by switching or substituting the ith column of our original matrix A with the right-hand side of our vector **z**.

In general terms and for 2 × 2 matrix if we have:

$$A = \begin{pmatrix} a & b \\ c & d \end{pmatrix}, \quad x = \begin{pmatrix} P_1 \\ P_2 \end{pmatrix} \quad \text{and} \quad z = \begin{pmatrix} e \\ f \end{pmatrix}$$

$$A_1 = \begin{pmatrix} e & b \\ f & d \end{pmatrix}$$

For A_1 we replace the *first* column in matrix A with the vector values from z: we swap 'a' and 'c' for 'e' and 'f'

and $A_2 = \begin{pmatrix} a & e \\ c & f \end{pmatrix}$

For A_2 we replace the *second* column in matrix A with the vector values from z: we swap 'b' and 'd' this time for 'e' and 'f'

We can use Cramer's rule to find out quickly the values of economic variables in a large matrix. It is useful because it is a relatively quick and neat way to get to the answers we want.

Example for a 2 × 2 matrix

We have price data on two commodities as follows:

$3P_1 - 2P_2 = -3$

$4P_1 - P_2 = 7$

$$A = \begin{pmatrix} 3 & -2 \\ 4 & -1 \end{pmatrix}, \; x = \begin{pmatrix} P_1 \\ P_2 \end{pmatrix}, \; z = \begin{pmatrix} -3 \\ 7 \end{pmatrix}$$

Using Cramer's rule:

$$P_1 = \frac{\det(A_1)}{\det(A)}$$

$A_1 = \begin{pmatrix} -3 & -2 \\ 7 & -1 \end{pmatrix}$ (we switch the '3' and the '4' for the '−3' and the '7')

$\det(A_1) = (-3 \times (1)) - (-2 \times 7) = 3 + 14 = 17$

$\det(A) = (3 \times (-1)) - (-2 \times 4) = -3 + 8 = 5$

$\Rightarrow P_1 = \dfrac{17}{5} = 3.4$

Using Cramer's rule:

$$P_2 = \frac{\det(A_2)}{\det(A)}$$

$A_2 = \begin{pmatrix} 3 & -3 \\ 4 & 7 \end{pmatrix}$ (we switch the second column this time)

$\det(A_2) = (3 \times 7) - (-3 \times 4) = 21 + 12 = 33$

We know from above that $\det(A) = 5$

$$P_2 = \frac{\det(A_2)}{\det(A)} = \frac{33}{5} = 6.6$$

Example for a 3 × 3 matrix

The principle is exactly the same for a 3 × 3 matrix although you might want to refer back to section 10.10 to remember how to calculate det(A) for a 3 × 3 matrix using cofactors etc.

We are told that:

$$p_1 + 2p_2 + 3p_3 = 17$$

$$3p_1 + 2p_2 + p_3 = 11$$

$$p_1 - 5p_2 + p_3 = -5$$

We set up using our usual notation:

$$A = \begin{pmatrix} 1 & 2 & 3 \\ 3 & 2 & 1 \\ 1 & -5 & 1 \end{pmatrix}, x = \begin{pmatrix} p_1 \\ p_2 \\ p_3 \end{pmatrix}, z = \begin{pmatrix} 17 \\ 11 \\ -5 \end{pmatrix}$$

$$\det(A) = 1 \times [(2 \times 1) - (1 \times (-5))] - 2 \times [(3 \times 1) - (1 \times 1)] + 3 \times [(3 \times (-5)) - (2 \times (-1))]$$
$$= 7 - 4 - 51 = 48$$

We will need to refer back to our answer for det(A).

Calculating p_1

Now,

$$A_1 = \begin{pmatrix} 17 & 2 & 3 \\ 11 & 2 & 1 \\ -5 & -5 & 1 \end{pmatrix} \quad \text{(replacing first column of A with vector z)}$$

$$\det(A_1) = 17 \times [(2 \times 1) - (1 \times (-5))] - 2 \times [(11 \times 1) - (1 \times (-5))] + 3 \times [(11 \times (-5)) - (2 \times (-5))]$$
$$= (17 \times 7) - (2 \times 16) + (3 \times (-45))$$
$$= 119 - 32 - 135 = -48$$

Going back to Cramer's rule that

$$x_i = \frac{\det(A_i)}{\det(A)}$$

$$\Rightarrow p_1 = \frac{\det(A_1)}{\det(A)} = \frac{-48}{-48} = 1$$

Calculating p_2

$$A_2 = \begin{pmatrix} 1 & 17 & 3 \\ 3 & 11 & 1 \\ 1 & -5 & 1 \end{pmatrix}$$

$$\det(A_2) = 1 \times [(11 \times 1) - (1 \times (-5))] - 17 \times [(3 \times 1) - (1 \times 1)] + 3 \times [(3 \times (-5)) - (11 \times 1)]$$
$$= (1 \times 16) - (17 \times 2) + (3 \times (-26))$$
$$= 16 - 34 - 78 = -96$$

$$p_2 = \frac{\det(P_2)}{\det(P)} = \frac{-96}{-48} = 2$$

Calculating p_3

$$A_3 = \begin{pmatrix} 1 & 2 & 17 \\ 3 & 2 & 11 \\ 1 & -5 & 5 \end{pmatrix}$$

$$\det(A_3) = 1 \times [(2 \times (-5)) - (11 \times (-5))] - 2 \times [(3 \times (-5)) - (11 \times 1)] + 17 \times [(3 \times (-5)) - (2 \times 1)]$$
$$= (1 \times 45) - (2 \times (-26)) + (17 \times (-17))$$
$$= 45 + 52 - 289 = -192$$

$$p_3 = \frac{\det(A_3)}{\det(A)} = \frac{-192}{-48} = 4$$

Quick problem 11

Task One

A statistician knows that $C + I = Y$ where C = consumption, I = investment and Y = national income. She reviews some recent economic data and concludes that

$7C + 3I = 15$

$-2C + 5I = 16$

(a) Using Cramer's rule find the values of C and I.

(b) Comment on your finding for I.

Task Two

The same statistician amends her work in light of revised data. She develops her economic model as follows:

$2C + 3I + G = 10$

$C - I + G = 4$

$4C - I - 5G = -8$

This model introduces government spending (G).
What are the values of C, I and G in this model of the economy?

Task Three

In another economy different economic equations are found as follows:

$3C - 2I + 2G = 4$

$-C + 3I + 2G = 2$

$2C + 4I - 6G = 1$

Use matrices and Cramer's rule to solve.

✔ **Learning outcome 11**

Answers to quick problems

Quick problem 1

Task One

$a_{22} = 6$

$a_{33} = 2$

$b_{11} = 1$

$b_{42} = 4$

Task Two

A is a 3×3 matrix.

B is a 4×4 matrix.

Task Three

b_{55} refers to the element in the fifth column and the fifth row. The matrix does not extend to a fifth column and/or a fifth row.

Quick problem 2

Task One

$$X^T = \begin{bmatrix} 12 & 3 \\ 11 & 2 \\ 3 & 1 \\ 7 & 1 \end{bmatrix}$$

Task Two

Statement 1: false

$$Y^T = \begin{bmatrix} 1 & 6 & 11 \\ 2 & 5 & 7 \\ 4 & 3 & 9 \end{bmatrix} \neq Z^T = \begin{bmatrix} 2 & 3 & 1 \\ 2 & 4 & 1 \\ 4 & 3 & 0 \end{bmatrix}$$

Statement 2: true

$$Z^T = \begin{bmatrix} 2 & 3 & 1 \\ 2 & 4 & 1 \\ 4 & 3 & 0 \end{bmatrix}$$

Statement 3: false

$$Y^T = \begin{bmatrix} 1 & 6 & 11 \\ 2 & 5 & 7 \\ 4 & 3 & 9 \end{bmatrix}$$

Quick problem 3

Task One
A vector can be identified if it is comprised of a single row *or* a single column of entries or elements.

Task Two
H, J and L are vectors: they have single rows/columns. Matrix L is a unique case: it has one entry and can be considered to be a single row or a single column.

Quick problem 4

(a) $A + B = \begin{pmatrix} 3 & 3 \\ 4 & 5 \end{pmatrix}$

(b) B + C cannot be calculated because the matrices are of a different order.

(c) G − E cannot be calculated because the matrices are of a different order.

(d) $C + E = \begin{pmatrix} 12 & 6 & 6 \\ 5 & 5 & 3 \\ 6 & 16 & 15 \end{pmatrix}$

(e) $E - C = \begin{pmatrix} 4 & -2 & -4 \\ -5 & -1 & -1 \\ -6 & 2 & -9 \end{pmatrix}$

(f) $G - D = \begin{pmatrix} 0 \\ -3 \end{pmatrix}$

(g) A + E cannot be calculated because the matrices are of a different order.

Quick problem 5

Task One

(a) $2X = \begin{pmatrix} 2 & 0 \\ 0 & 2 \end{pmatrix}$

(b) $3Y = \begin{pmatrix} 6 \\ -6 \end{pmatrix}$

(c) $\frac{1}{2}Z = \begin{pmatrix} \frac{3}{2} & \frac{7}{2} & 3 \\ 2 & \frac{7}{2} & \frac{3}{2} \\ \frac{5}{2} & -1 & \frac{7}{2} \end{pmatrix}$

Task Two

Statement 1 is true since

$$2X = \begin{pmatrix} 2 & 0 \\ 0 & 2 \end{pmatrix}$$

$$2(2X) = \begin{pmatrix} 4 & 0 \\ 0 & 4 \end{pmatrix}$$

and equally

$$4X = 4 \times X = 4 \times \begin{pmatrix} 1 & 0 \\ 0 & 1 \end{pmatrix} = \begin{pmatrix} 4 & 0 \\ 0 & 4 \end{pmatrix}$$

Statement 2 is false because the expression cannot be evaluated: the matrices are of a different order.

Statement 3 is false

$$3Z = \begin{pmatrix} 3 \times 3 & 7 \times 3 & 6 \times 3 \\ 4 \times 3 & 7 \times 3 & 3 \times 3 \\ 5 \times 3 & -2 \times 3 & 7 \times 3 \end{pmatrix} = \begin{pmatrix} 9 & 21 & 18 \\ 12 & 21 & 9 \\ 15 & -6 & 21 \end{pmatrix} \neq \begin{pmatrix} 9 & 21 & 18 \\ 12 & 14 & 6 \\ 15 & 6 & 21 \end{pmatrix}$$

Statement 4 is true since

$$5Y = 5 \times \begin{pmatrix} 2 \\ -2 \end{pmatrix} = \begin{pmatrix} 10 \\ -10 \end{pmatrix}$$

and

$$\begin{pmatrix} 12 \\ 6 \end{pmatrix} - \begin{pmatrix} 6 \\ 16 \end{pmatrix} = \begin{pmatrix} 10 \\ -10 \end{pmatrix}$$

Quick problem 6

(a) $AD = \begin{pmatrix} 2 & -1 \\ -1 & 2 \end{pmatrix}$

(b) $BE = (5 \quad 8 \quad 9 \quad -4)$

(c) AF cannot be found because the rows and columns do not match.

(d) DC cannot be found because the rows and columns do not match.

Quick problem 7

Task One

(a)

$\det(A) = 2$

$\det(B) = 0$

$\det(C) = 23$

(b) Since $\det(A)$ and $\det(C)$ are both not equal to zero, matrix A and matrix C are non-singular. Since $\det(B) = 0$, matrix B is singular.

Task Two

$$A^{-1} = \begin{pmatrix} 1/2 & 3/2 \\ -1/2 & -1/2 \end{pmatrix}$$

B^{-1} cannot be calculated since B is a singular matrix

$$C^{-1} = \begin{pmatrix} 7/23 & 1/23 \\ 2/23 & 3/23 \end{pmatrix}$$

Quick problem 8

Task One

$$p_a = 1$$

$$p_b = -\frac{2}{3}$$

Task Two

p_a value does not make sense: you cannot have a negative price unless the consumer is being paid by the producer to take the product which seems implausible.

Task Three

The values do change and, at the very least, the signs of the figures now make sense.

$$p_a = \frac{7}{10}$$

$$p_b = \frac{1}{10}$$

Quick problem 9

Task One

$$A^{-1} = \frac{1}{8}\begin{pmatrix} 7 & -5 & 1 \\ -5 & 7 & -3 \\ -1 & 3 & 1 \end{pmatrix}$$

$$B^{-1} = \frac{1}{3}\begin{pmatrix} 1 & -3 & 2 \\ 0 & 3 & -3 \\ 1 & 9 & 11 \end{pmatrix}$$

Task Two

The matrix D is a singular matrix and the inverse cannot be calculated. The reason why the matrix is singular is because its determinant is zero.

Quick problem 10

Task One

$P_1 = 5$

$P_2 = -3$, i.e., a loss

$P_3 = 1$

Note change in solutions again the same problem.

Task Two

$P_1 = -1$

$P_2 = 3$

$P_3 = 2$

Quick problem 11

Task One

(a) $C = 3, I = -2$

(b) The figure for I is negative. Negative investment means that overall the assets of the economy are depreciating without any renewal or improvement. Firms may very pessimistic about the future and so not invest in new plant and machinery.

Task Two

$C = 2, I = 1$ and $G = 3$.

Task Three

$C = -122/(-94) = 1.30$

$I = -60/(-94) = 0.64$

$G = -65/(-94) = 0.69$

Index

Page numbers for figures have suffix **f**, those with equations have suffix **e**, and those with tables have suffix **t**

A

Abramovich, Ramon, 118
alternative price (P$_a$), 52, 67
annuities, 138–140
Apple Corporation, 118
arithmetic progressions, 119–123
  defined, 119
autonomous consumption, 77, 81
  defined, 77
autonomous saving, 79, 202
autonomous spending, 78
AVC *see* average variable cost
average revenue defined, 196
average variable cost (AVC), 71

C

capital (K), 14, 198, 199, 229
chain rule in differentiation, 186–187
Cobb-Douglas production function, 15e, 199e, 200, 201
consumer's income (M), 67
consumers total income (Y), 52, 53, 223
Cramer's rule, 300–303

D

demand (Q$_d$), 66, 67
determinant of the matrix (det(A)), 289
difference rule in differentiation, 180–182
differentiation, 173–187 *see also* partial differentiation
  chain rule, 186–187
    examples, 186–187
    general form, 186–187
    used when one function is encased within another, 186
  product rule, 182–184

    differentiating a function that has two terms mutiplied together, 182
    examples of typical operations, 182–184
    general form, 182
  quotient rule, 185–186
    general form, 185
  simple derivative, 173–180
    example find slope of line with given coordinates, 174–177
    derivative of f(x) denotes the slope of the function, 174–177
    graphs of the quadratic function, 175f
    slope calculated and plotted with tangent, 174f
    example sketch function, 177–179
    graph, 177f
    slope of function illustrated, 178f
    examples of differentiation of six different functions, 179–180
    gradient is change of y (Δy) divided by change of x(Δx), 173
  sum rule and difference rule, 180–182
    differentiating a function that has terms that are added or subtracted frolm each other, 180–182
    examples of typical functions, 181–182
    general form of rules, 181

E

economic data, 9
economic growth, 140–143, 151
economic theory, 39, 76, 157
economic variables, 11, 118, 300
economics, 2, 4, 30, 44, 98, 105, 106, 112, 154, 163, 173, 235
Excel (software), 277

F

factorization, 160–163
FC *see* fixed costs
feasible region defined, 95
finance and growth, 118–144
  arithmetic progressions, 119–123
    based on addition of a common difference, 119
    calculating a term, 119–123
    equation, 120e
    calculating the sum of terms, 120–121
    example, 120, 121t
    defined, 119
  economic growth, 140–143
    average annual compunded growth rate, 142e, 143
    equation for growth rate over period, 142e
    plot of UK gross domestic product, 141f
    table of annual GDP growth rate, 141t
  geometric progression, 123–128
    based on common multiplication by a common ratio, 123
    example, 123t, 124
    calculating the sum of terms, 126–128
    example of economy growing at 9% per annum, 127
    check on results, 127t
    equation for total value, 127e
    calculating the value of a term, 124
    example calculation of value of a bank account, 125t
    flow chart for identifying whether a series is arithmetical or geometrical, 128f
  investment appraisal, 132–140
    annuities, 138–140

finance and growth (*continued*)
  defined, 138
  example to estimate total
    present value of annuity
    (TPVA), 139e
  internal rate of return (IRR),
    137
  defined, 137
  example check offer of high
    rate of return, 137
  net present value (NPV),
    135–136
  allows for the cost of the
    investment, 135–136
  present value, 133–134
  equation for the future value
    of an investment after n
    years, 133e
  example about pension,
    133–134
  wide-ranging evaluation of
    opportunities, 132
fixed costs (FC), 54, 71
functions of two variables,
  216–217

G

G *see* Global Electrics PLC
GDP *see* gross domestic
  product
geometric progression, 123–128
Global Electrics PLC (G), 276
goverment spending, 82
gradient of line, 173
gross domestic product (GDP),
  10, 140

I

integration, 248–268
  applying definite integrals,
    265–268
    consumer surplus, 265–266
      calculation of consumer
        surplus, 266
      equilibrium supply and
        demand, 265f–266
      example of coffee supply
        and demand, 265
    producer surplus, 267
      method as for consumer
        surplus, 267
  definite integrals, 260–264,
    267–268
    analysing consumer surplus,
      262–263

example, 263
    supply and demand
      curves, 262f
    analysing producer surplus,
      263–264
    supply and demand
      curves, 264f
    areas under the curves, 260f
    definition, 260
    example, 261f
    use of limits, 260
    using exponentials, 267–268
    example, 268
  indefinite integration, 249–251,
    255–259
    defined, 249
    example, 251
    reversing differentiation,
      249–251
    understanding cost
      functions, 255–259
      examples of marginal
        costs, 256–259
      graph of cost curves, 256f
    integrating expressions with
      multiple terms, 254
      examples, 254
    integrating using exponentials,
      253–254
      examples, 253–254
    integrating where power of the
      function is −1 can be done
      with natural logarithms,
      252
      examples, 252
    summary of the process of
      integration, 250f
    use of integration by
      economists, 248
internal rate of return (IRR), 137
investment appraisal, 132–140
IRR *see* internal rate of return
isoquant is where different
  combinations of capital and
  labour give the same output,
  229

K

K *see* capital

L

labour (L), 14, 198
lagrange multipliers, 240–241
law of diminishing marginal
  utility, 227–231

law of diminishing returns, 199
linear equations, 28–85 *see also*
  linear programming
  applications of linear equations
    in economics, 44–55
    break-even point, 54–55
      total costs made up of
        fixed costs (FC) and
        variable costs (VC), 54
      equation, 54e
      example, production needed to
        break even, 54
      graph of the point of
        intersection, 55f
    budget constraints, 44–48
      calculating the slope of the
        budget constraint,
        47–48
      equation, 45e
      example, budget split
        between two products,
        45–46
      graph of split budget, 46f
    demand function, 52–53
      additional factors in
        demand function, 52
      consumer's total income (Y),
        52
      effect of a rise in income, 53t
      equation, 52e
      price of an alternative good
        (P'), 52
    supply and demand, 48–52
      coordinates for supply and
        demand, 49t
      deriving the demand and
        supply equations,
        49e–50e
      find the equilibrium point,
        51
      supply and demand graph,
        49f
      supply curve and demand
        curve defined, 48t
      table of chocolate bars
        supply and demand, 48t
  co-ordinates, 28–29
    location relative to origin
      defined by co-ordinates,
      28f, 29
  cost, volume and profit
    analysis, 71–73
    example find an expression
      for profit from input data,
      71–72

graph of break-even point,
72f
relationships of cost, volume
and profit, 71
effects of a per unit tax, 73–76
equations, 73e
example illustrate the effect
of tax, 73–76
supply and demand
curves, 74f, 76f
equation of a line, 34, 35e,
36–38
examples, 36–38
intercept (c), 36
slope (m) defined, 34
types of slope illustrated, 34f
finding points of intersection,
38–44
equating the equations,
41–42
example, 41–42
graphically, 39–41
examples, 39, 40f, 41f
row operation, 43–44
examples, 43–44
substitution, 42–43
example, 42–43
linear form, 29–33
examples of linear equation,
30, 31f, 32f, 33f
form of linear equation,
29–30e
market equilibrium and
changes in supply or
demand, 66–70
example effect of 20%
increase in demand, 68
supply and demand
curves, 68f, 69f
example of calculating
market equilibrium, 66
example of increase in
consumer income by 40%,
70
shift in demand curve,
70f
shift in demand curve due to
changes in variables, 67f
simultaneous linear equations
with more than two
unknowns, 60–66
steps needed to solve
problems, 61
example A, 61–63
equations, 61e

example B, 64–66
equations, 64e
linear programming, 90–112 *see
also* linear equations
application of linear
programming in
economics, 105–112
example A, 106–108
Apex manufactures car
radios, model S and
Model D, 106
calculation and
conclusion, 108
constraints on plastic
components and on
metal components, 107
graphical solution, 107f
objective function is to
maximise profit,
106–108
example B, 108–112
calculation and
conclusion, 111–112
constraints on time and
space, 109
florist grows roses (R) and
poppies (P), 108–109
graphical solutions, 109f,
110f
objective function is to
maximise profit,
109–110
graphing inequalities, 90–95
examples of inequalities, 93,
94f, 95f
expressing a linear
inequality, 91
graph of line, 90f
graphs illustrate the original
inequality, 91, 92f
linear equation, 90e
graphing simultaneous linear
inequalities, 95–98
example of two inequalities
on the same graph, 95, 96f
feasible region within the
points of intersection,
97f
feasible region defined, 95
objective function, 98–104
examples maximising the
objective function,
98–104
graph four constraints,
100f

graph three inequalities,
99f
plot two lines to identify
the feasible region, 102f
objective function defined,
98
practical applications to simple
and compound interest,
129–131
compound interest, 129–130
link between compound
interest and geometric
progression, 130
example of application of
compound interest, 130,
131t
table shows interest earned
yearly, 130t
simple interest defined in
two ways, 129
unbounded feasible regions,
104–105
example of cases which do
not have a complete
solution, 104–105

M

M *see* trade imports
macroeconomics, 76–85
economic theory and analysis
on the national level, 76
firm consumption and
investment, 81–82
equilibrium level between
income and consumption,
81f
government activity taxation
and trade, 82–85
government spending (G),
82
equation, 82e
taxation (T), 82–83
equation, 82e
example, 82–83
trade, exports (X) and
imports (M), 83–84
equation, 83f
example, determine
equilibrium level of
national income,
84–85
household consumption and
saving, 77–80
consumption function, 77e
income identity, 77e

macroeconomics (*continued*)
marginal propensity to consume (MPC), 77–80
savings function, 80f
relationship between households and firms, 77f
marginal concepts, 192–204
consumption and savings, 202–203
consumption function, 202e
example, 203e
marginal propensity to consume (MPC), 202e
demand, total revenue and marginal revenue, 193–196
example and explanation, 193e, 194e
graphical link between demand, total revenue and marginal revenue, 195, 196f
illustration of solution, 195f
illustration of total revenue function, 194f
marginal revenue defined, 193
marginal functions, 192
differentiation of quadratic equation produces marginal function, 192
table of total and marginal functions, 192t
total revenue is product of price and quantity, 192e
production, 198–201
calculation using production function, 199e
graph of production function, 201f
increasing, constant or decreasing returns to scale, 200f
law of diminishing returns, 199
second order derivatives, 203–204
defined, 203e–204e
examples, 204e
total and marginal cost, 197–198
example of marginal cost, 197–198e
marginal cost defined, 197e
marginal cost defined, 197e
marginal cost (MC), 197, 257

marginal propensity to consume (MPC), 77, 81, 202
marginal propensity to import (MPM), 84
marginal propensity to save (MPS), 79, 202
mathematical review, 2–21
algebra, 17–21
example of Martian robot, 19f
calculations, 19–20ft
typical uses, 17–18
arithmetic operators, 2–4
addition, subtraction, multiplication and division, 2
fractions, 4–7
example of fraction re-expressed using highest common denominator, 5t
'proper fractions' and 'improper' fractions, 4
used to express probabilities, 6
logarithms, 16–17
diagram of uses in business, 16f
percentages, 7–11
benefits in using percentages, 8
defined, 7
example of highest tax rate, 8
table of economic data, 9t
example based on data, 10
powers, 12–15
defined, 12ef
production function, 14e–15
Cobb-Douglas function, 15e
typical uses, 12
matrices, 276–303
adding and subtracting matrices, 280–282
procedures, 280–281
application of 3x3 matrices and inversions to economics, 296–299, 297–299
example, 297–299
application of 2x2 matrices to economic problems, 290–292
equations for prices of goods, 290e

examples, 290–291
dealing with 'zero matrices,' 282
definitions, notation and operations, 276–279
data in table expressed as a matrix, 276t
example of Global Electrics PLC, 276
transposing a matrix, 277–279
inversions of 3x3 matrices, 292–296
example, 293–296
transposing to find the adjoint, 293
use of cofactors, 292–293
matrix inversion
defined, 287, 288–289
determinant of the matrix (det(A)), 289
example, 288
identity matrix defined, 288, 289
singular and non-singular matrices, 289
multiplying matrices, 284–287
example of mobile phone manufacturer, 284–287
profit calculation, 285
sales data, 285t
MC *see* marginal cost
MPC *see* marginal propensity to consume
MPM *see* marginal propensity to import
MPS *see* marginal propensity to save

N
net present value (NPV), 135–136
non-linear equations, 154–173
economics applications of quadratic equations, 168–173
relationship between quadratic equations and market equilibriums, 168
equations, 168e–172e
examples, 168–173
illustrations, 169f–170f
factorization, 160–163
factorizing the quadratic expression, 160

finding the value for x that makes the function zero, 160
process steps, 160e–163e
functions with more than one independent variable, 154–160
  cubic functions, 157
    equation, 157e
    graph, 157f
  graphing a quadratic function, 158–160
    equation, 158e
    example, 158–160
    graph, 159f
  quadratic functions, 154–157
    equation, 154e
    example, 155, 156
    graph, 155f, 156f
quadratic formula, 163–173
  example A, 164–165
    graph, 165f
    two posible solutions, 165
  example B, 166–167
    graphs of the functions, 166f, 167f
    values of x making the function zero, 166
  quadratic formula, 163e
NPV see net present value

O

objective function, 90, 98–104, 106, 108, 110, 237, 239, 241, 243
objective function defined, 98
Office of National Statistics, 140, 141
optimisation, 205–212
  calculating maxima and minima, 205
  constrained optimisation improves realism, 205
  example, 205e
  finding critical values and value of inflection point, 205
  second order derivative calculation, 207e
  examples, 208e
    check for inflexion points, 209e
    evaluate the function, 209e
    find critical values, 208e
    graph the function, 208f
    test for concavity, 208e

graph of function, 207f
table summarising minimum and maximum, 206
use in economics, 210e–212e
  examples, 210e–212e

P

P see price per unit
P_a see alternative price
partial derivatives, 217–219
partial differentiation, 216–243
  see also differentiation
  changes to independent and dependent variables, 221–223
    change to two variables simultaneously is called small increments formula, 222
    example find first-order partial derivatives for given function, 221–223
  constrained optimization, 237–239
    firm's cost constraint, 238
    objective function to be made more relalistic, 237
    values of goods purchased must equal total income, 238f, 239f
  functions of two variables, 216–217
    dependent and independent varaibles, 216
    examples of calculations, 217
    $f(x.y)=2xy-5x$ is simple function in two variables, 216–217
  lagrange multipliers, 240–243
    application to an objective function, 240
    defined, 240
    economic application, 242–243
    examples, 240–243
  law of diminishing marginal utility, 227–231
    indifference curves are downward sloping, 228
    production functions, 229–231
      isoquant is where different combinations of capital and labour give the same output, 229, 230f

marginal rate of technical substitution, 231
second-order derivative of utility function graphed, 227, 228f
slope of curve is the marginal rate of substitution, 228
partial derivatives, 217–219
  defined, 217
  examples find all partial derivatives of given functions, 218–219
  partial derivative of f with respect to x is f_x, 218
partial differentiation and marginal functions, 225–231
  utility functions, 225–227
    exercise, 226–227
    utility (U) represents levels of satisfaction, 226
partial elasticity, 223–225
  demand function is $Q_1=f(P_1, P_2, Y)$, 223–225
  cross-price elasticity of demand, 224
    formula E_{p2}=percentage change in Q_1/percentage change in P_2, 224
  income elasticity of demand, 224
    formula E_Y=percentage change in Q_1/percentage change in Y, 224
  own price elasticity of demand, 223
    formula E_p=percentage change in Q_1/percentage change in P_1, 223
  income and own price elasticity of demand can be positive or negative, 224
    example, 225
second-order partial derivatives, 219–221
  examples find all partial derivatives of given functions, 220–221
  four second order derivatives for function with two variables, 219
unconstrained optimization, 231–237
  application to economics, 235–237

partial differentiation (*continued*)
  for a given function utility U should be as large as possible, 235
  funding available is a constraint, 235
  example, 235–237
  finding the maximum and minimum points for a given function, 231–232
  example, 233–234
  similar for two variables, 232
  for single variable solve for the derivative of the function and set to zero, 232
partial elasticity, 223–225
percentage change defined, 10e
powers defined, 12ef
present value, 133–134
price per unit (P), 30, 49, 54, 71, 192, 223
product rule in differentiation, 182–184

Q

Q *see* quantity
Q_d *see* demand
Q_s *see* supply
quadratic equation, 154, 160, 161, 162, 163, 165, 166, 168, 171, 175, 207
quadratic formula, 163–173, 211
quadratic function, 154, 157, 158, 160, 174, 205
quantity (Q), 14, 30, 49, 52, 54, 71, 192, 198, 223
quick problems
  allocation of production to maximise profit, 112
  analyse bases for given costs and revenues, 259
  arithmetic progression of taxpayers, 120
  calculate
    budget constraints, 48
    common ratio for series, 124
    effect of 4.5% growth on global economy, 126
    given matrices, 289
    and graph total revenue and costs, 55
    income using algebraic equation, 21

the inverse of 3x3 matrices, 296
  supply and demand for lamps, 52t
  calculations about present value of investment, 134–135
  calculations on specific geometrical progressions, 127–128
  check rate of return on capital against competing rates, 138
  complete the figure on page 250 on the uses of integration to economists, 250
  definite integral calculations, 266
  from demand curve write expression for consumer surplus, 263
  determine firm's equilibrium levels of income and consumption, 82
  determine savings functions, 80
  differentiate
    several functions, 180
    typical expressions, 187
    typical functions, 186
  differentiating functions, 182
  differentiation of functions, 184
  economic analysis of given data, 258
  effect of 25% increase in demand, 70
  equilibrium level of national income, 83, 85
  estimate present value of annuity and check comparative proposals, 140
  evaluate definite integrals, 262
  evaluate functions with two variables, 217
  evaluating matrices, 284
  evaluation of
    definite integrals, 268
    functions, 217
    matrices, 282
  expression to calculate producer surplus, 264
  filling-in missing operators, 3t

find
  all first and second order partial derivatives for given functions, 221
  equation of line through each set of coordinates, 38
  expression for profit using input data, 73
  expressions for the marginal product of capital, marginal product of labour, and marginal rate of technical substitution, 231
  first-order partial derivatives for given function, 223
  indefinite integrals of given functions, 251
  integrals of given functions, 253
  intersection by
    all four methods, 44
    equating the equations, 42
    row operation, 44
    substitution, 43
  maximum profit for firm with specified functions, 243
  partial derivatives, 219
given a demand function calculate elasticity of demand, 225
given a utility function calculate the marginal rate of substitution, 229
from given data assess tasks using matrices, 292
for given equation find maximum profit, 237
given existing supply and demand curves, illustrate the new curves, 76
for a given function find critical values, 234
graphs of linear equations, 34
growth rates based on GDP in China, 143t
identify data in a matrix, 277
identify market equilibria, 170
illustrating inequalities, 95
integrate the given expressions, 255
Lagrange multipliers used to optimize given function, 242

logarithms used in example, 17

maximising and minimizing, 104, 105

maximising the production function, 239

multiplying matrices, 287

plotting co-ordinates, 29

prediction of GDP assuming data in arithmetic progression, 122

production function examples, 15

quadratic formula used to solve equations, 167e

re-expression of figures in table, 6f

show effect of increased price with graphs, 53

simple interest table, 129t

sketch function $f(x)=x^2$, 179

sketching inequalities and feasibel regions, 98

solve three simultaneous equations, 66

solving quadratic equations using factorization, 163

tasks
  about powers, 13e
  based on table of economic data, 9t, 11
  with matrices, 278–279
  with vectors, 280

time for interest to increase to a set value, 132

total cost schedule calculation, 173

using fractions and estimating areas, 6–7

quotient rule in differentiation, 185–186

S

scalar multiplication, 282–284
  defined, 283
  example, 283

second order derivatives defined, 203e–204e

second-order partial derivatives, 219–221

slope (m) defined, 34

small increments formula, 222

student notes
  adding and subtracting matrices, 280–281

associated coordinates must be kept together, 35

autonomous savings is also autonomous consumption, 79

average revenue defined, 196

basic rules of algebra, 18–19

budget constraint graph is straight line, 45

calculation
  of revenue2, 59
  for sum of terms in geometric progression, 126
  of terms in arithmetic progression, 122–123

characteristics of a function, 218

co-ordinates define location relative to origin, 29

combining terms for simplicity, 79

compound interest calculation, 130

consider notation when function has two or more variables, 216

constraints in inequalities illustrated, 96f

coordinates must represent a specific point on the line, 36

defnite integrals, 261

demand and supply equation, 30e

determinant of the matrix, defined, 289

equation for present value of an annuity, 138, 139e

examples in economics are generally positive, 47

expression for producer surplus, 264

finding the value for x that makes a quadratic function zero, 163

form of equation for slope of budget constraint, 47

goods can lead to positive or negative elasticity of demand, 224

graph of quadratic function, 155f

graphing inequalities, 91

identity matrix, 289

if $y=x^3$ identifies a cubed function, then dy/dx identies a derivative, 177

illustration of inequalities, 93f

importance of the tangent line to a quadratic curve, 176

indifference curve and isoquant are different, 239

integrating
  expressions with multiple terms, 255
  using exponentials, 253, 254
  where power of the function is −1 can be done with natural logarithms, 252

integration and the process of reversing differentiation, 250

integration of exponential functions, 267

intersection shows the point at which demand meets supply, 39f

isoquant is where different colmbinations of capital and labour give the same output, 230f

key terms used in investment appraisal, 132

labels of axes should represent the data, 33

limitations of graphing a quadratic function, 159

marginal propensity to import (MPM), 84

matrix is a table array of information, 277

maxima and minima summarised, 206

meaning of first and second order derivatives, 204

multiply equation by 1.2 to increase demand by 20%, 69

multiplying matrices, 286

NPV is the value of an investment less the investment cost, 135e

parallel lines never intersect, 41

percentage change defined, 10e

percentages and taxation rates, 9

positive relationships consumption/income and savings/income, 202

partial differentiation (*continued*)

progression is a sequence of numbers which change by a common factor, 119

quadratic formula provides two solutions, 164

quantity can be expressed as function of price by re-arranging equations, 51

rates of return compared by rearranging equation, 137

reformulating matrix equations, 291

relationships of cost, volume and profit, 71

rules about powers, 12e, 14e

rules for logarithms, 16

saddle point is both a stationary point and a point of inflexion, 232f

scaling a matrix, 283

signs and powers in differentiation, 179

simple interest calculation, 129

slope of supply function has the same value as the slope of the demand function, 50

solving a problem where three variables are linked, 297

solving quadratic equations, 171

steps needed to solve problems with more than two variables, 61

maintain consistency throughout the calculation, 63

multiply through the whole equation by the chosen value, 62

use operations needed to eliminate one unknown, 62

steps to relate linear programming to economics, 106

steps to work out the inverse of a 3x3 matrix, 293

straight line graph needs only two points, 31

summary of non-linear equations, 158

synonyms and symbols for arithmetic operators, 2f

total revenue is price times quantity, 172

transposing a matrix, 278

typical basic calculations and use of fractions, 4–5

use of the quadratic formula, 164

value of a term in a geometric progression, 125

value of rate of percentage change, 11

value of slope for different lines, 35

when slope of consumption and savings functions are similar they have a positive relationship, 80

sum rule in differentiation, 180–182

supply and demand, 49f

supply (Q_s), 66

T

taxation (T), 82

total cost (TC), 71, 255

total fixed costs (TFC), 255

total present value of annuity (TPVA), 139e

total revenue (TR), 54, 71, 192

total variable cost (TVC), 255

TPVA *see* total present value of annuity

TR *see* total revenue

trade exports (X), 82, 84

trade imports (M), 82, 84

U

utility (U), 226, 235

V

variable costs (VC), 54, 71

vectors, defined, 279

X

X *see* trade exports

Y

Y *see* consumers total income

Z

'zero matrices', 282